To Natasha and Sawyer, the two most important people in my life.
Today, tomorrow, always.

To the three who will always be ...
in my memory, in my heart, in my soul.

RED ✚ BLACK
BOOKS

redandblackbooks.com

Copyright© 2009 by Red & Black Books, L.L.C.
Published by Red & Black Books, L.L.C.

10   9   8   7   6   5   4   3   2   1

Library of Congress Cataloging-in-Publication Data on file with Publisher.
Pennington, Tina W., 1962-
Williams, Mandy S., 1957-

ISBN 978-0-984096-70-1

Special Thanks To:

Bright Sky Press as consulting publisher for making this project not only polished, but possible.

Mike Guillory Design and Illustration for giving our trademark a needed nose job
and adding a sense of style to all our illustrations.

Kleis Design for taking pages and pages of words and designing a book that surpassed all our expectations.

Printed in the United States of America.

What I Learned About Life
When My Husband Got Fired!

a real approach to personal finance
and prioritizing your life

By

real sisters. real life.

table of contents

prologue
Help — I Have A Crisis On My Hands!

E-mail From: Red
To: Black
Importance: High
Subject: Nick
Sent: Friday, January 23, 9:43 PM

I need to talk to you about Nick as soon as possible! It's serious.

E-mail From: Black
To: Red
Importance: High
Subject: Nick
Sent: Friday, January 23, 10:57 PM

Is Nick sick? Call me as soon as you get this e-mail. Regardless of the time!

I was grateful my sister, Black, wasn't online until late that Friday evening, as I really wasn't sure how I'd have responded. I was still trying to grasp the enormity of what had just happened. My husband was fired. No warning. This morning he had a great job with a great company that he dedicated his life to for almost 25 years. This evening that was all gone.

I thought my life was happy and secure. Two beautiful, healthy daughters. A marriage to a husband who was a wonderful father and who I knew loved me. Sure, there were things I wanted to change. But that's normal.

But at 5:00 on a rainy Friday afternoon in January my life was changed in an instant. Forget about long-term plans and dreams for the future. How were we going to get through today and tomorrow and next week?

I was terrified. I was devastated. Emotionally I was a wreck. I could have killed my husband for doing this to the family. Yet I felt incredibly sad for him. His entire career had been dedicated to the Company, and he didn't deserve this. I was ashamed. Yet, I had to be strong and put on a brave face for Nick and our daughters, Natasha and Sawyer, who were only 5 and 1-1/2 years old.

And what was I going to tell people? I decided I would eventually figure that out, but first, I had to tell my sister — the one person who knows everything about my life and who I talk to almost every day. I thought I was a strong person and well-educated, but I wasn't sure I had the skills to handle this.

E-mail From: Red
To: Black
Importance: High
Subject: Nick
Sent: Saturday, January 24 5:58 AM

Nick was fired. I'm sorry — I didn't mean to scare you. No one's sick.

E-mail From: Black
To: Red
Importance: High
Subject: Nick
Sent: Saturday, January 24 5:59 AM

What happened?

E-mail From: Red
To: Black
Importance: High
Subject: Nick
Sent: Saturday, January 24 6:02 AM

Good question. I don't know. I always thought Nick would work for the Company until he retired, and by then we would have a second home and would live the happily ever after. I never thought anything would change that plan. Yesterday everything was perfect; today my life is a living nightmare.

E-mail From: Black
To: Red
Importance: High
Subject: Nick
Sent: Saturday, January 24 6:03 AM

Take a deep breath ... we'll go through it ... and you'll get through it. Things happen for a reason.

Has he talked to an attorney? Did he sign anything? Can you get away from the house and call me? You need to distance yourself from the house and your emotions.

E-mail From: Red
To: Black
Importance: High
Subject: Nick
Sent: Saturday, January 24 6:07 AM

Give me about 30 minutes, and I'll call you from the car. Thanks.

With everyone still asleep, feeling sick to my stomach, I didn't want to face Nick, yet alone this situation. I left him a note telling him I was going off for my usual early morning Saturday grocery run. I got into my Jaguar, wishing I could escape into its luxurious world of leather and exotic wood. Instead, I drove for 20 minutes in the pouring rain, trying to fight back tears, mustering up the courage to call Black. I parked in a shopping center, less than two minutes from Black's house, took a deep breath and called her.

introduction

When my husband Nick lost his job, I realized not only did I not understand the ins-and-outs of corporate life and how he could suddenly be fired, but even worse that I didn't know the first thing about our finances. Scared and confused, I turned to my sister Black for advice. Her lessons about how to get a grip on money matters helped me prioritize my whole life in just three months. We want to share what we (mainly I) learned, in the hope that it helps you look at your own life in a new way.

There are many people who are experts in a given field. Suze Orman can get you straight on financial matters, Dr. Phil can enlighten you about relationships, and if you want to improve your lifestyle, there's Martha Stewart. Then there are people, like Oprah, who are extremely resourceful facilitators. We are none of those things. Black and I are sisters, real people who are not experts in any given area. But, working together, we are becoming experts in our own lives.

What follows are our exchanges, recreated to the best of our abilities and memory, from those three months, dirty laundry and all. Eavesdrop on our conversations, read our e-mails and walk in our shoes. (Mine are more affordable and definitely more comfortable than Black's, but hers are certainly beautiful.) We hope that a better understanding of finances and priorities will unfold for you, as it did for me when Black pointed out all the things my life had failed to teach me. And if you laugh at us along the way, that's great. We won't take it personally. We laugh at ourselves all the time.

You would be hard-pressed to find two sisters as different as Black and I. We bring completely different points of view to the table — about everything! I'm warm and fuzzy, while Black is ultimately pragmatic.

Let's get introduced, and then I'll tell you everything that happened after my husband got fired.

Red:

I'm five years younger than Black, and for as long as I can remember she has called me Red. I have long red hair, so this isn't surprising. Since my mother hated it when anyone called me "Red," it ensured that Black would rarely call me anything else. Sisters are like that. So are mothers and daughters. But I digress.

As a child, I always tried to please my parents. I liked the harmony of agreement, and especially hated confrontation, so I rarely caused problems. I made good grades and earned a scholarship to college. After graduation I lived with my parents for five years and commuted to work in New York City. I was sheltered from real life — things like renting an apartment, living expenses, insurance. I didn't even have to buy a car. At this point, someone should have kicked me out of my parents' house and told me to get a life. But, unfortunately, no one did.

Instead, I married Nick, an Englishman who worked in international marketing for a large oil company. I won't go into the details of our courtship, including the two engagements, but it's probably important you know that initially he was Black's first fiancé. The point is that I went from living in my parents' house to living in my husband's house. I followed him around the world, living in such exotic places as Hong Kong and Shanghai, as well as The Netherlands and England. We waited ten years to start a family and had two wonderful, red-headed daughters, first Natasha and then, four years later, Sawyer. To complete the family, Black bought us a red Labradoodle we named Woof.

I lived in a fairy tale. Life was easy for me. Looking back, it was too easy. I managed to avoid many learning experiences that would have served me well. But that all changed one January afternoon. Thank goodness I had Black. I suppose I should tell you a little about her, too.

Black has dark brunette, almost black, hair, but I never called her Black until a few years ago when she started leaving phone messages to the effect of "Red, this is Black ..." And, since then, we've been "Red and Black" in every way.

Black lives life to the fullest — damn the consequences! She makes her opinions known, sometimes tactfully, sometimes not. She has never been afraid of a little confrontation; in fact, I think she welcomes the verbal and mental challenge. Black obviously likes more excitement in her life than I do. She isn't emotional. She isn't touchy-feely. But she's genuine, honest and smart. And, as you'll see, she has a huge heart — just don't mention it in her presence, because she'll argue with you.

Black established her independence early and always seemed to have ambition and a plan. She went to college when she was 16 and graduated less than four years later with an economics degree. By the time she was 21, she had worked full time for a brokerage firm, gone to school in New York City and London and earned a masters in business administration in international finance. Talk about being in a rush!

Although she had a fascinating professional career, I'm going to fast forward to when she was 39. After marrying her second husband, Larry, a brilliant engineer who took his ideas and turned them into a mega-million-dollar business, she gave up her highly successful career. Black had become the personification of the professional career woman in the male-dominated oil and gas industry, and she had amassed an impressive personal net worth — at least it was impressive to me! Her married life seemed less demanding, although she was overseeing a private family partnership, designing several houses, and being a stepmom to two young girls, Brittney and Chelsea. And there was also Jeff, Larry's adult son from his first marriage, who had children of his own. (I guess that makes her a grandmother, too!) If all this wasn't enough, she started racing Porsches and then Ferraris.

Black and I became close ever since I had Natasha, and especially after Nick and I moved to Houston. We shared life's daily activities and thoughts. Before that, our conversations were infrequent and brief. More along the lines of checking up on one another vs. truly sharing our lives. We always loved one another and would have dropped everything if the other called for help, but since Black went off to college when I was only eleven, our lives basically separated years ago.

From the time we were little, she was the older, worldlier sister, and I was the innocent baby. I had mixed feelings about her — she was both a great example to follow as well as a great example of what not to do. I was very good at riding her coattails when it served my purpose; otherwise, I denied being her sister. And, at times, I was envious. She was constantly bringing home new boyfriends. She wasn't beautiful, but something about her made her attractive. Maybe it was her fashion sense. Or maybe her flirtatious personality. My relationship with my sister was basically no different than most — maybe just a little more extreme. Because Black was a little more extreme.

I think a great deal of my desire to avoid confrontation and to be an ideal daughter stemmed from witnessing so many heated arguments between Black and our mom. Their personalities were so similar – opinionated, forceful, energetic — and the result was a constant state of agitation and conflict in our house.

One argument stands out and best sums up many of my conflicting emotions and opinions about Black. We were eating dinner at IHOP. It was the early seventies, so Black was probably about 15. Mom's conversation veered towards the teenage use of marijuana. She proclaimed (which to her meant there was no other correct opinion) that marijuana was evil, that those who smoked marijuana were immoral, and there was no way her girls would ever touch the stuff. Immediately, Black announced, quite calmly, that she had smoked marijuana. Several times. I have no idea if it was true, but Black certainly was enjoying herself.

As the earthquake erupted in the restaurant and continued rocking our car on the drive home, I realized I never wanted to have this sort of confrontational argument with anyone. I hated it. It was obviously better to leave uncomfortable topics buried. The next morning I woke up to find a letter from Black on my pillow. She said she was sorry I had to witness the fight, and she hoped I wouldn't think any less of her. (I wish I still had that letter.) I was too much of a wimp to tell her that, to the contrary, that night made me love and respect her even more. No matter what her true beliefs about marijuana, she didn't take the easy path. She didn't care what other people thought. She didn't shy away from conflict. She was strong.

It's curious. Black and I were raised with the same morals, values and expectations by the same parents in the same house. But that's where the similarities end. As Black often tells me, I'm warm and fuzzy, and she's purely practical. There are many times that, not only have I questioned if we have the same parents, I have wondered if we're from the same planet. Black's fond of saying that with her designer clothes and expensive cars she lives in "La-La Land." But the truth is Black not only recognized the realities of life, she dealt with them head on. And now when my world changed, I realized it was me, not her, who lived in a fantasy world.

But, as usual, I'm going on and on. I'll stop and let Black give you her take on our relationship.

Black:

Enough of the blah-blah-blah ... let me sum it up this way, our differences are:

	Red	Black
Born	1962, New York	1957, New York
Hair Color	Red	Black
Personality	Warm & Fuzzy	Painfully Blunt
Marital Status	Married	Married/TBD
Children	2	0
Pets	Labradoodle	0
Current Career	Mother & Wife	Management of $100MM portfolio
Prior Careers	Wife, Administrative positions in PR and Art Industries	Executive in Male-Dominated Industries (Oil & Gas, Offshore Construction), Retired at age 39 with net worth in excess of $1MM
# Years Lived Alone	0	14
# Romantic Relationships	Count on one hand	Lost count
# Countries Lived in	5	1
# Years in Texas	Less than 5	Over 20
Highest Level of Education	B.A. — Theater Arts	MBA — International Finance
Collects	Sheep (non-real), Books	Wine, Art
Other Interests	Piano, Cooking	The Make-A-Wish Foundation, Racing Cars

I

How Did A Smart Person Like Me End Up In A Mess Like This?

📱 I don't know where to start. I don't know what to do. I can't believe this is happening.

☎ Calm down: Start at the beginning. What happened?

📱 Nick came home last night and told me he was fired. He tried to explain, but I couldn't follow his logic. There didn't seem to be a valid reason.

☎ Did he say anything else?

📱 Not really. He was unusually quiet. I have a thousand questions I'm afraid to ask. What are we supposed to do? When can he get another job? What am I going to do?

☎ Calm down. Everything will be OK.

📱 That's easy for you to say. I cried myself to sleep last night, hoping I would wake up and find this was all a bad dream. But it's not. Instead, I feel sick to my stomach. And scared. And stupid.

☎ Why stupid?

📱 Because I should have known better. How could I have not seen this coming?!

☎ If you can predict the future, then I need you to pick some stocks for me. Stop being so hard on yourself.

📱 I always thought I was a fairly smart person. Now I have no idea what I'm supposed to do. I can't deal with this.

☎ Stop! I know it seems overwhelming, but I promise, you will get through this. Take it one step at a time. Start by calming down; otherwise, you will wear yourself out before you even start.

📱 It's too late! I'm already exhausted. How did this happen?

☎ Let me point out the obvious — it is too late to change the past, so save that analysis for later. Now you have work to do.

I understand, but I don't know what to do. That is the problem. And another reason why I feel so stupid.

 Hey, if it makes it easier, "pull a Freud" and blame it on Mom. There are things you never learned. Sometime we will sit down and have a long talk about our childhoods, and I promise you will even laugh at some of it. Go home and we can talk later.

Laugh? She must be kidding. I was desperately trying to hold back tears. What's that quote about seeing light at the end of the tunnel? Well, when your husband is fired, it's a very long, very dark tunnel. Instead of facing a typical easygoing Saturday — the girls would wake up as I was unpacking groceries, have their swim lesson and then we would go out to lunch and run errands — my life was turned inside out.

I followed Black's advice, although I picked up a few groceries so nothing would look amiss. I then watched the girls from my bedroom window that overlooked the pool, partially so as not to distract them, but more so that no one could see me. And once again I found myself fighting back tears. As a stay-at-home mom, my "job" is to make sure my family is comfortable and happy. Not to worry about financial things. How could I have been so naïve?

I guess it just never occurred to me that I needed to be involved. Plus it made my life easier to let Nick handle most things. I also think I was happy living in my fantasy. The truth is no one actually wants to know the cost of a fantasy, let alone have to pay the price. But I realized, whatever the reasons and whatever the situation, I couldn't do this alone. But I was lucky. Very lucky. I had Black.

You Can Run Away From Home — Not Reality

IM Help! I think we're in serious trouble.

IM Can you be a little more specific?

IM I was telling Nick how upset I was about him being fired, especially since he had worked so hard for the Company for almost 20 years. I said that at least he was paid well and so we should be OK for a while. Instead of comforting me, he started talking in circles about our finances. I asked if he could give me a straight-forward answer, and he got red in the face, muttered under his breath and stormed out of the room.

IM Then what happened?

IM When I tried to find out if he was mad at me for asking or mad at the situation, we started talking. The bottom line is I don't think he knows where we stand financially. Now I'm really scared.

IM If Nick does not know your financial position, how do you know you are in serious trouble? Can I borrow your crystal ball?

IM I don't know it as a fact, but based on some of Nick's roundabout comments, I have a sickening feeling that we don't have any savings. If it wasn't for the girls, I'd get in my car and run away.

IM Run from reality. That is always a good solution. If you calm down, I can help you figure out where you stand financially.

IM How can I calm down? I thought it was bad enough when Nick came home and told me he was fired. But now he's telling me, or rather, not telling me, that we're facing financial ruin. What are we going to use for money? How do I provide for the girls?

IM You have to try and be a little less emotional … and a lot more practical.

IM That's easy for you to say — you have financial security. You don't know what it's like to worry about money. And you don't have any children. I do.

IM I understand the situation. And I understand why you are so upset. But you need to calm down. We will work through this one step at a time. And I promise that you and the girls, and even Nick, will be OK.

IM Maybe I need to take the girls and go visit Emily and Ken in Florida for a month and let Nick sort out this mess. After all, he's responsible for it.

IM STOP! You are not listening. You need to suck it up, grow up and face reality. Your family, which includes Nick, needs you now more than ever. And they need you to help deal with the situation. Not point blame. Not hide from the truth.

IM How am I supposed to help? I haven't worked in years.

IM If you can calm down long enough to accept my help, which will also mean taking your head out of the sand, there is a lot you can do. And not everything is about money. Right now it is late, and you are tired and not thinking clearly. Try to get some sleep and we can start fresh tomorrow. I will call you first thing in the morning.

After that conversation, I wasn't sure I wanted to talk to Black. I was starting to feel embarrassed that I had gone from living in my parents' home to moving to my husband's home. I didn't want to admit that I was a grown woman over the age of 40 who always had the luxury of letting someone else handle all the finances. In fact, if there had been a financial crisis or situation, I not only managed to avoid having to deal with it, I had also managed to avoid even knowing about it.

Nick and I shared almost everything — our feelings, our opinions, our daily lives. But we didn't share financial information or responsibility. He made the money — he managed the money. I trusted him entirely with the financial aspects of the house, although I handled most of the other household responsibilities. I thought I had a sense of things. Now I wasn't so sure.

2
Why Can't Money Grow On Trees?

☎ Good morning. Is this a good time to talk?

☎ As good as any. I'm thinking about going out to buy some lottery tickets. The jackpot's close to $50 million. That would solve all my problems.

☎ Not really. It would only create different ones. Regardless, the odds of winning the lottery are not in your favor, so you need another plan.

☎ How about going to Barnes & Noble and getting a "Get Rich Quick" book?

☎ If I thought you were serious, I would recommend a few books that would help you understand your finances. However, you must know there are no quick fixes, so the only reason you would read a book is to postpone having to deal with your situation.

☎ Actually, I'm hoping that Nick will come up with some miracle.

☎ Is Nick working on a plan? From conversations Nick and I have had over the years, I know finance is not one of his favorite subjects. In fact, he has never shown any interest in financial matters. Do you want me to call him and offer to help?

☎ No! That would make matters even worse. Nick's still in a state of shock and disbelief. And his English pride won't let him ask for help. He'd be embarrassed even talking to you about it.

☎ Men and their precious egos. They could be on their way to the poorhouse and would not stop to ask for directions.

☎ You know Nick well.

☎ I was not talking specifically about Nick; I was referring to just about every man I have ever known. Do you think you could convince Nick to let you help him, and I will help you? Nick will know you are turning to me for help, but it will let him maintain appearances. Now is not the time to kick sand in his face.

☎ Great. Nick gets the sympathy, and I do the work.

☎ Sympathy will not get you out of this mess. Advice and guidance will. Your choice. And speaking of advice, do you know if Nick has spoken with an attorney?

☎ Not that he has mentioned. Why?

☎ Although Texas is a right-to-work state, there may be some legal issues if he had an employment contract or any other relevant labor issues. Rather than making you the middleman on this, too, can I send Nick an e-mail suggesting he might want legal counsel and then recommend an attorney "just in case."

Although I welcomed Black's help, I wasn't sure how Nick would feel about having her come into our lives in such an extremely personal way. It's funny — no matter how well you know someone, no matter how close family or friends might be, when it comes to money, things get weird. You can talk about sports, you can talk about the weather, you can talk about sex, you can, contrary to public opinion, talk about politics. It's all fair game. But discussing personal finances? That's entirely a different matter. A very private matter.

Why Can't I Buy A "Get Rich Quick" Book And Solve All My Problems?

I knew Black was right – I wasn't going to win the lottery. There was no book that would instantly solve my financial problems. And as Black bluntly told me, sympathy wasn't going to help either. She also made it painfully clear that although I wanted to keep my head in the sand, I needed to face reality. That left me with no choice, but to get on with it. And so I decided I had to do it Black's way. She was doing her best to help me clear my head of the emotional aspects of the situation, trying instead to make me look coldly and honestly at the critical issues we were facing.

I knew we were in a huge financial mess, not because of the specific details of our situation, but because neither Nick nor I really knew where we stood. And as uncomfortable as it was, I decided to offer to help Nick with our financial matters. This "transfer of responsibility" was tricky because I didn't have any financial experience. Although I had worked for a number of years before I got married, I never had to spend my money on necessities because I lived with my parents until the day I married Nick. For the next 15 years nothing much changed except Nick paid the bills instead of my Mom and Dad. Then suddenly, I'm being forced to deal with the financial well-being of my family.

IM Quick update before I go to bed. I offered to help Nick out, and we agreed that I'd start doing all the day-to-day financial stuff: paying bills, balancing the checkbook, reviewing bank statements, etc.

IM I thought you were already paying all the bills.

IM No, just small personal stuff that comes out of my secret savings account. For the first time in our marriage, I'll have some idea of our financial picture. But, I don't think I'll like what I see.

IM Welcome to my world, Martha Stewart.

IM At least Martha knows how to run a business empire.

IM True. Just do not ask her advice on personal investments; you could end up in jail.

IM Thanks. I need words of wisdom, and you offer flippant remarks.

IM Lighten up. The point I was trying to make is even smart people make careless mistakes when it comes to money. Enjoy your last night off; tomorrow, you start your new job.

IM Do I have to?

IM Yes, because you need to take responsibility for your financial life. First thing we will do is start to identify and organize your finances. Then we can review everything. But be prepared — you may not like the questions, and you will probably hate the answers. However, down the road you will thank me.

IM Gee — sounds like fun. I can't wait.

Talk about a daunting concept. I was finally going to learn about our finances, which was long overdue, but I was going to do so in the midst of a financial crisis. Not knowing when we'd have any new income meant there was no room for mistakes. I know I had volunteered to help, but I wasn't sure I was in the right frame of mind to make such an overwhelming change to my life. Not to mention the distinct possibility that I might have bitten off more than I could chew.

First Step: Find And Face Financial Facts

E-mail From: Black
Subject: **Finance 101**
Sent: Tuesday, January 27

Good morning. Let me know when you get this and are ready for your first class. I think it would be best to do this by e-mail so you have everything written down in case you want to refer back to a topic.

E-mail From: Red
Subject: **Finance 101**
Sent: Tuesday, January 27

I guess I'm as ready as I'll ever be. Why didn't someone tell me to take some business classes in college? How did I let myself get to this point in life without ever having to deal with any of this? Can you please explain that to me?

You forgot to ask why Mom taught you about the "birds and the bees" instead of about "dollars and sense." I finally get your ostrich head out of the sand, and you want to look backwards. Stop stalling! You are here now. You need to focus on your current situation and move forward.

FIRST, YOU NEED TO DETERMINE:

Money You Have Today

- How much cash do you and Nick have? Checking accounts, savings accounts and investment accounts. Not total assets (we will look at that later) but cash and other liquid assets you can withdraw from the bank.

Additional Money Coming In

- Nick's severance package – how much does he get and for how long?
- Any other money coming in? Expense account reimbursements? Stock option plans?
- Is Nick eligible for unemployment benefits?

Money Going Out

- Reoccurring bills: What bills are currently due? What will be coming in? Is anything past due?
- What are the essentials (food, rent, insurance, utilities) vs. discretionary expenses (dining out, entertainment)?

After you gather all the numbers, we will be able to determine how long the money will last and whether you have saved sufficiently for a rainy day.

E-mail From: Red
Subject: **Finance 101**
Sent: Tuesday, January 27

Apparently Mommy neglected to tell me about a lot of things. Why do you think that is? Do you think it was intentional?

E-mail From: Black
Subject: **Finance 101**
Sent: Tuesday, January 27

Stop stalling and focus on the finance lesson.

E-mail From: Red
Subject: **Finance 101**
Sent: Tuesday, January 27

I'd rather not. I know those are supposed to be straight-forward questions, but I keep re-reading them and (I hate to admit this) I don't have the answers. And I'm not sure where to find them. Let me think about it and get back to you.

E-mail From: Black
Subject: Finance 101
Sent: Tuesday, January 27

No. We are going to do this now! Do you have any financial statements, worksheets or budgets that we can use as a starting point?

E-mail From: Red
Subject: Finance 101
Sent: Tuesday, January 27

You must be kidding! Nick's in marketing and sales, not accounting. I think that was part of why he got so mad at me when I tried to talk to him about it. He must have been embarrassed he didn't have a better handle on our finances.

E-mail From: Black
Subject: Finance 101: Quick & Dirty
Sent: Tuesday, January 27

Nothing to be embarrassed about. Many people do not actively manage their personal finances. Some are very wealthy and have financial advisors, and others, like you, think they will never have to face a financial crisis.

Regardless of your income level, there are two main concepts: Cash Flow (cash in vs. cash out) and Net Worth (assets vs. liabilities — more simply put, what you own vs. what you owe). I will go into more detail later, but right now you need to gather all the relevant information, and then we can do some "quick and dirty" calculations.

You probably have most of this information already so it is merely a matter of getting it accumulated and organized. Grab some file folders or Ziploc bags and start separating financial information into the following categories:

- ❍ Bank Statements
- ❍ Investment Account Statements
- ❍ Severance Package & Other Company Documents
- ❍ Bills: Paid
- ❍ Bills: Due
- ❍ Credit Card Statements
- ❍ Loans and Other Liabilities
- ❍ Other/Miscellaneous

It should not take you long to gather the information. If there is anything that you think might be finance-related, but are not sure, put it in the "other" file. Do not waste time trying to figure it out now. We will go through it in more detail as soon as everything is sorted. Later, I would recommend you start a loose-leaf binder for all the financial documents.

Initially, we need to figure out how much money you have access to immediately — cash as well as other liquid assets, such as stocks and bonds. Other assets, like cars and real estate, we will deal with later. It is critical to get all the financial terms of Nick's severance package.

At the same time, you have to figure out how much you need to pay your monthly bills and any liabilities that have payments due in the next few months.

E-mail From: Red
Subject: Finance 101: Quick & Dirty
Sent: Tuesday, January 27

You call this "quick and dirty?" I think this is overwhelming! I'm not sure I can do this. And I know I can't confront Nick.

E-mail From: Black
Subject: Finance 101: You need the facts
Sent: Tuesday, January 27

Yes, you can. You need to stop thinking you cannot do this and start doing it. At this point I am only asking you to gather information. No technical training required. And as far as "confronting" Nick, you need to change your attitude. You are helping him figure out your finances, so it is only reasonable that you ask him to provide the information you need. Print out the e-mail above and use it as a checklist. And then tell him what information you are missing and ask if he can help find it. If Nick thinks he is providing supporting documents vs. defending himself, he will be more willing to help.

I wondered if Black was bordering on the "warm and fuzzy" by being so protective of Nick's feelings, but then I realized she was being her typical logical self and merely using a clever approach to solve a problem. Our finances would have been a very difficult subject to broach with Nick in good times, let alone bad ones. I think I assumed everything was OK because he never indicated anything to the contrary. But even if I had any doubts, I don't think I would have questioned him, let alone ask him for documentation.

Black was right. If I presented it as a request for information — not a request for explanation — he might be more receptive. And when I finally gathered up the nerve to ask Nick for financial information (and I must confess I didn't have the guts to actually face him, so I sent him an e-mail) he quickly provided it. Interestingly, he seemed relieved.

But the surprise was the immediate feeling of confidence that I experienced merely by asking Nick for financial information. I felt I had overcome a huge emotional hurdle. Black's assurance that I was more than capable of accumulating and organizing all our financial information helped, and I started to think that maybe, just maybe, I could handle this new responsibility in my life.

E-mail From: Red
Subject: Finance 101: You need the facts
Sent: Wednesday, January 28

Believe it or not, Nick provided me with the financial statements I needed. And he contacted the Company to get up-to-date balances on his retirement account. I should have that information in a week or so, and then we can start looking at the bills.

E-mail From: Black
Subject: Finance 101: You need the facts
Sent: Wednesday, January 28

You are still stalling. The list I provided was everything you need to determine immediately. Just because you do not know what your total assets are has nothing to do with figuring out how much money you need to cover expenses.

E-mail From: Red
Subject: Finance 101: You need the facts
Sent: Wednesday, January 28

What's the big rush? A week or two won't make a huge difference. All we're going to do is calculate exactly when we'll be broke!

I know you keep telling me I'm an ostrich, and I need to stop hiding from reality, but I'll be honest with you — I'm not sure I want to. Ignorance is bliss!

E-mail From: Black
Subject: Finance 101: Face the facts ... NOW!
Sent: Wednesday, January 28

No, ignorance is ignorance. You may not like what you will find, but I can promise you that keeping your head in the sand will NOT help the situation. You keep asking me what you can do and I am trying to tell you. If you do not take control of your financial reality, who will? I am willing to help you if you are willing to learn, but remember ... patience is not one of my strong suits.

E-mail From: Red
Subject: Finance 101: Face the facts ... NOW!
Sent: Wednesday, January 28

Obviously, I'm not getting any sympathy from you. And since you're not going to let me ignore the situation, I guess I don't have many alternatives, do I? I know figuring out how much money we have will be the easy part. Not much — which is the problem. But how do I figure out what we need on a monthly basis?

E-mail From: Black
Subject: Finance 101: A Starting Point
Sent: Wednesday, January 28

Since you already have accumulated most of your financial documents, we should be able to get a feel for what you have been spending on a monthly basis. It will at least be a good starting point, although it is highly unlikely you need to maintain that same level of spending.

Let's get the easy part done first, which is listing your assets, and as you gather more information on your expenses, that will help us identify all your liabilities.

Black may have thought sorting out our assets and liabilities was the "easy part." But I didn't. In fact, I didn't understand why it was something we had to do at all. I really didn't understand the relevance or the need to look at our total assets and liabilities when all I was interested in knowing was what money we had available to pay bills in the coming months. The rest, I hoped, would sort itself out with time. At this point I was willing to try and deal with reality, but only for the short-term. Once we got through the crisis, I planned to go back to my blissful ignorance.

Assets And Liabilities — Own Vs. Owe

I was confused. I thought Black had said there were two main concepts – Cash Flow and Net Worth. It seemed to me she was mixing them together, and although I could see where they might be related, I really wanted to tackle one thing at a time. Trying to look at everything at once seemed overwhelming. And was giving me a huge headache.

E-mail From: Red
Subject: **Finance 101: A Starting Point**
Sent: Wednesday, January 28

Can't I just figure out what our monthly bills are and then look at our checking and savings accounts and see how long our money will last? Are you sure I have to figure out our total assets and liabilities?

E-mail From: Black
Subject: **Finance 101: A Starting Point**
Sent: Wednesday, January 28

Yes to both questions. I will explain in more detail as we go along, but right now I need to know what we are working with in terms of what you have vs. what you owe.

E-mail From: Red
Subject: **Finance 101: A Starting Point**
Sent: Wednesday, January 28

You said we were going to do "quick and dirty" calculations. This seems more like "slow and tedious." I know you're the financial expert, but it seems like this could wait.

E-mail From: Black
Subject: **Finance 101: Quick & Dirty – Part 2**
Sent: Wednesday, January 28

Good idea ... we can wait until your checks start bouncing.

The "quick and dirty" referred to looking at the big picture vs. analyzing all the details. And that is basically comparing required monthly expenses vs. cash and other liquid assets. However, you cannot make intelligent decisions about your finances until you know the entire picture. Just because you have enough money in your checking account to pay the next few months of bills does not mean things are OK. On the other hand, you may have very little in your checking account, but if there are investments or assets residing elsewhere, then your situation may not be as dire as you think. That is why you need to uncover and identify everything now. Not later.

Make sense?

At first, no. Upon re-reading, yes. Maybe I didn't want to do the work. More likely, I didn't want to know the answers. But I finally gave up the fight and worked with Black on figuring out our assets and liabilities. And she was right about the assets being the easy part. Once I sat down and actually started reviewing the bank statements line-by-line, everything became more obvious. I was able to total up the amount of cash we had available in all our accounts, and although I had some questions regarding money market accounts vs. checking accounts, everything was less complicated than I had expected. I had not yet received the retirement account statements, but since the severance package provided for three months of continued salary, I knew we would be okay for at least the next few months. It didn't provide for long term security, but knowing we had a little time to sort things out made life a bit more bearable.

> **IM** What are you working on at this hour?

> **IM** Miscellaneous paper work. I just finished filing bank statements in a loose-leaf binder. And I even highlighted the balances so I could easily calculate how much money we have available.

> **IM** Have you gotten the retirement account statements yet?

> **IM** No, but I'm sure as soon as they arrive, I'll have questions, so you'll know when they get here.

> **IM** That's fine. At some point we need to start identifying your other assets since we have never really talked about them. Things like houses and cars.

> **IM** As you know, we don't own our house, we rent it; otherwise, that would have been a big plus on the asset side.

> **IM** Yes, it would have been an asset, but keep in mind that the mortgage would be an offsetting liability, so the net value would basically be the difference between the market value of the house and the balance on the mortgage.

> **IM** Oh. I never thought about it that way. Same thing with the cars?

IM Yes. Your Jaguar is an asset because I bought it for you as a gift, and you own it outright. But since Nick has a car loan, it is a function of which is larger — the market value of the car or the loan balance.

IM You mean you can owe more than a car is worth?

IM Yes, it is called being upside-down. It usually happens when people buy more car than they can really afford and structure the loan to minimize the payments. The amount of the payments applied against the price of the car (vs. the interest) does not keep up with the amount the car is depreciating in value. That was probably more information than you wanted. Sorry. But if you send me the details (year, model, mileage) on both cars, I will get estimated market values.

IM I'm not sure I understood all that, but I can manage sending you those details.

IM I really was not going to take the time to do all the other assets right now, but since we are already talking about it ... Do you own any real estate in England? Or any foreign bank accounts?

IM No real estate. We sold the house in England when we moved to The Netherlands and I think I have identified all of our bank accounts. I found a few small accounts that aren't active and basically are remnants of accounts from when we lived in various countries. Any other assets you can think of?

IM Jewelry. And your paintings and antiques are assets. At this point include them on the assets side, but do not spend any time trying to establish a value because most of the items are not easily turned into cash. And although you could sell some of your jewelry, you would be very unhappy with the price you would receive. Sounds like you have a handle on the assets, so go get some sleep.

Sell my jewelry and furniture? Just the thought gave me a feeling of panic. Did Black really think things were going to get so bad that we were going to have to sell our "things" to pay our bills? Or was I just overreacting to a simple comment? I wasn't sure, and I decided not to ask since I might not like the answer.

☎ Good morning. Checking in on my financial student. Now that you have identified all your assets, are you ready to focus on liabilities?

☎ Not really. Can we take a day off? I don't think I'm ready to face the truth.

☎ Think the numbers will be prettier tomorrow? You have probably uncovered everything already anyway; you have just not calculated a total. Right now I am only interested in the liabilities to be able to determine what expenses we need to plan for in the coming months. Later we will go through them in detail as to interest rates and other terms. So put together a complete list of the liabilities and the monthly payments. You do not have to total them. Yet.

☎ Should I include my husband on the list? At the moment he seems like my biggest liability.

☎ You might think so, but in reality he is your greatest asset.

☎ Really? I'm not sure you can convince me of that.

☎ Nick has the ability to generate income, so unless you plan on getting a job, he is a very valuable asset. Now back to liabilities. What have you found?

☎ The lease on the house is on a month-by-month basis and is horribly expensive now that Nick's no longer receiving a housing allowance. We have Nick's car loan and the note on the piano. And if that wasn't bad enough, I just discovered a personal bank loan.

☎ The house was always expensive, but when it was other people's money, you did not notice. Nothing we can do about the other items. What about credit cards?

☎ Almost too many to count. And offers for more cards seem to arrive almost daily.

☎ Save the offers. Start a separate Ziploc bag for them. Meanwhile, you need to determine how many active charge accounts you have and their current balances.

☎ I already did that. In fact, I was curious the other night about how many credit cards I have, and so I did a quick count. Including bank cards, store cards, gas cards, etc., the number was close to 20! Isn't that ridiculous?! And I haven't even asked Nick how many he has, though I know they make his wallet very fat. I don't think I want to know the total — of either the number of cards or the amount owed on each!

☎ Not knowing will not change the amount. Right now you need to stop all unnecessary spending, especially on credit, so you and Nick need to take as many credit cards as possible out of your wallets and put them somewhere safe.

☎ I know we can't afford to keep charging stuff. But I'm afraid we can't afford to pay for everything we have already charged. I'll be happy if we can afford to pay the minimums until the balances are paid off.

☎ I understand. Right now pay only the minimum amount due. Sometime in the next few weeks you will need to determine how much you owe on all your credit cards so we can make intelligent decisions regarding all your debt. But be prepared. Most people carry way too much debt, and it will drag you down ... both financially and emotionally.

☎ So I have permission to keep my head in the sand a little longer?

☎ Yes. At least until we figure out your monthly expenses. Once we've done that, I want to go back and analyze your debt in detail. For now just list the liability and the monthly payment.

Wow — I had permission to ignore the truth. But as I started listing each liability and the monthly payment, I couldn't avoid also looking at the outstanding balance. And so I started another column on my worksheet. After several hours, and some very upsetting investigation, I finally had to admit the truth to Black. I knew things weren't going to be pretty, but I didn't realize how ugly it could turn out. For the amount we owed on our credit cards we could have bought Nick's car outright and never had a car note. I don't know whether to scream or cry! Or both!

IM I'm so glad you're online. I'm too upset to talk.

IM Is everyone OK?

IM Physically, yes. Financially, no. We're sick. Very sick. I think almost terminal.

IM Can you be a little more specific?

IM I was working on our monthly liability worksheet. I listed the liabilities I knew about, including credit cards. Then I went back to fill in the monthly payments. I couldn't help but notice the balance amounts on the statements and so I added those up too. The number is unbelievable. We owe so much money. I feel sick.

IM I understand. But we can and will work through this. Remember you do not have to pay off everything immediately.

IM Immediately? I don't know how we're ever going to get ourselves out of debt. This could take years and years to pay off. How did this happen? What are we going to do? Can you be worse than broke?

IM Take a deep breath and calm down. Although you obviously do not like the number, at least you know what you are facing. And some of the liabilities, like Nick's car and the piano, have offsetting assets, so it is not as bad as it looks.

IM Trust me, it still looks bad. How are we ever going to deal with all this debt?

IM No, you trust me. We will deal with your debt, but we will do it later. At the moment I am more concerned about the associated monthly expenses than I am about the total amount of debt. Now may be a good time for you to take a break and go spend some time with the girls.

IM Maybe now is the time to take the girls and go visit Emily and Ken.

IM That will not solve anything. But a trip to the park might be good for everyone. I may even try and swing by. And if it makes you feel any better, remember you are not alone.

IM That's true. And I do appreciate all your help with this.

IM Thanks, but I was actually talking about the fact you were not alone in terms of the debt. Many people today carry too much debt, and never realize the extent of it until it reaches crisis proportions.

That's Black, all facts and no emotion. I wasn't sure I was prepared to continue working on this. The amount of debt we had was a staggering amount, and the thought of trying to figure out how to pay it all off was overwhelming. I wasn't sure there was a way out. I wasn't sure there would have been even if Nick hadn't been fired. I began to realize that Nick and I looked like we had money because we had a lot of expensive assets. The reality was we also had a huge amount of debt. We really only gave an impression of wealth. The numbers proved otherwise. Sadly, our lifestyle was an image, it wasn't reality.

I took Black's advice to go to the park. As I watched Natasha and Sawyer on the swings, and, hearing their laughter, I realized that although I didn't like our financial picture, I had to deal with it. If not for myself, then for my daughters. I knew we could cut back on our spending, although that wouldn't solve much, as the damage had already been done. I hoped Black had some magic words of wisdom. And then, almost magically, she appeared, except of course you couldn't help but hear her Ferrari before you could actually see her. And as I watched her walk towards me in her perfectly pressed designer jeans and crisp white shirt, I couldn't help but laugh to myself as I wondered if we were really related. And then I asked her my million-dollar question, "What do we do now?" And she casually told me to enjoy the afternoon with the girls.

Where Has All Our Money Gone?

IM Thanks for coming by the park this afternoon. The girls were thrilled to see you, and it was a nice break for me.

IM No problem. You needed it. Should I ask why you are online this late or leave well enough alone?

IM I just made myself a cup of tea, and although I'm not sure how long it will be until we're out of money, I'm paying bills.

IM If I had known tea calmed you down, I would have had a case delivered days ago.

IM Very funny. No, I think it's because there are only five bills and they're all small. I'll worry about the big ones when they arrive.

IM OK. Good night and pleasant dreams.

That was an easy conversation with Black since she didn't give me grief for not being concerned about the big bills. I wasn't sure why she didn't, but I decided to enjoy the guilt-free evening. I finished the bills and enjoyed my tea. And the quiet of the house. I tried not to worry about tomorrow but wasn't very successful. I had this hollow feeling in the pit of my stomach and tried to escape by watching an old movie on TV, but even that didn't help. I had a feeling I'd be worrying about tomorrows for a very long time.

☎ Good morning. Just checking in. What are your plans for the day?

☎ Don't know. I figured you'd have more of your financial torture tests for me.

☎ You are doing great. Putting together your list of assets and liabilities may not have been a pleasant task, but it is an extremely important one. Now you need to identify and review your expenses.

☎ Not to sound stupid, but how do I do that?

☎ I knew you were going to ask that, so I already put together a detailed e-mail. It is waiting for you.

☎ I have a few things I need to do this morning before I get on the computer. Can you give me a sneak preview so I don't panic when I get online?

☎ Quit overreacting. First step is more information-gathering. We are going to analyze your bills and spending habits by going through the details of your checking account, credit card statements and any other paper trails we can find.

☎ Sounds like I am going to need a whole bunch of Ziploc bags to get through this nightmare.

☎ And different colored highlighters. Oh, and some ledger paper, too!

☎ Ledger paper? Do I need one of those green-shade visors and rubber bands for my sleeves like in a Dickens novel? There has got to be a better way to do this. Can't we do this on the computer?

☎ We can use ledger paper, computer spreadsheets or even computer programs specifically designed for personal finances, but the bottom line is you need to understand where your money is going. I am hoping you have enough of a paper trail to reconstruct the last six months of cash flow.

☎ Correct me if I'm wrong, but what has been spent is gone. Nothing we can do about it now. I need to figure out how to deal with today's bills. And tomorrow's. And the day after.

☎ That is what I am trying to do, if you will let me. By looking at recent history we will identify all your reoccurring expenses to try and avoid surprises. Or in your case, panic. And, even more importantly, it will allow you to see where your money has gone which will help you make informed decisions regarding future expenditures.

☎ As long as we're going to look backwards, can we discuss why all this is so new to me? Until this week I've never even looked at a financial statement, yet alone tried to understand one.

☎ We do not have the luxury of time to go that far backwards. We need to focus on the past six months, not return to your childhood.

☎ My childhood?

☎ Yes. But we are not going there now.

☎ Maybe you don't need to talk about personal history, but I do. If not today, soon. Meanwhile, will you do me a favor? You've made a career of dealing with numbers and finances. In fact, I bet you used ledger paper instead of drawing paper when you were a kid. Rather than make me figure this out on my own, would you please send me a cheatsheet or checklist?

☎ I already did. That is the e-mail I told you was waiting for you. But now, I need you to do me a favor. Stop being so hard on yourself for not knowing how to do something that you were never exposed to or even told was important to understand.

That was all fine and good, but I still had this nagging feeling that I needed to understand how I got here.

3
Things I Wasn't Taught And
The Lessons I Learned All Too Well!

IM Good to see you finally got online today. Are you working on my "Where is Your Money Going?" E-mail?

IM No. It's overwhelming, and I'm in a really bad mood. And extremely angry.

IM At Nick? You need to cut him some slack. It is not as if he asked to be fired. He is going through his own hell right now.

IM Glad you have sympathy for Nick, but I'm not mad at him. Well I am, but he's not the target at the moment. I'm mad at myself for being so incredibly stupid.

IM You sound like a broken record this morning. You are not stupid. However, you have been living in a fairy tale, and now it is time to enter the big-bad world.

IM I really am NOT in the mood for your clever comments. It's very easy for you to be a know-it-all because financially you do know it all. I, on the other hand, am merely your dumb kid sister. For someone with a great education and smart parents, I seem to be clueless about so many things.

IM Done venting?

IM No! How did I get to my age without understanding what was going on? How could my life — and my family's life — be such a mess? How could I be so stupid?

IM Are you done now?

IM For the moment.

IM When we were kids, I might have thought you were my dumb kid sister, but I have grown up — a little — since then. You are many things, but stupid is not one of them. The main difference between us, even though we started at the same place, is we traveled very different roads and were exposed to very different things.

IM It seems to me that I picked the wrong road, and now I'm at a dead end.

IM If it makes you feel any better, you were led down the road you traveled. And you are not at a dead end, but rather a crossroad. However, where you go next will be up to you.

IM Thanks for the philosophy. Using your logic means I'm really in trouble. If I'm not able to figure out how I got here, or who led me down this road, then I'm obviously not going to be able to figure out where to go next.

IM This is not very productive. We are getting nowhere fast. We need to discuss this before you make yourself sick. Call me.

Until recently, I had thought that my life and the path that I had taken were right for me. I had the chance to travel the world and enjoy all the benefits of being a corporate wife, without having to juggle my own career. Once we settled in the States, we moved into a beautiful house in a premier neighborhood. The best part is we have two beautiful and healthy daughters, and I have enjoyed the luxury of being a stay-at-home mom. But now I felt like I had made some very wrong turns. All of a sudden my life was extremely frightening. Although the circumstances that brought me down this road weren't my fault (or even Nick's), I still felt I had significantly contributed to our current misery by not being aware of our finances.

Looking Forward To The Past

I wasn't sure I was ready for another conversation with Black. She wouldn't let me wallow in self-pity, although I felt like I deserved the right to feel sorry for myself. Especially since I was willing to take the blame for much of our current predicament. But I also knew that I wouldn't be able to avoid her, so I took a deep breath and dialed.

☎ Is this a good time to talk?

☎ You tell me. You sound desperate.

☎ Sorry. I'm just overwhelmed. I go from being incredibly mad to crying to back to being mad. Excluding Nick, who's currently in his own little world, you're the only person who knows what's going on and I can talk to.

☎ Aren't I special? I was hoping that once you started working on the finances and focused on moving forward you would be OK, but you keep wanting to blame yourself for the situation. Unless we can get past the past, we are going to have a hard time moving forward.

☎ But I keep questioning how I got here. And I feel very guilty.

☎ You are Jewish. Guilt trips are a way of life. As far as how you got here, to me that does not seem as important as where you go next. Which brings us back to looking at your financial situation. But it is your call whether we look backward or forward.

☎ I really need to understand how I got here, but I don't want you to accuse me of stalling. Can we make a deal? Can we discuss this today if I promise to focus on the finances tomorrow?

☎ Tomorrow is Saturday. If you are willing to spend your Saturday doing finances, then I am willing to spend my Friday traveling down memory lane. However, you need to remember that I majored in economics and international finance. Not philosophy and child psychology.

☎ Well, I wish I had majored in finance instead of theater arts. I might not have enjoyed it as much, but at least I wouldn't be in this predicament today.

☎ Really? Remember, Nick and I went to the same business school. Has his MBA made any difference to your financial situation? It is not as much a function of what you studied, but rather how you approach life. It is your experiences and the decisions you make along the way, not your college degree. Although a few accounting courses would not have hurt you. But as I said early this morning, it also goes back to your childhood.

☎ So you're saying I have spent my life doing the wrong things and making the wrong decisions? Great. I feel so much better now. Thanks.

☎ Stop with the drama. It is not an issue of right or wrong. It is about choices and experiences. Think of life as a journey, not a destination. We took different roads.

☎ I know I was the one who wanted this discussion, but if you don't mind, I need more specifics and less tee-shirt slogans.

☎ Fine. Then think about how we grew up and the differences in our personalities. I was hard-headed and independent and off to conquer the world. You, on the other hand, were the "good daughter" who valued a family life. You chose a fairly traditional path; therefore, many decisions were already made for you. I chose a life that forced me to learn how to survive on my own. We went in opposite directions. We learned different things.

☎ Yes, but it seems to me that you learned the most important life lessons. The ones about money and handling your finances.

☎ I had no choice. Unlike you, no one was taking care of me. But how to handle money is not a life lesson, as you call it, but a practical application. The life lesson would be learning the true value of money. And it took me years to learn that.

☎ Right now, I need to focus on how best to handle money. I don't have the time, nor the desire, to figure out the value of money.

☎ You will, but for now I think it is safe to say this is probably the first time in your life you have stopped to think about any of these things.

☎ You're right. You left home at 16. I was protected, maybe overprotected, at home until I was 26. And then I got married, moved overseas and let Nick take care of everything.

Which, if you fast forward 15 years, leads me to my current predicament. How could I have been so stupid?

☎ Sheltered is a better word. The fact Mom and Daddy subsidized and stabilized your early 20's did not help, although you were already accustomed to having them do things, make decisions and take responsibility. But, it was not a deliberate plan to make your later life miserable. And remember, you did not ask to be the baby of the family!

You Can't Pick Your Parents, But Can You Blame Them?

Although I liked the idea of shifting the responsibility to someone else, I wasn't sure that I approved of our parents taking the blame. It didn't seem fair. They did a good job of raising both Black and me.

☎ So am I supposed to blame Mommy and Daddy?

☎ No. This is not about placing blame, but about realizing that so much of how we approach finances as adults is a result of our childhoods.

☎ This is going to be very philosophical, isn't it?

☎ Yes, which is why I really did not want to do this. I would prefer to spend the time on more practical topics. Or at least ones where you can see the results of your efforts. What we are talking about now has no definitive answers, only things to think about. For centuries people have philosophized whether our values are inherited, taught or learned through experience. I do not pretend to know the answer, but I believe values, and not just those related to finances, are firmly established during childhood. Our parents had a lot to do with them.

☎ But we learned good things from them, not bad. They gave us a good home and there's no question that they loved us.

☎ And how did you learn things from Mom and Daddy? By listening to their words? Or watching their actions?

☎ Should I lie down on a couch before I answer, Dr. Black? I don't know. Probably both. But overall more from what they did, than what they said. Especially Daddy. He was such a quiet, gentle man who never said very much. In fact, I am not sure I can even remember any specific conversations. But he was always there to listen.

☎ And what about Mom?

☎ I think this is a trick question. Her strong personality and outspoken nature meant I always knew where she stood on a subject. Ranging from topics as uninteresting, at least to me, about how much money Mrs. Kay spent on clothing and maids to her strong opinions on how other parents were not raising their children properly. So I change my initial response. I learned from Mommy by listening to her words, not her actions.

☎ Next question. Off the top of your head, if you had to name one value you learned from Daddy, what would it be?

☎ That's easy. Love is unconditional.

☎ And from Mom?

☎ Even easier. Money can buy happiness.

☎ Interesting.

☎ Is that all you are going to say? And what about you?

☎ This is not about me. Over the years I have had to make some difficult decisions and so I have done a lot of soul-searching. I have had time to contemplate these questions. For now, I think it would be useful for you to think about your answers and call me when you want to talk further. Then I might tell you what my answers were.

So I made myself a very large cup of tea and sat down. For the first time I truly began to think about how my parents influenced me. I started with my father, since he was clearly the least complicated parent. He was a very quiet man, who was kind and extraordinarily good-natured. I have wonderful memories of him and things we did together, such as watching reruns of *Benny Hill* and *Monty Python* and laughing out loud. Although we didn't have conversations about important topics, he was always there for me, always supportive and caring. His love was unconditional, and he taught me through his actions — like taking me to school in the mornings or asking me about my day and truly listening to my replies — that it was important to be there for the people you loved and that words weren't always necessary. I had never stopped to think about any of this before, and now that I did, I was amazed by the values I learned from him without ever realizing it.

My Mom, on the other hand, is a far more complex person. The more I thought about our relationship, the more confused I became. And I was concerned that the most memorable lesson I had learned from her was "money could buy happiness." It wasn't as if it was any specific conversations we had; it was her overall attitude. Looking back, there were countless examples of "things" and "stuff" she wanted (mink coats, a house in the Hamptons, a Mercedes) that she claimed would have made her happy. At the time it seemed logical, but now it sounded so superficial. I wanted to discuss all this with Black, but first I wanted to learn a little more about me.

☎ I have always thought my personality was very much like Daddy's and yours was more like Mommy's. Do you think personalities are inherited?

☎ The question of nature vs. nurture has been debated for years. Next, you will want to know if birth order had anything to do with your situation. And before you ask, there are certain characteristics attributed to youngest children. And they are very different that those used to describe first-born or middle-born. And you are the baby of the family. And it sounds like you are stalling.

☎ No, I am trying to figure myself out. I am trying to understand why I shied away from potentially difficult conversations, and why I just accepted everything I was told without asking any questions. Plus I wonder if witnessing all those heated battles between you and Mommy would explain why I hate confrontation?

☎ Possibly. Probably. Hell, I do not know. All I know is there are a lot of contributing factors to how you become who you are. And different combinations result in different people. Think of yourself as an end result.

☎ But what would explain why you're so different than me? And approach life so differently?

☎ Death is the reason we approach life so differently.

☎ Excuse me?!

☎ When I was growing up, two people I dearly loved — Gary and Uncle David — died very young. In retrospect, I think it dramatically influenced how I looked at everything. The future was not a guarantee, but merely an incentive. And that changed my priorities. And how I approached life. End of discussion. Now can we get back to you?

☎ Yes, but first I need to put in a load of laundry. I'll call you back in a few minutes.

I couldn't get my mind off her death comment. I was too young to remember Gary in any detail, but I knew he was the stereotypical boy-next-door, and was probably Black's first crush. Uncle David, Mom's kid brother, was very much part of our family. To Black, he was the older brother she always wanted, and she idolized him. I can still remember her screams early in the morning when she was the one to get the phone call saying he was dead. (She answered the phone and the other person mistakenly thought it Mom and told her the devastating news.) The powerful impact death had made on Black would explain a lot of her "devil-may-care" attitude and why she sees things differently than most people.

Does Mother Always Know Best?

I realized I needed to honestly think about my relationship with my Mom. When I became a mother at the age of 35, there was a dramatic change in our relationship, but for most of my life we had been very close. Mom and Black were almost always at odds with one another, but I tended to be more doting and accepting.

☎ I'm back. First load is in. Only two more after that. Funny how Nick getting fired changed things. I used to think I'd love to have someone do all the housework. Now I'm just going to miss having somebody come in once a week to do the heavy cleaning.

☎ Now you sound like Mom.

☎ Really? She always complained about having to do housework. She used to tell me it wasn't that she couldn't afford a maid, but rather that they would never clean to her satisfaction. And she was certain they would steal something.

☎ When you were very young, we had a cleaning woman who came only a few times before Mom decided to fire her. For the exact reasons you stated, which is my point. Mom focused on the negative, not the positive. Mom takes the "half-full glass" to a new extreme, in that she thinks it is not only half-empty but someone spit in it.

☎ You're being very hard on her. And remember your financial circumstances are very different. Can you even remember the last time you cleaned your own house?

☎ 1980. But you are missing the point. I am trying to make you think about what you have listened to your whole life. For as long as I can remember, Mom has focused on what she thinks she missed — a college education, a career or having enough money to buy whatever she wanted. She never seemed to appreciate what she had.

☎ I know she always seemed to think the grass was greener everywhere else, but now that you mention it, I can't think of any time she seemed grateful for anything she had. Or even content.

☎ No. She has managed to convince herself, and you, that the things that are "missing" would have brought her great happiness.

☎ I think they would have. She always talked about wanting to go to college, and have a career, and nice clothing and expensive vacations.

☎ Maybe the education and the career would have made her happy, but not the "things."

☎ How do you know? You have ALL those things.

☎ Experience. I tested her theory. When I was growing up, Mom kept telling me if she had a Mercedes, a full-length mink coat and expensive clothing, she would have been happy. She constantly told me I should make sure that I get those things, although she neglected to mention that what she really meant was that I should find a man to buy those things for me. So by the time I was 21, I had entered the corporate world and was working late almost every night, struggling to overcome the barriers of being a woman in a man's industry. However, I did buy my first Mercedes, my first mink, and I started to accumulate clothing and other things. And guess what? They did not make me any happier.

☎ Are you crazy? I'd have been thrilled.

☎ Maybe for a short time; then the newness wears off, and you start looking for something else to acquire. You can never be content with your acquisitions because you are never done. Trust me, I have spent most of my adult life accumulating things, and they do not bring you happiness.

☎ Sorry, but it's very easy for someone with lots of money to say money won't buy happiness. Us mere mortals don't see things the same way, especially those of us whose husbands have just lost their jobs.

☎ I understand, but I am talking about things that go beyond the basic need for food, shelter and clothing. I am saying non-essential things — expensive cars, bigger houses and designer clothing — will not make you happy. Big bank accounts give you peace of mind and security, which may make you happy, but that is a totally different issue.

☎ OK. If I admit money won't buy happiness, will you at least admit it makes life much easier?

☎ Absolutely! Money definitely makes misery more acceptable. And that is another theory I have tested extensively.

I wasn't sure I totally agreed with Black's opinion. However, given our current financial crisis, I didn't think it made sense to argue the point with her. I knew better than to try to debate the issue with her when she could fall back on experience, and I could only defend myself with theory.

☎ OK. You tell me that acquiring the things Mommy dreamed of didn't bring you everlasting happiness. But at least her values pushed you towards a successful career. For me, it led to years of making bad decisions in terms of buying things. I thought things were important and would make me happy, so I bought lots of stuff. And along the way I also managed to acquire lots of debt. And I didn't save enough. All of which have brought me to my current state of misery.

☎ The big difference was you returned home after graduating from college and Mom loaned you money to buy clothing and shoes, rather than suggesting you rent an apartment and learn how to support yourself. And then you married Nick and let him take care of things. I spent a lot of money when I first started working. And because I was making good money, that meant I could buy more expensive things and get into bigger debt.

☎ Well, in a sick kind of way, I feel better knowing you made the same mistakes.

☎ Misery loves company. Happy to help.

☎ Another tee-shirt? Got any more?

☎ How about the cliché ... Do as I say, not as I do ... did Mom ever use that on you?

☎ Yes. A lot. Why?

☎ I heard it all the time and it always pissed me off. And although I cross-examined her on many issues, I never did when it came to material possessions. I should have. Mom talked about all the things that would make her happy, but she never bought them. With the exception of the mortgage, they had no debt. Granted this was in large part due to her generation's experience with the Depression, but the bottom line is that she chose financial security over buying things. Things that she said would bring her happiness.

☎ That's true. And she also saved money. Now I feel really miserable. You're saying that if I had paid more attention to her actions, saving rather than spending, we'd be in a much better financial position today. So it really does go back to being my fault.

☎ Stop with the guilt! It is not a blame game. I am trying to help you understand how you got to where you are so you can make smart decisions starting now. Besides, Mom was a secret saver. It was not until after Daddy died that we ever knew how much money she had saved. Listening to Mom, it always sounded like they could never afford to do things, and that was why she was unhappy.

☎ Why do think she did that?

☎ Not sure. In fact, when Daddy died, she really did not want me to know all the details. But since I was handling all the legal and financial matters, she had no choice.

☎ I understand not wanting anyone to know your financial secrets. But why didn't she use some of the money to buy herself some happiness?

☎ Not sure about that, either. But I am not interested enough to ask her. Are you?

☎ You must be kidding. I avoid confrontation at all costs! I think I'll do something safe and check on the laundry.

Theoretically We Need More Practical Knowledge

Black got me thinking about the fact we grew up without ever really talking about what money is and isn't, and what it can and can't do — either in philosophical or practical terms. I began to wonder why. I knew it was too big a topic to broach at this point, but it didn't stop me from questioning my own personal experiences — or lack thereof.

☎ OK. I'm back. Your comment about Mommy being a secret saver really bothers me. Now that I think more about it, I realize she was very involved with the family finances. Daddy made the money, but she wrote all the checks so she obviously understood the basics of finance. Or at least bookkeeping. Why didn't she ever teach me about any of this?

☎ I have no idea. Ask her.

☎ No thanks. I'd rather guess at her answer. Which I'm sure would first be a complaint that she had to do it instead of Daddy, and then she would blame the school system, saying they should have taught me.

☎ Agree. And she would probably be right.

☎ About Daddy or the schools?

☎ Maybe both. For some reason, people think men should be inherently good at dealing with money, just like they are supposed to be good at sex, yet nobody tells them how to do it. They are just expected to know.

☎ I'm not sure I understand your analogy. Sex is pretty straight-forward and was explained in health class. However, dealing with money was never taught in school to either the girls or the boys!

☎ Forget about the sex comment. I forgot how sheltered you were. Are. However, the point I was making was how could you expect anyone, male or female, to be automatically good at something that is a learned skill.

☎ So you think the schools are to blame?

☎ There you go with the blame game again, but in this case I might agree with you. I hated school. With the exception of the 3R's — reading, 'riting and 'rithemetic — I could never figure out why we had to waste time on everything else. I spent more time figuring out how to get out of doing assignments than I would have spent actually doing them. But the upside was I learned other skills, like debating and negotiating, which proved very useful in my career.

☎ And I was an exemplary student. I loved school and learning about history and studying literature, and look where it got me. Why is that, anyway? You learn all this stuff in school and very little of it has any practical application once you're in the real world. It would have been very helpful if they had taught, or at least introduced us to, some life lessons in the school program.

☎ Life lessons involve value judgments. Whose values are you going to teach? Especially when there is a separation of church and state and you cannot bring religion into the picture. Sounds like you are trying to delegate parental responsibilities to the teachers. Teachers who are already overworked and underpaid.

☎ Sorry. I never expected such a strong reaction from you. It's not like you have children.

☎ The educational system is one of my pet peeves. I think it is a political nightmare. We entrust our teachers with our children — our future — but do not give them the resources and support to be successful. It is despicable.

☎ So forget about life lessons. How about adding some practical, financial applications? Would that be asking too much?

☎ Mom used to joke that the reason I excelled in math was because I substituted dollars for apples and oranges. Why not do that as part of the curriculum? Learning to balance a checkbook is really only addition and subtraction.

☎ I'm not sure the normal kid would be any more interested in money than apples and oranges.

☎ You mean Natasha would have no preference between counting apples and oranges and figuring out how much money she has to save to buy a new Barbie? Later you could introduce the concept of budgeting, which is only a comparison of which numbers are bigger — the money you have or the money you want to spend. And what things have to be eliminated to make the numbers equal? This would also introduce the concept of priorities. There are always ways to use realistic examples to teach fundamental concepts.

☎ What a shame that schools don't teach math your way.

☎ I agree. But there is nothing that stops you from teaching the basics of money to the girls.

☎ I will. As soon as I understand them myself.

I started thinking about my formal education, both public school and college, and although I knew there was value in all the subjects I studied, I also knew that if just a fraction of my schooling had been about practical subjects, I'd have been much better off today. But I decided not to focus on what had been "missing" from my education and instead concentrate on the fact I had inadvertently stumbled across a way to better prepare my children.

I See My Reflection In My Car

📱 I know you're probably tired of talking to me today, but I had to call you. I'm sitting here at the end of the school pick-up line. I got here late, so I'm stuck for a while, and started thinking.

☎ And now you want to kill time talking to me. Thanks. Are you thinking about the fact you will probably need to send Natasha to public school next year?

📱 No, I was actually thinking about cars. I hadn't thought about Natasha's schooling for next year since this semester is already paid for, but thanks for bringing it up. More bad news.

☎ Sorry. Go back to the cars. You know it is one of my favorite subjects, but not something I ever thought you cared about. At least not once I bought you your beloved Jaguar.

📱 I know, but I'm sitting here and looking at an amazing collection of cars. There's probably a million dollars worth sitting in this line!

☎ And you are surprised? You are in a carpool line at an expensive, private school. Any great sports cars?

📱 Obviously you're not a mom. Kids are supposed to ride in the back seat, which rules out sports cars since there are no back seats. However, between the carpool line and the parking lot there's a showroom full of Range Rovers and other huge SUVs. Not to mention a full assortment of Mercedes.

☎ I am impressed you can identify the cars. Is this going somewhere?

📱 Yes. Until a few days ago I assumed the person with the more expensive car had more money. Now, thanks to you, I realize the mom who drives the Mercedes could be carrying a large car loan while the mom who drives the Toyota may own it outright. In that case, the mom with the less expensive car may actually be "richer."

☎ Or vice versa. And your point is?

📱 I wanted you to know that your efforts haven't been wasted and that I'm starting to look at material things differently. And sitting here, I realized the car you drive doesn't necessarily represent who you really are, either in financial or personal terms.

☎ Idealistically, you are correct. But cars are probably a poor example to use.

📱 Why?

☎ As you already figured out, sometimes people's cars do not honestly reflect their financial situation. Which means people do not necessarily buy what they need, but instead may buy what they think is a reflection of who they are or who they want to be. But if you analyze it carefully, cars are usually an accurate reflection of people's values.

📱 I thought you'd agree with me, not start a philosophical discussion.

☎ Sorry, but you started it. And it is important for you to realize we live in a very commercial and status-conscious society. And whether you like it or not, "things" have become status symbols. And cars are probably the most common status symbol, as almost everyone has one. Or more.

📱 Says the woman who has how many cars? Including more than one Ferrari!

☎ This conversation is not about me. But for the record, Larry bought all but one of my cars and all of them are paid for and in my name. And without going into details, the way his attorney structured the prenuptial agreement almost forces me to collect expensive cars. Not to mention other "things." But that is another topic entirely and, although interesting and even amusing, not relevant to this conversation.

📱 But that doesn't change the fact you drive a Ferrari.

☎ I admit I am a "motor head." As a kid I dreamed of owning a Corvette. Now I drive a Ferrari. Same dream, different price point.

📱 Then I am confused. Again. You rationalize your Ferrari, yet accuse other people of buying cars as status symbols.

☎ I am talking in general terms, and you are looking at a specific example. I know some very wealthy people who could afford to write a check for an entire car dealership, yet choose to drive modest cars. It is a function of what is important to you. Think about what Mom and Daddy drove when we were growing up.

📱 Mom drove the Caddy and Daddy drove an old Olds.

☎ Do you remember when Daddy bought the Cadillac?

📱 No, I was too young. But I do remember Mommy always complaining that for what they had paid for the Caddy, she could have had a Mercedes.

☎ Did she ever tell you the whole story?

📱 Only that Daddy wanted a Cadillac, not a Mercedes.

☎ Daddy had dreamed of owning a Cadillac since he was a little boy. For him, it represented success. When one of his childhood friends died unexpectedly, he decided to finally buy the Cadillac. It was the first brand-new car they ever owned. He was very proud of that car. And the fact he could write a check for it.

📱 Do you think the car made him happy?

☎ Hard to say. There have been many times I have thought about it and wished I had asked him. But I am certain listening to Mom wish they had bought a Mercedes probably spoiled his excitement.

📱 If they were the same price, I would have picked the Mercedes over the Cadillac, too.

☎ They probably were close in price at that time. But Mom knew nothing about cars, so she wanted it purely for the prestige. Daddy wanted to fulfill a childhood dream.

📱 That's an interesting point. Even if I had thought about any of this, which I never have, I'd never have looked at it that way.

☎ We all value things differently. Unfortunately, sometimes our values get off track. We buy things because we think they will make us happy. Or because we feel the need to keep up with the Joneses. Or sometimes to prove we are better than the Joneses.

📱 We? I'm glad you include yourself in this because you do more than your fair share of supporting the economy.

☎ Years ago, when I was playing the corporate game, I went through a stage of unnecessary spending because I thought it would enhance my image as a successful executive.

📱 And today you rationalize your excessive spending how?

☎ Excessive is a relative term. But I rationalize my spending because I do not have an incentive to save. The prenuptial agreement has created a "use it or lose it" situation. But this is still not about me. I know why I buy things. Do you?

📱 I thought I did, but now I'm starting to question a lot of our decisions. We probably have wasted a lot of money trying to keep up with the Joneses, and I'm not even sure who the Joneses are. That's pretty stupid, isn't it?

☎ It is not my place to pass judgment. Each person has to decide for themselves what is important. It is one thing if you truly enjoy the prestige value. It is a totally different thing if you are doing it because of peer pressure or to be accepted by society. The key is to decide what is important in your life. The right financial decisions, and purchases, will follow.

📱 One quick question because I'm getting close to the front of the line. Is it wrong to want nice things?

☎ Nothing is wrong with wanting them. And nothing is wrong with working hard to achieve them. The problem is with thinking they will bring you happiness. But society, with a lot of help from Madison Avenue, has convinced us you can buy happiness. Not only "statement" cars, but big houses, expensive jewelry, designer clothing. The list is endless. Think about all the status symbols. The one I find most amusing is the concept of trophy wives. That pretty much sums up the ultimate in conspicuous consumption.

📱 Well, that's one thing I don't have to worry about. You may be Larry's trophy wife, but no one would ever accuse me of that. But I wouldn't be insulted if someone called me a trophy mom. Got to go, I can see Natasha waving at me.

I realized that I had never thought about my values and what shaped them. I knew that society, as well as my Mom, put a high value on accumulating things, but I had never realized the huge impact this had on our financial and personal decision-making. I had a hard time with the idea that perhaps we had been letting our possessions define us. Little did I realize it went even further than material possessions.

Who Are The "Joneses?" And Why Are We Trying To Keep Up With Them?

I remembered a conversation I had overheard a few weeks ago at the school playground about potty training. One mom was saying how her daughter had been potty trained at an earlier age. The tone of her voice implied her daughter had "won" and was smarter. However, given the subject matter, and knowing the smart-ass comments I'd get back in return, I decided not to mention this to Black.

☎ I just tried calling the house and Nick said you and the girls were still out. Have a minute?

📱 Yup. We're at McDonald's. And before you say anything, I only bought some fries for them, and they've been playing for over an hour. Pretty cost-effective, don't you think?

☎ Yes. Something you said got me thinking.

📱 Now there's role reversal.

☎ Do you really think Larry sees me as a trophy? I personally think I am not attractive enough and I am much too independent and stubborn to be a trophy wife. But that would explain many things.

📱 I hate to burst your bubble, but I was just trying to be funny. You may not be a trophy wife, but if it makes you feel better, you're certainly an expensive wife.

☎ Thanks. Anything else before I hang up on you?

📱 Yes. Do you think there's such a thing as a trophy kid?

☎ Never thought about it, but obviously you have. Why do you ask?

📱 Because it seems like some parents are always trying to compare their kids to other kids to show how much better they are.

☎ I am not sure they are really saying their children are better. They may be trying to prove they are better parents. Think about it. The only proof you will have of how good you did as a parent is when you see how your children turn out later in life. We are a fast-food society. We want instant gratification. So parents have to come up with ways to measure their success. For example, Mom still brags I was reading *The New York Times* in third grade. So what?

📱 She reminds me of that every time the topic of Natasha and reading comes up. It's as if you being an advanced reader proves she was a good mother, and I have to measure up to that standard. Yet, I can remember growing up and her telling me, "I'm raising my kids, not racing them." Seems like a contradiction.

☎ You want consistency from a woman who preached: "Do as I say, not as I do?"

📱 True. How silly of me!

☎ In any event, it is human nature to try and find a way to prove you are good at what you do.

📱 But using kids as benchmarks? That's just not right.

☎ I agree. Just because some people think parenting is a competitive sport does not mean you have to participate.

📱 I don't! But why do some people?

☎ In a status-conscious society, everything is competitive, and things like consumer goods and grades are tangibles that are easy to measure and compare. And if the mother is used to a competitive work environment, then her ability to perform in some measurable way probably takes on added importance.

📱 Sounds like the kids are pawns, not people.

☎ Which would explain Cheerleader Moms and Little League Dads. They are achievement-oriented. Plus it is much easier to see results when you are focused on winning vs. sportsmanship and teamwork.

📱 Child-raising and spending are way too much to think about in a single day. I think Natasha and Sawyer are ready to go home so I'll scoop up my non-trophy daughters, who are my most treasured possessions, and put them in my top-of-the-line Jaguar and return to our too-expensive home in our upscale neighborhood.

☎ Sounds like a plan!

I didn't think possessions were the most important things in life or that as parents we should be comparing our children and encouraging them to win at all costs. But the fact was that these misguided priorities were contaminating our lives. And I started to notice these values everywhere — in conversations with other parents, school activities, television commercials (aimed at kids as well as those aimed at adults), magazine advertisements, the list went on and on!

I had been exposed to these messages for years but never stopped to process them until Black got me thinking. But when I combined the status-conscious messages that bombarded me daily along with my Mom's materialistic values and Black's extravagant lifestyle, it was easy to see how I could get off-track. And this didn't even take into consideration Nick's upbringing or his corporate lifestyle. The combination of "all of the above" created a false environment in which I was supposed to be able to distinguish what values were real. No wonder I felt lost. The street signs were all wrong!

IM You were online early this morning. And now you are online late tonight. I am impressed.

IM Don't be. I'm just printing out your "Where is Your Money Going?" e-mail so I can be prepared for tomorrow.

IM Glad to see you remembered your pact with the devil.

IM I knew the devil wouldn't let me forget. By the way, thanks for today. It really helped.

IM Whatever. Anything else before I say good night?

IM Yes. You never told me the values you learned from Mommy and Daddy.

IM No, I never did. Good night.

It was a good night. Because it had been a good day, although I know Black probably thought it was a wasted day. Black once told me that school taught her book knowledge and social skills, but that she really learned about life by living it. I now understand what she meant.

Today allowed me to better understand my background and how maybe I came to be who I am. But rather than play the blame game, as Black so succinctly put it, I decided that night that I would accept, albeit with some trepidation, the opportunity that now lay ahead of me.

4

Rearranging The Deck Chairs On The Titanic

IM Good morning. Just checking in. I saw you were online earlier this morning, but left you alone. I figured you needed the quiet time to focus on things without any interruptions.

IM That had been my plan, but I made the mistake of checking e-mails. I managed to waste over 30 minutes. Then I started to pay a few bills, but first had to go through the stacks on my desk and that wasted an hour.

IM I thought you had sorted everything on your desk during the week.

IM I did, but I was looking for so many different types of financial documents to address your Finance 101 e-mail that I was afraid I might not have caught everything. Turns out I had missed a few bills. By the time I looked up, it was time to go to my weigh-in at Weight Watchers. I have accomplished nothing this morning. Absolutely nothing!

IM At least you got to escape to Weight Watchers.

IM So far that is my only good news. I managed to lose almost two pounds since last Saturday. Maybe I should start a new diet plan — stress out and lose weight!

IM How about … quit eating and save money?

Life Gets In The Way Of Plans

IM Cute. Anyway, now all I need to do is see if Nick has any unpaid bills lost in the piles on his desk. But I only have another 15 minutes before Natasha's swim lesson.

IM You should have told me to leave you alone.

IM Never thought of that since it doesn't work on anyone else in this family.

IM Is everyone else bothering you, too?

IM Not really. Just being themselves. Sawyer is Sawyer. She got into the kitchen cabinets, and just as I was about to reprimand her, she put a colander on her head. It is difficult to be stern when you are laughing. Natasha's watching TV, but it's just a matter of time before she starts pestering me about plans for the day. Nick's wandering around the house trying to be helpful but mostly getting in my way. All that's missing is a phone call from Mommy!

IM In other words, it's your typical chaotic Saturday.

IM Exactly. Some things never change.

IM Is Nick going to do something with the girls this afternoon?

IM Not unless I plan it. Why?

IM So how do you intend to work on the "Money" e-mail today? In five-minute increments between interruptions? Or are you going to wait until tonight when everyone is asleep and you are exhausted and frustrated?

IM Just what I needed — more of your sarcastic attitude. Now my morning is complete! Thanks.

IM You know I am always happy to help. And you must admit that I do have an uncanny grasp of the obvious. Do you want to guess where Larry and I are going to eat dinner tonight?

IM Could it possibly be Tony's since that's where you eat every Saturday night? And what does that have to do with anything?

IM Just pointing out my Saturdays are very predictable, too.

IM Regardless, I made a deal with you yesterday that I'd focus on your "Money" e-mail today. Now I doubt it will happen. Sorry.

IM News flash — I knew that. I knew it yesterday before you even made the deal, but I thought it best not to let it influence your decision. Your weekends are always spent doing things as a family. I did not expect that to change.

IM So you already knew today was going to be a wasted day?

IM I never said "wasted." You might find time to look at some of the documents listed in my e-mail, but being able to focus on the detail will not happen today. And probably not tomorrow either. However, time spent with your family is not "wasted." Your finances will not change dramatically between now and Monday unless you do something stupid this weekend.

IM I don't have the luxury of time to relax all weekend. You haven't seen the piles on my desk. And my list of things to do is growing so fast than I don't have enough time to write everything down.

IM Calm down. I did not say to sit around doing nothing all weekend. I am only trying to explain that sometimes reality changes our plans for the day. And that you need to be realistic about what you can accomplish in any given day.

For any given day? My reality had changed everything in my life! All I wanted to do was put together a list of what needed to be done and then start crossing things off the list. I had made up my mind that I was going to work on finances today, and didn't want to admit that I ignored the reality of what my weekends were really like. It annoyed me when Black pointed out the obvious.

It's Not Always About Money

At least I could start thinking about the reality of the changes we had to make — both in terms of our attitude and how we spend money. I thought I could begin by making some obvious decisions regarding expenditures that could be quickly eliminated. It turned out things were not as obvious as I thought.

☎ Have a few minutes?

☎ Sure.

☎ I want to talk to you about Natasha and her swim lesson. She loves the lessons and talks about them and her teacher, Miss Chris, all week long. I hate to cancel them, but I don't know if we can afford them anymore. To play it safe I plan on making up something to tell Miss Chris after today's lesson about why we have to cancel for a while. I called to ask if you had any ideas, other than telling the truth.

☎ Yes. Do nothing. I know it is important to cut out all unnecessary spending immediately, but right now making sure the girls' lives are not needlessly disrupted is far more important than saving the money. Once we have a chance to review all your spending, I am sure we can find a way to cut back enough in other areas. Natasha's swimming lesson is important and should be a priority even though it may not be essential. Does this make sense?

☎ Yes, I think so. But how do I figure out what is important spending and what is stupid spending?

☎ Would it be too sarcastic if I said, "Think before you spend?"

☎ Yes, it would! Right now I have so much going through my mind I can't think straight about anything. I have never thought much about spending in the past and now I'm obsessed with it. And since I have no idea how long our money is going to last, I feel like I shouldn't spend anything.

☎ OK. Sorry. Calm down. This will all become much clearer next week when we analyze how you spent money in the past. When you look at actual numbers, the trade-offs and priorities will become obvious, as will all the ways you can cut back on expenses. For now, feel free to call and get my permission before you make any expenditures.

☎ Cute. Any documents I should submit first?

☎ No. I can review your request over the phone.

It was getting on my nerves that Black thought everything was obvious, or almost everything, because surely she didn't see how uncertain I was of everything. I knew I was questioning everything. And on the rare occasion I felt like I had an answer, I wasn't sure if it was the right one or for the right reason.

☎ Got a minute? I'm making the girls soup and sandwiches for lunch and I need your advice.

☎ You put the mayo on before you cut the sandwich.

☎ I'll ignore that. Natasha keeps asking me to take her to Mad Potter. It's a place where they paint pottery. I know she really enjoys it, but it can get expensive, and I'd rather not spend the money right now.

☎ Did you tell her you would take her?

☎ No. I keep saying, "We'll see."

☎ Well, if it is not a matter of you keeping your word, then she probably would be happy doing something else. Why not offer to spend some time painting together? And include Nick, since he is the artist in the family.

☎ I don't know. She paints at school, so I don't think painting at home would be anything special. It's not that I mind taking her to Mad Potter; it's a pretty cool place. It's just about the money.

☎ Humor me and ask her. You might be surprised.

Surprised? I was shocked. Natasha screamed "yes" so loudly that I'm sure Black could hear her across Houston. We cleared the kitchen table of everything and put down newspapers, and Nick and Sawyer joined in the fun. My drawing abilities are limited to stick figures, whereas Nick does phenomenal pen-and-ink drawings. Natasha took great pleasure in her Dad helping her, and in turn, she showed me how to do it. It was a really fun painting session that filled the afternoon with laughter. Black stopped by the house on her way to dinner and admired the new artwork scattered around the kitchen. I'm sure it took everything in her not to tell me, "I told you so."

Establishing Financial Priorities

E-mail From: Red
Subject: Better Computers?
Sent: Saturday, January 31

I know you're probably still at dinner being part of the "see and be seen" crowd, but I'd appreciate it if you could get back to me in the morning. Nick started talking about computers tonight, and I need your opinion. Knowing Nick, he may be at the computer store when it opens. Here's where we are:

New Computer For Nick: Nick had to turn in his company computer, so he has been using an old one that he still had from before we moved back to the States. Now he wants to buy a new one with more speed and power. I'm concerned we don't have the money, but Nick figures we can either put it on one of our credit cards or get store financing.

Upgrade My Computer: Since I'm going to be doing all the bills and other stuff, I was wondering if maybe I should think about a new computer. Nick said prices have come down so much that we could probably get me something much better than my current laptop (your Dell hand-me-down) for a minimal amount of money. He also thinks we might get a better deal if we're buying two computers.

Part of me says we shouldn't spend anything. Part of me thinks some of what Nick's saying makes sense. And, of course, most of me doesn't even want to deal with the issue.

P.S. — How was dinner?

E-mail From: Black
Subject: Better Computers?
Sent: Saturday, January 31

Easy answer first. Dinner was the usual — excellent food, minimal conversation, too much wine and home by 8:30.

Re: Computers: Both "parts" of you are right. And "most of you" is predictable. I know you want something more specific, but first I must confess that since Larry's son is a computer genius I have him do all my computer work.

New Computer For Nick: I agree Nick needs his own computer — both from a practical and a psychological viewpoint. However, the general tendency for all of us is to buy more computer than we need. We look at whatever the "latest and greatest" is, which is a moving target since the technology seems to change daily. My recommendation would be for him to spec out his own Dell computer (which is what I have always used for all my "workhorse" computers, but Jeff does the specs) so he can get exactly what he needs. I know you want him to spend as little as possible. If you can get him to wait a few days until you finish working out your finances, that might help with the decisions, such as what you can really afford as well as whether to put it on a credit card or take advantage of Dell's financing or leasing options. Keep in mind this may be one of those battles it is best to let Nick win.

Upgrade Your Computer: This is where the part of you that does not want to spend any money is right. Even if you ignore the obvious — buying something you do not need with money you do not have — ask yourself if you have the time (or desire) to set-up and learn a new computer. If you want to do something for yourself, treat yourself to the movies and a huge bucket of popcorn.

Hope that helps.

That all made sense. And I could see a trend here. I had been looking at things by asking myself "should we spend the money" — and given our circumstances, every answer was an obvious "no." Now I was beginning to understand the important question was "WHY should we spend the money?" Which meant the financial decisions were intertwined with the personal priorities. And was what Black had said yesterday — the key was to decide what was important in our life and then the right decisions and purchases would follow.

IM Good morning. Got your "Computer" e-mail. Thanks.

IM Did it make sense?

IM Absolutely. It seemed obvious in the light of day. Are all financial decisions that straight-forward?

IM I hate to burst your bubble, but you were only deciding whether to buy a computer. You did not figure out how much you should spend, whether to lease or purchase or what other expenses may need to be reduced or eliminated.

IM I thought it was too easy. How do I do all that? Or will you and Nick do it?

IM Not to sound like a broken record, but that is why the "Where is Your Money Going?" e-mail is so important. It will help you identify your financial priorities. Not just the immediate ones, but also the long-term goals.

IM Right now I'm only concerned about the short-term. I'll worry about the long-term later.

IM I understand, but your short-term decisions should at least be pointed in the same direction as your long-term goals. And how do you do that if you do not know where you are headed?

IM You are talking in circles. Give me an example.

IM If your goal is to buy a home, you might decide not to redecorate your rental and save the money. Or if your goal is to take a vacation, you might cut back on the numbers of dinners eaten out. You think about what is important to you and the family and what is worth spending money on. And what is not.

IM That's great, but since at the moment I don't think we can even afford the house we're renting, let alone buying a home, and I know a vacation isn't going to happen anytime soon, it's a little hard for me to relate to those examples.

IM I understand. For many people, a financial priority is being able to pay for food and utilities until the next paycheck. But I am trying to get you to understand the concept of trade-offs. For now that might mean deciding between Natasha's swimming lesson or a week of Starbucks. Next week it might mean downgrading one or both of your cars so that you could pay off debt.

IM That makes more sense. So I need to decide where best to spend my money, assuming that I have any. Or, hopefully, where and how to spend it once I have some again.

IM Bingo!

IM And let me guess — this will become clearer when I finally get around to working on your "Money" e-mail.

IM We have another Bingo!

Prioritizing Life

In the past, my focus had always been on the non-financial aspects of a happy home life, specifically trying to be a good mom to Natasha and Sawyer. Now I was focused almost exclusively on the financial implications of each and every decision. Until Black brought it to my attention, I did not even recognize my newest problem — I was neglecting to find a balance between the two. For example, Natasha's swim lesson. I was so focused on the cost, I neglected to see the bigger picture — minimizing the disruptions to the girls' life. I did the same thing with Mad Potter. I was focused on not spending money vs. the fact Natasha and Sawyer just wanted to spend time with Nick and me. It was the old adage of not seeing the forest for the trees.

☎ Got a minute? I need help.

☎ And the topic is?

☎ Lists. I understand I'll need to focus 100% on your "Money" e-mail tomorrow so I was trying to organize all my other things to do. Each item seems to lead to five more items. The list is growing quicker than I can write it. Yesterday morning I felt like I was making no progress. Today I feel like I'm going backwards. I figured you would have a suggestion on how to do it better.

☎ Stop making lists.

☎ You must be joking. I'll forget things I need to do without a list. Plus, I feel in control when I check things off.

☎ I understand. But right now, as you are finding out, your list is going to be so long that you are going to feel frustrated and out of control. You will not even know where to start. Not to mention how much time you will waste just writing the list.

☎ Sounds like a Catch-22. If I don't make a list, I don't know what I have to do. If I make a list, I'll be overwhelmed and won't know where to start. So what do you suggest? Because right now I feel like I'm rearranging the deck chairs on the Titanic!

☎ Think calmly and rationally and try to decide what is most important and what can wait.

You need to figure out what critical things need to happen and how much time they will take. You cannot procrastinate on something that needs a lot of lead time.

☎ What are you talking about? Give me an example.

☎ OK. When I am on a racetrack, I am constantly looking way ahead. Not just one corner, but as far as I can see because you set up for corners a long time before you ever get to them. By the time you get to them, you are already committed and moving too fast to make any major adjustment.

☎ The only part of that which makes sense to me is the moving too fast. I feel like I'm running around putting out flash fires.

☎ Ok, using your analogies — would you waste time with little self-contained fires or would you focus on the one that has the potential to get out of control and burn the house down? Or using your Titanic analogy, and forget the deck chairs, would you stop to pack your suitcase before you went looking for a lifeboat?

☎ Is there a real-life example, and I mean my life, not yours, that you can give me?

☎ Yes, but I do not think you are going to like it. I was going to let this topic wait until tomorrow, but it is the perfect example. You are renting a house which means you are at the mercy of the landlord if you fail to pay the rent. Legally, it does not count as a homestead, so if you have to declare bankruptcy, you can be forced to move. Since you were starting to think about buying a house just before Nick was fired, I think one of your first priorities should be to figure out if and how you can buy a house. And to start this process immediately since it is not a one-day project.

I panicked because I thought Black was assuming we were going to have to declare bankruptcy, but then I thought about it in light of the conversation. She was looking at our needs in a rational and calm manner and knew securing a homestead was critical. (I can remember Black trying to convince us to buy a house when we first moved to the States, but in my own ignorance I was thinking Texas was merely a stopping point and not a permanent home. I didn't understand, or even think to ask, about the financial argument she had tried to make.) Buying a home now made sense to me, for an assortment of very important reasons, but I knew it wasn't going to happen overnight.

☎ You're right. Now that the company's housing allowance is gone, we can't possibly afford this house. Maybe we should focus on that tomorrow instead of your "Money" e-mail.

☎ No, because we still need to determine how much you can afford to pay every month. But the good news is you have already pulled together your assets and liabilities. That will be a key consideration for the mortgage company.

☎ And how will we find a mortgage company that will lend money to us now that Nick's unemployed?

☎ We can find a mortgage company. In fact, think about people you already know. You may have friends in the banking industry that can point you in the right direction. Not to mention, I know a lot of people. But the first thing you need to do is talk to Nick and decide your priorities.

☎ A large house with a big yard, in a good neighborhood with excellent schools, that's reasonably priced.

☎ Dream on. But at least it is a starting point from which you can decide your trade-offs. If schools are the priority, that will narrow down the options quickly. I can send you a map indicating the better school districts, and you can start driving the neighborhoods.

☎ More trade-offs?

☎ Yes. And not only in terms of money. But back to the discussion of your lists. Do not try to figure out everything you need to do, but instead, focus on what is critical. As things that demand your time come up, ask yourself if it is truly important or if it can wait. If you only list the important things, then it will be easier to focus on them. And the priorities will become more obvious if you try to think about what your goals are rather than just choosing random tasks.

All this made sense, but putting it into practice was going to be an entirely different matter. I spent the balance of the day looking at the real estate section of the Sunday paper. It didn't help the piles on my desk, and in fact it started a new one, but at least I felt like I was doing something productive; and with a specific goal in mind.

Don't Ignore The Obvious!

But as the day turned into evening, I had to face the fact that tomorrow would be spent dealing with the "Money" e-mail. Our financial reality was that many of the wonderful houses I looked at today would be out of our price range by tomorrow. And then I slipped back into self-pity and frustration. I wanted a step-by-step "how-to" book. Nick should have gotten an "exit manual." When you start a new job, the human resources department gives you lots of information telling you about the company and your benefits. But when you leave, there's no guide to tell you what to do. It doesn't seem fair that they don't help you when you need it the most.

E-mail From: Red
Subject: I Need to Vent!
Sent: Sunday, February 1

I need an accountant. I need a financial analyst. I may need a lawyer. I need a nanny. I need to understand what to do and how to do it. I need to scream. I need to escape! But if nothing else, I need to vent which is why I didn't call. Plus, I figured you were at dinner. No need to respond.

E-mail From: Black
Subject: Can I Vent Too?
Sent: Sunday, February 1

I know you did not want a response, but I am bored and have nothing else to do. Like you do to me when you are in the carpool line. Went out to eat like we do every night. Dinner was good. Conversation was minimal. Too much wine. Home by 8:00 p.m. Husband snoring on couch within 30 minutes. I need a new routine. I need something to do in the evenings. I need a life!

E-mail From: Red
Subject: Can I Vent Too?
Sent: Sunday, February 1

Sorry, no sympathy for you. You live in a great house that you own — no mortgage or landlord to worry about. You have a successful husband who never has to worry about getting fired because he owns the company. AND you have plenty of money. You don't have any real problems. It wouldn't kill you to be a little more sympathetic.

E-mail From: Black
Subject: Sorry ...
Sent: Sunday, February 1

You are right, so I will make you a deal: I will be more sympathetic if you are less emotional. Since it is difficult to break habits "cold turkey," we can ease into it. I will say warm and fuzzy things for an hour a day if you try and think calmly for one hour a day. I will start.

Red, your personal and underlying priorities are all wonderful. Your financial decisions have been a little confused, but that is only temporary. You are a very smart person who (with a little guidance from someone who knows more about life than you do) will be able to fight all your fires, and even learn to prevent fires in the future.

You are married to a caring man who is a loving father and husband, but at the moment must feel like the captain of the Titanic just after it hit the iceberg. However, you being the sweet and loving wife and mother that you are, will have sympathy and understanding for him and will wake up tomorrow morning and bring him coffee and the want ads of the newspaper.

How am I doing?

E-mail From: Red
Subject: Sorry ...
Sent: Sunday, February 1

Awful. But it made me laugh. It's good to know there are some things you aren't good at! Warm and fuzzy appears to be at the top of that list.

E-mail From: Black
Subject: Good Night!
Sent: Sunday, February 1

Happy to help. Get some sleep and we will conquer the world in the morning.

The good thing about having a non-emotional sister is that you can get away with saying whatever you want, particularly when you're stressed. Black won't go off in a huff with wounded feelings as I'd have done. She's not very sensitive, and sometimes this bothers me. But there's certainly an upside to her personality — you can discard with the time and effort of sugar-coating situations and emotions and just get to the point. There's no "woe is me." It's straight to the point and then she responds with constructive suggestions or sometimes just smart-ass comments that bring you back to your senses.

5

Open Your Eyes Before Your Wallet

IM Good morning.

IM It is 5:00 a.m.! I am impressed.

IM Yup. I thought I'd try your approach and get up early. But for the record, I think this is an insane hour.

IM Quite the contrary. It is an extremely sane hour. Everything is quiet and calm.

IM That's what I'm hoping for. I have finally summoned up the courage to seriously look at your "Money" e-mail. In a strange sort of way, I went to bed last night almost looking forward to this morning.

IM Great. Then I will leave you alone so you can get started.

IM OK. But first, I have one question. I know you keep telling me I need to understand the history of how we spent money so we can make smart decisions in the future. And you keep saying everything will become obvious. But what if it doesn't? Nothing financial seems obvious to me.

IM Trust me, it will. Even to you. But if I am wrong, which I am NOT, all you are risking is some time. Both yours and mine. So stop procrastinating and get started.

Where Was Our Money Going?

Trust her? How could I not? Especially on finance-related issues. The past three days proved invaluable in helping me to understand how I became the person I am, especially in terms of my finances, as well as coming to grips with priorities in life. And yet, I was still hesitant to jump into Black's e-mail. I knew that the moment I started working on it, I'd have to leave all my philosophizing behind and face reality. But, I knew I had no choice, so I took a deep breath, re-read her e-mail from last week and took a huge step forward towards a new financial life. One based on reality and knowledge.

Warning: People seem more comfortable discussing their sex lives than their financial lives. I personally do not care how much money you have or how you spend it, or even how much you piss away. However, in order for me to be able to help you, we are going to have to look at everything you and Nick spend money on. And I mean everything.

I have identified six major steps. I do not want to overwhelm you with budgeting and long-term planning issues at this point, but I want you to understand that is where we are heading. The first two steps are basically organization and analysis, and should go fairly quickly. The third step is going to be the rude awakening, but probably also the most important. Once we get through those, you will be comfortable with the general concepts, and then you will be ready (and I bet willing) to address the last items.

1. Identify All the Ways You Spend Money

- Checking Accounts — Checkbook or Ledger Detail
- Savings Accounts — Withdrawals and Transfers
- Credit Card Statements
- Household Bills (Rent, Utility, Insurance — probably included in one of the above)
- Cash Receipts (if you save them)

2. Categorize the Expenditures

As you go through the details, you will need to start organizing the expenses into types and categories of things. I developed (and attached) a Microsoft Excel spreadsheet you can use or you can use ledger paper. It is important to separate your expenditures into as many useful and detailed categories as possible. If you lump too much into a miscellaneous category, you will never figure it out.

3. Review Each Category

Once everything is categorized, then you can review them and see what is required (such as groceries, utilities and insurance) vs. what is discretionary (such as eating out and vacations). The good news is that without even seeing the details, I can guarantee there is money being wasted which means there is room to reduce spending painlessly. We will look at the largest numbers first, as small percentages of savings on them will have the greatest impact. But remember, pennies add up, so we will eventually need to review everything.

4. Develop a Realistic Budget

Obviously, the discretionary items can be either eliminated or greatly reduced. And keep in mind just because something is required — for example, groceries — it does not mean the amount you have been spending is required. Once you have the details, you will be able to identify ways to reduce many of these expenses.

5. Budget Review Process

6. Establish Goals and Objectives

Questions/Comments: Similar to when we were working on your assets and liabilities, I recommend we use e-mails so you have everything written down in case you want to refer back to a topic.

E-mail From: Red
Subject: CHECKLIST: Where Is Your Money Going?
Sent: Monday, February 2

Please tell me you're kidding. It will take me weeks to do everything that you've outlined. We'll be out of money before I have figured out where the money went. There must be a simpler — and faster — way of doing this. And keep in mind I want to figure out our finances, not become a financial analyst.

E-mail From: Black
Subject: CHECKLIST: Where Is Your Money Going?
Sent: Monday, February 2

As usual, you are overreacting. Go back and re-read the second paragraph. You are going to do this one step at a time. Think of it like eating an elephant — you can do it, just not all at once.

E-mail From: Red
Subject: CHECKLIST: Where Is Your Money Going?
Sent: Monday, February 2

Eating an elephant? Where do you come up with this stuff? I'm overwhelmed because all this finance stuff is unknown territory.

E-mail From: Black
Subject: CHECKLIST: Step One
Sent: Monday, February 2

I understand. So would be the idea of eating an entire elephant, but it could be done in small servings.

Focus on Step One: Identify All the Ways You Spend Money. This is merely accumulating all your bank account and credit card statements, monthly household bills and any other receipts. Most of this should already be in those files or Ziploc bags you started when we were working on assets and liabilities. Ideally, you will have statements going back six months, but if not, you can contact the companies and get them. For now, we will work with whatever you have and fill in the blanks later.

E-mail From: Red
Subject: CHECKLIST: Step One
Sent: Monday, February 2

I actually have almost everything on the list going back a few years. Mommy always saved all those things in manila folders. Then once I saw you had expensive leather loose-leaf binders I did an economy version and filed the papers in vinyl binders.

No cash receipts. And the checkbook is a disaster! When I started writing checks, I noticed Nick didn't always keep a record of the checks he wrote. Or the deposits. I'm not even sure the balance is correct. It could take forever to try and figure it out.

E-mail From: Black
Subject: CHECKLIST: Step One is done ... On to Two
Sent: Monday, February 2

For now, the most important aspect of the checkbook is making sure you are not bouncing checks. Call the bank and determine your current balance.

There is no way to recreate your cash receipts, so we will forget that aspect of the past.

Looks like we can move to Step Two: Categorize the Expenditures. This will probably be the most tedious step as it means going through the statements and categorizing each line item. The Microsoft Excel spreadsheet I sent lists all the major categories and subcategories I could think would apply to you, but I left space for any we may need to add. Although the spreadsheet is set up to capture expenditures by month for a year, you will only need to focus on the last six months. In fact, if you start backwards, we might have enough detail once we get the past four months.

E-mail From: Red
Subject: CHECKLIST: Step One is done ... On to Two
Sent: Monday, February 2

So how do I do this? Go through each statement line by line and note the category? There are too many categories to color-code them with highlighters. And then what? How do I subtotal the stuff so I can fill in the boxes on the spreadsheet?

P.S. — Your spreadsheet is very "cool," as Natasha would say. Maybe one day I'll be able to create something like that, but for now I feel more comfortable with pencils, erasers and calculators.

E-mail From: Black
Subject: Step Two ... Pick your Poison
Sent: Monday, February 2

Whatever method you pick, you are going to have to invest some time categorizing and analyzing all your expenditures. Obviously, you could manually fill in the spreadsheet, but that is not very efficient. Since you liked the spreadsheet, I could show you how to use Microsoft Excel, which will automatically do the math for you and allow you to organize and sort all your expenditures. It is very easy to use.

Or you can buy software specifically designed for this purpose. I have been using Microsoft Money for years and find it indispensable, both for personal finances and also small business applications. I use it to write checks, but more importantly, to consolidate activity on all my accounts. Then I can look at spending by category and payee, do cash flow statements, generate reports for the tax accountants and a multitude of other uses. I even download my American Express statements into Microsoft Money.

E-mail From: Red
Subject: Step Two ... Pick your Poison
Sent: Monday, February 2

Stop! I only need to do personal finances. And, as you already know, I'm a computer idiot. I think I have enough on my "elephant plate" at the moment without learning a new computer program. I might let you show me how to use Microsoft Excel since it looks relatively simple, plus it's already on my computer, so I wouldn't have to spend any money. I don't think I need or want to learn a program like Microsoft Money right now. Maybe later.

E-mail From: Black
Subject: Step Two ... Pick your Poison
Sent: Monday, February 2

You are not looking at a major expenditure. In fact, Microsoft Money is probably not much more expensive than buying ledger paper and assorted highlighters.

And as long as you are going to have to learn something new, combined with the fact you are going to invest time inputting history, I think your time would be best spent with Microsoft Money. It will not only generate checks and schedule bills, but since it is specifically designed for personal finances it already has account types (checking, savings, credit cards) and spending categories set up. All this will immediately save you time and help speed up your learning process. Plus, it automatically generates reports and budgets which you will find useful down the line. I promise it will make your life easier, not more difficult.

Pick a time you can come by the house, and I will show you how to use it. It is not difficult, and inputting the historical information will be a great way to learn the program. Bring your computer and we can download a trial copy so you can use it before you have to decide whether or not you want to buy it.

Bottom line: All I am asking is you invest 30 minutes of your time to try it. I am convinced you will like it, but if not, I will show you how to use Microsoft Excel.

E-mail From: Red
Subject: Step Two ... Pick your Poison
Sent: Monday, February 2

Enough already. I'll make sure I have everything up-to-date in the binders and then I'll call you and let you know when I'm ready to come over for my lesson. I can't believe I'm doing this. I hate computers. I'd rather go for root canal work.

E-mail From: Black
Subject: Prefer the Dentist?
Sent: Monday, February 2

Root canal? Funny you should say that ... I remember reading about a bank survey that indicated about one-third of the respondents rather go to the dentist than balance a checkbook. At the time I thought that extreme, but maybe not.

Gee, computers and finance. My two least-favorite things, and I was going to deal with them both simultaneously. I could hardly wait! I checked off most of the boxes under Step One and felt a sense of accomplishment. I started to review the savings account statements and realized the activity was minimal — no recent deposits, nominal interest income and the safety deposit rental. I highlighted them. The utility and insurance bills were straight-forward, so I merely highlighted the monthly amount. However, I noticed they also indicated the last payment, and I figured I could use that information to fill in some of the blanks in the checkbook, so I circled them.

When I got to the credit card statements, I realized categorizing all this was going to be a full-time job. All the bank cards had an assortment of charges, plus there were just too many damn credit cards. All I did was circle the amounts paid each month so I could try and fill in more of the missing data in the checkbook. The rest would wait.

And now I had run out of financial things to do. Although Black told me not to worry about the checkbook, I decided to go back and use the payments from the various statements to try and identify the checks written. I felt like a detective trying to solve a crime — or at least recreate the crime scene. Good news was it wasn't a murder scene, although I did want to kill Nick for his sloppy bookkeeping. But, surprisingly, I was able to match up almost everything. So with that done, I felt like I had eaten a little more of that elephant.

Smart People Spending Without Thinking

☎ Catch you at a bad time?

📱 No — Sawyer and I are grabbing a Jamba Juice before picking Natasha up at school. Anything important?

☎ No. I was calling to see if you had any idea when you might be coming over. By the way, any idea how much you spend on smoothies every month?

📱 No, I don't. But if you don't mind, I'd like to enjoy my Jamba Juice in peace. Unless you have something important to tell me, I'll talk to you another time.

I thought it best to end the conversation as quickly as possible before I said something nasty. Black's question really annoyed me. I was going through a major crisis; I had been working hard this morning, and she was giving me grief about taking a few quiet minutes and enjoying a smoothie! But then, after I calmed down, I started thinking about what she had said. And I got annoyed again. Because it was a valid question.

I did go to Jamba Juice three or four times a week. At almost $5 each, my smoothies were an expensive habit. I figured if I cut back my visits to twice a week, I could easily save over $600 a year! My habit got me thinking that Nick was probably guilty of doing the same thing at Starbucks. Although he didn't have an office to go to now, I wanted to make sure he wasn't continuing his morning Starbucks run. In the past, I'd have tried to subtly bring up the topic, but I felt I'd earned the right to ask him how he was spending "our" money, so I talked to him about it when I got home. He agreed that it would be easy to make a pot of coffee at home.

IM I was hoping you'd be online. I want to apologize for being so short with you earlier this afternoon. I was really pissed off at you and didn't want to say so.

IM Really? I may not be overly sensitive, but I did pick up on your tone of voice.

IM I was feeling sorry for myself. Anyway, once I settled down and thought about it, I realized that I do spend too much money on smoothies. That got me thinking about Nick and his coffee, and so I confronted him about his Starbucks habit.

IM Great. So you decided if I made you mad, you were going to share it with Nick. I am sure he was thrilled.

IM Actually he was fairly accepting. I guess he realizes I'm at my wit's end and scared about finances.

IM You do make it pretty obvious. But keep in mind my question was trying to make you understand where your money is going, not decide how you should spend it.

IM I know. And we're wasting money without even realizing it.

IM Neither you nor Nick smoke, but think about how much smokers spend every week to support their habit. Or the person who stops for a drink on the way home from work. The point is spending should be based on conscious decisions, not habits.

IM Be patient. I'm trying to figure all this out, but there's so much to consider. If it's OK with you, I'd like to come by tonight for my Microsoft Money lesson. Unless that interferes with your dinner plans.

IM And our conscious decision to drink an expensive bottle of wine every night? No problem. I will talk less and drink faster, and we will be home by 7:30. See you then.

I knew that if Jamba Juices were not a habit, but rather were a conscious decision, I would enjoy them more, as I'd look forward to them. And I could use it as a special treat for the girls. But on Saturdays I would continue to use it as part of my Weight Watchers routine. (I would buy it on the way to the meeting, but since nothing passed my lips until after weigh-in, I would savor it throughout the meeting.)

History May Surprise You

IM   Good morning.

IM   It is 5:00 a.m. Two days in a row. Now I am really impressed.

IM   I thought you'd be. But my next comment is going to impress you even more! After I got home from our Microsoft Money class last night, the house was quiet, and so I stayed up past midnight inputting data. I'm almost done!

IM   Whoever is on Red's computer ... please identify yourself. Immediately!

IM   And I'm determined to get the rest of it input this morning, so unless you have something specific to tell me, I have more important things to do than sit here IMing with you.

I was glad that Black was right about Microsoft Money being easy to learn, although I'd prefer to claim I was a computer prodigy. The lesson went quickly because everything was logical. Even to a non-finance person like me.

Reconstructing the history of our spending wasn't as difficult or even as time-consuming as I thought it was going to be. In fact, learning Microsoft Money was actually fun once I allowed myself not to be intimidated by a computer program devoted to money management. And once I got all the data into the system, I felt another sense of accomplishment. I was working away at that elephant.

☎   Believe it or not, I think I have everything loaded into Microsoft Money. And it took only four months of history to see we're consistent with our spending.

☎   Great!

☎   Not really. We're consistently spending a lot of money.

☎   Across the board or just on specific categories? Have you started to look at the detail yet?

☎   The answer to the first question is "both." And yes, I have started to look at some of the detail. Can you say, "Red, why do you spend so much money on groceries?"

☎   Do you? You and Nick do not seem the extravagant type. I can not picture you eating Russian caviar and sipping vintage champagne.

☎   Maybe lox and bagels and fresh orange juice, but even that wouldn't explain the astronomical amount we spend on groceries. I can't believe how much we spend at just Whole Foods, not to mention all the other grocery stores we use.

☎   Do you realize that Whole Foods is probably the most expensive grocery store in your neighborhood? Their nickname is "Whole Paycheck."

☎ Who nicknames a grocery store?

☎ Probably the same people who call Neiman Marcus "Needless Mark-up." Regardless, I have seen it in articles from *The Wall Street Journal* and heard it from friends.

☎ Do you think it's an accurate nickname?

☎ I am not a grocery store expert, but as far as Neiman Marcus, I do not think they mark up prices more than other retailers; they just carry more upscale merchandise.

☎ Same with Whole Foods. Their produce and meats are more expensive than other stores because they're a better quality. Plus they have organic products.

☎ So then it was a conscious decision.

☎ Yes and no. It was for certain items, but I also shopped there because it was close to the house, and I loved the look and feel of the store. The lighting and layout are so much nicer than your average grocery store. I'm embarrassed that I never thought about their prices, not even when Mommy would make snide remarks. Why didn't I ever bother to stop and think?

☎ But you already said you use other grocery stores, too.

☎ Yes. I also use another convenient and expensive, I might add, grocery store for basic items, like paper products and most of my staple pantry items. I can't believe I never thought about the prices. I know those items are cheaper elsewhere.

☎ Do not cry over spilt milk. Now you understand you paid a price for convenience. We could discuss the history and evolution of the business side of the food-selling industry, and mega-stores like Target, which is fascinating, but the bottom line is different stores have different prices on different items.

☎ I know that. I just never did anything about it. I have separate shopping lists for three or four different stores based on their product selection, and while I am there, I buy whatever other groceries are on my general list. I never thought about having separate shopping lists based on price. What an idiot I have been.

☎ Let me see if I understand this. You have multiple grocery lists?

☎ You wouldn't understand. You order all your groceries online and have them delivered. Not to mention you eat out every night. I end up shopping at different stores because one may have better produce. Another may carry a specific brand or product I can't find elsewhere. I have different lists for different stores. The problem is I never thought about who had the best prices, especially for basic items like toilet paper or laundry detergent. I'm saying I need to have lists based on price too.

☎ Now I understand. And for the record, we do not eat out every night. Once a month, Larry barbecues steak for the girls.

I had another embarrassing confession, but I kept it to myself. Not only didn't I pay attention to the prices of groceries from store-to-store, but I didn't even look at the weekly specials or use coupons. I had always been amused by my Mom and her envelopes full of coupons, but I never paid serious attention to them before. I shopped like a mindless idiot who seemed to have all the money in the world. But all that had to change.

IM Glad you're on IM. How was dinner?

IM That is why you are glad I am on IM? To ask me about dinner?

IM No, I was trying to be nice. Sorry. I'll get to the point. I was looking at our checking account statements and saw that Nick and I are on very familiar terms with the ATM. We seem to withdraw a significant amount of cash, and I don't have a clue where all this money is going. Any ideas or suggestions?

IM You already told me you do not have any cash receipts, so unless you have a phenomenal memory it will probably remain a mystery. Can you identify the main uses of cash?

IM Starbucks, Jamba Juice and baby-sitters. But there's no way that the amount of cash that has gone out has been for just those items. The total is significant. Or at least it's significant for us. How do you track cash expenditures?

IM As a percentage of my spending, cash is not even a rounding error, so I ignore it. Almost everything I do is either by check or credit card.

IM Writing checks for small purchases around town really isn't practical, and the last thing we need is to use our credit cards more. So any other suggestions?

IM A couple. You could come up with a weekly cash amount that is acceptable and write yourselves checks for cash and lock up the ATM cards. If you do that, you might want to consider starting a "Cash Account" on Microsoft Money and then making a deliberate attempt to save all your cash receipts.

IM That sounds great, but the hard part will be getting Nick and me into the habit of getting receipts. You said you had a couple of ideas. What's the other?

IM I am almost afraid to make the next suggestion, but another option is to start using your American Express for those cash purchases. Since you have to pay off the balance every month, it will not increase your debt level and will give you a paper trail. But you have to make sure you think before you charge. That may be a harder habit to get into than asking for cash receipts.

I knew I had absolutely no way of ever figuring out where all that money had gone. The amount of cash we went through in the last four months was significant, and I couldn't help but think about how much it added up to each year. Year after year. I couldn't do anything about the past, but I certainly could do things differently in the future.

I decided I would start using my American Express for everything that I could, rather than cash, so I could track how we were spending money. At the same time I decided to make a major effort to keep cash receipts. And I would ask Nick to do the same, although I doubted it would happen. The bottom line was that most spending was easy to track. The million dollar question was "How could it be reduced?"

Discretionary Expenditures Are Called That For A Reason

Black had said to look at the biggest numbers first, but with the exception of groceries, most of them were fixed costs like rent, insurance, and Nick's car note. Instead, I decided to focus on all the discretionary items because by definition they weren't required, and I figured they could be reduced or eliminated without any major upheaval to our lifestyle. As I was proudly printing a Microsoft Money report, I glanced over and saw a two-foot pile of magazines in the corner. I couldn't believe how tall it was, so I actually got up and measured it!

IM You still there?

IM No.

IM Very funny. How many magazines do you subscribe to?

IM I would guess about 12-15. Mostly car-related, a few fashion, a few art, one business, one wine. Why? Which ones do you want when I am done with them?

IM None! I just figured out how much I spend on magazine subscriptions. Magazines, I might add, that I never get a chance to read. They just pile up in the corner of my workroom, a constant reminder that I don't have enough free time in my life.

IM Well that would explain how you dress ... you obviously are not reading your Vogue.

IM Thanks. I didn't IM you to get fashion advice. And personally, I prefer InStyle. That and Vanity Fair are the only two magazines I make time to read. But I never get to the rest of them, so every six months or so I end up quickly flipping through them and throwing them in the recycling bin or giving them away.

IM If they are six months old, why even take the time to look through them? Just get rid of them. Where does it say you are required to read them?

IM But that would be wasting money.

IM So you would rather waste your time? Go through the pile, save only the ones you really want to read. And if you ever run out of magazines, let me know and I will share mine with you, although I have a hard time picturing you with AutoWeek, Fortune or Wine Spectator. Meanwhile, unless you have something important to talk about, I am going to bed. Catch you in the morning.

I decided to keep only a handful of my favorite magazines and cancel or at least not renew the rest. It was funny — besides the financial savings, I liked the feeling of capturing back time in my life.

I now started to review the discretionary expenditures, and immediately spotted the category called "Dining." Up until Nick was fired, we'd have lunch at family-friendly restaurants every Saturday and Sunday. I'm not even sure the girls enjoyed it. The more I thought about it, the more I realized I'm not sure I even enjoyed it. I usually felt like I was inhaling my food while playing social director, or sometimes referee with the girls. Cutting back was an easy decision because both Nick and I enjoy cooking and the girls enjoy "helping." In addition to saving us a substantial amount of money, it would give us more time together.

E-mail From: Red
Subject: Cutting Back and Cutting Out
Sent: Tuesday, February 3

I know you're asleep, but I had to e-mail you. After our IM session I started going through all my discretionary spending categories. I mean really looking closely at stuff. I couldn't believe what I could either cut out entirely or reduce significantly. I know this sounds crazy, but it's fun. It's a challenge to see how much I can save and not even miss.

I'm going to bed now, but I feel really good that I'm starting to take hold of our finances. I wanted to share that with you and to thank you for all of your help. Night-night.

Spending Habits Can Become Very Expensive

E-mail From: Black
Subject: Cutting Back and Cutting Out
Sent: Wednesday, February 4

Good morning.

Glad you are having fun. Maybe we should write a book. "Fun with Finances" would make a great title, although I am guessing most people would think it fiction. Not me, of course! And now, maybe not you either.

I know you think the whole issue of finances is overwhelming, and if I had initially told you "when you start controlling your expenses instead of them controlling you, it feels good" you would have thought I was crazy. But I am thrilled you are starting to understand.

Now that you have gone through your discretionary spending categories, you need to review the non-discretionary or required expenses. Obviously, the rent number is going to change (hopefully to a mortgage payment, but that will mean there will be taxes and increased homeowners insurance), but we will look at that after we are done analyzing all your expenses to determine what you can afford. We also need to sit down and analyze your credit cards, but that is a topic unto itself.

If you review the remaining required items this morning, then you will be done with Step 3.

E-mail From: Red
Subject: Cutting Back and Cutting Out
Sent: Wednesday, February 4

Done! There was not much left to analyze after you exclude the house-related expenses and credit cards. The debt (Nick's car loan, the personal note and the piano financing) and insurance are straight-forward. The only other things were utilities and routine services.

I know it was just a small savings, but I noticed on our TV cable bill that we were paying for the most expensive "everything included" plan, so I called them and changed it to one that was more in line with our viewing habits. I also made phone calls to our telephone provider and cell phone companies and found there were more economical packages for those services, too. I plan to call the utility companies later this week and will talk to the landscapers and pool guys to see if there is any room to cut back there.

This was really a revelation. I just figured because these categories were non-discretionary they were fixed amounts. Looking back to yesterday's rude awakening about groceries, I should have expected there'd be more opportunities to save — even with "required" items.

E-mail From: Black
Subject: Habits Are Expensive
Sent: Wednesday, February 4

So things are becoming obvious? Is this where I get to say, "I told you so?" Spending habits can become very expensive, because the more you become accustomed to something, the less you think about it. And the cost is cumulative. It adds up over time.

E-mail From: Red
Subject: Habits Are Expensive
Sent: Wednesday, February 4

Like your shopping?

E-mail From: Black
Subject: From the Shopping Queen
Sent: Wednesday, February 4

It is all relative to what you can afford to spend and why you spend. I do not shop out of habit, I shop out of boredom. But this is not about me. It is about you. And I think it is great that you are truly beginning to take control of your finances and spending.

I knew Black would be fully aware of her spending habits, but I always thought that she spent so much because she liked to shop. But out of boredom? I found that a very curious comment. Anyway, I did feel good about understanding and taking control of our financial situation. It wasn't difficult — once I had the facts about how we spent our money — to eliminate or reduce spending in a lot of areas. Black was lucky that she didn't have to worry about the thousands she spent shopping. I, on the other hand, had to watch every penny.

IM I was thinking about your comment about spending money out of habit and went back and looked at all the categories again. Guilty as charged! I found several more expenses that were truly habits, not conscious decisions.

IM You may not remember, but last week I tried to explain how you can never be content with your acquisitions because there is always something else to acquire. That holds true for spending levels too.

IM You're talking in circles.

IM You get used to a certain way of life and then it becomes your baseline. And then before you know it, you add or upgrade a few things and that becomes your new baseline. And then a few more. It can eventually get out of hand, but it happens so gradually, you do not realize it. But the dollars add up.

IM You mean like you and your Hermes handbags?

IM Where did that come from?

IM You've always had a handbag fetish. In fact, you've always been a clotheshorse. Over the years I watched in amazement and amusement as your spending reached new levels in terms of the labels. Now you only buy designer clothing and you collect Hermes handbags.

IM I can rationalize my Hermes handbags because they are classics and will never go out of style. Not to mention there is a strong resale market for them, so I consider them investments. But I see your point as far as the rest of my clothing. I have always bought classics, but over the years I have upgraded the labels.

IM So you admit it? You're just as guilty as the rest of us!

IM Guilty of spending money on things I do not need? YES. Guilty of not being aware? NO. Guilty of spending money I need to use for something more important? NO.

IM Damn, I thought I had you! Well, back to real life. How do Nick and I control things so they don't start creeping up without us noticing it until it's too late?

IM This is where I get to say, "I told you so." Go back to my "Money" e-mail. You just completed Step 3. And in the second paragraph I said once we finished the first three steps, you would be ready and willing to move to Step 4: Develop a Realistic Budget.

IM You couldn't just say, "Develop a budget?" You had to point out you were right? Again.

IM Sorry. That would not have been as much fun. And now ... it is Budget Time!

IM Obviously, you're more excited about that than I am. I'll call you after I drop Natasha off at school. And I promise I'm not procrastinating.

Budgeting 101

A budget. What a novel concept! At least for us. I wondered why we had never done one. Then I wondered how many people actually did. I'm not sure I ever would have thought about it if it hadn't been for this crisis. I started to think about how much money we wasted. But I knew Black would have told me that it was no good worrying about what we did or didn't do yesterday. What was important was to start taking the right steps today. And so I did.

☎ OK. I'm ready to tackle Step 4. Is this something we can do via e-mail or do I need to come over and see how you do your budget?

☎ Here is where I have to say, "Do as I say, not as I do," because I have not done a personal budget in years. But I can remember my first one.

☎ You remember your first budget? You have a strange collection of fond memories!

☎ It was when Mom put me on a clothing budget. She gave me an amount I could spend every year and wrote it on a big manila envelope. Every time I bought something, I would deduct that amount from the total and put the receipt in the envelope. I always knew how much was left in my budget, so I never had to ask if I could buy something. Mom was brilliant!

☎ [Silence for 5 seconds, followed by a burst of laughter.] You're kidding, right?

☎ No, it was brilliant.

☎ No, it was a punishment! It wasn't Mommy's way of teaching you about money; it was her way of controlling you. She was tired of you constantly wanting to buy clothing, and so she did it to shut you up.

☎ Are you sure?

☎ Very. Mommy told me the story many times. You loved expensive clothing, so she came up with a number that was less than she was willing to spend and told you that was your "budget." I only liked cheap stuff, so she never gave me a budget.

☎ Then she did you a huge disservice, because whatever the ulterior motive, it was brilliant. Besides teaching me how to budget, it taught me to save for future purchases and motivated me to get part-time jobs in high school so I would have more money.

Which all probably contributed towards making me feel comfortable with finances. I ended up being one of the few women in graduate school majoring in finance and spent the first half of my corporate career in financial planning and budgets.

☎ Fine. You live a charmed life! You're the only person I know who could turn a punishment into a career.

☎ But remember, I had no idea it was a punishment. Until today.

☎ Which I find hilarious. Especially since everything is usually so damn obvious to you.

I was amused, and amazed, that Black never realized she was being punished. But the fact remained — she had been taught a very valuable lesson, and I too could learn from her "punishment."

I now had a history of expenditures in detailed categories that I could use as a starting point for predicting what to expect in the future. I printed out one of the standardized reports from Microsoft Money that indicated expenses by category by month. I knew there would be a way to computerize this, but decided to do it manually so I could work it through in my mind. First, I went through and highlighted all the items that were required and fixed, such as the rent (for now) and Nick's car note and ran a subtotal. Next, I highlighted (in a different color) items that were required, but might have room for improvement, such as groceries and utilities. For budgeting purposes I used the current level of expenditures, unless I was certain I could cut costs. I then ran another subtotal.

Talk about being naïve! I totaled these two subtotals and was shocked. As a middle-aged, college-educated woman, this is embarrassing to admit, but I never realized there were so many monthly expenses. And that was before I got to the third group, which was discretionary items. Although they weren't required expenditures and therefore could theoretically be eliminated, I doubted they would totally disappear.

IM It's 9:30. You're late getting back from dinner.

IM No. I am late getting back on the computer. Checking up on me?

IM No. I'm just so excited I couldn't wait to tell you that I did it! I put together a monthly budget. It's a bit alarming to actually see the total, but at least I now know the truth.

IM I am impressed. When I did not hear from you, I figured you were procrastinating.

IM That might have been the answer in the past, but I was determined to figure it out on my own. I'm sure there was a better way to do it, but I used highlighters and a calculator.

IM Whatever works. The key is the thought process. I pushed you to automate the sorting and the straight math, but you are the one that has to analyze the numbers and then make the decisions.

IM I'm starting to understand that.

IM You can computerize a "most-likely" budget based on history, but it will not take into account how you are going to change the future. The one question I have for you is — did you use historical numbers or wishful thinking amounts?

IM Neither. I used realistic numbers based on history. Or at least I think I did. The fixed-cost items were obvious. I reduced other expenses, like groceries, to levels I think are reasonable, although it won't be easy. But I wasn't exactly sure how to budget for discretionary things, like eating out and miscellaneous cash. I guessed at those. And we still need to look at the credit card debt.

IM Now I am REALLY impressed. You are my best student. Ever.

IM I'm also your only student.

IM Minor detail. You did a great job and you are almost done with Step 4. Now you can start thinking about Step 5, which is the budget review process. Just remember — you will need to monitor the items that are goals or guesses a little more closely than the fixed amount categories.

IM Monitor them?

IM Yes. The secret to successful budgeting is not only putting together a realistic budget, but sticking to it. This means you need to review your spending to make sure you stay on track. Typically it would be at the end of the month, but since all of this is new, plus some of these items are guesses, I would review them more often.

IM I guess it was wishful thinking to hope that once I did our budget I'd be done.

IM Yes, it was. But look how quickly you were able to load months of history into Microsoft Money. It will be easy to keep current, especially if you are going to use it to generate checks. The critical item is how to track your credit card and cash expenditures. Those are the things that can throw even the most well-intentioned budget off track.

IM Makes sense. I talked to Nick about the "missing" cash, and we're both going to try our best to minimize our ATM withdrawals and save as many of the cash receipts as possible. And I can input credit card charges every few days.

IM I already told you, you can automatically download your American Express charges.

IM I prefer to manually input them because makes me aware of where the money's going. I want everything to be a conscious decision, so a few painful reminders may be necessary.

IM OK. Keep in mind that you will probably have to add items to your budget since you may have missed some things when you put your budget together today. Some items are not routine occurrences and others may only be annual payments and so may not yet have appeared on your radar.

IM I'd prefer no more surprises. Since I only input the last four months of data, tomorrow I will go back and look at the various statements to see if I missed any large charges or categories. And then I may need help setting up budget spreadsheets. I don't want to automate everything, but I'd like to retire my calculator, if possible.

IM Computerizing the budget spreadsheets will be the easy part.

I was amazed when I realized it had only been a few days since my first Microsoft Money lesson. It seemed like years given how much I had learned this week.

Outing The Ostrich

E-mail From: Red
Subject: Thank you
Sent: Wednesday, February 6

I know you don't want any formal thank you, but I wanted you to know that I really appreciate everything you did to make me not only face our financial situation, but more importantly to understand it. The lessons you've taught me are far more valuable than anything I learned in school, and I never could have done it without you. Thank you.

E-mail From: Black
Subject: Invoice to follow ...
Sent: Thursday, February 7

My warm and fuzzy response is, "Well that is what sisters are for," but I cannot even type it with a straight face. However, I can send you a bill for services rendered.

E-mail From: Red
Subject: Invoice to follow ...
Sent: Thursday, February 7

I can't afford you. I'd need a new budget category: ridiculously overpriced bills never to be paid.

The most important lesson I learned about finances in the past week was that common sense things, like developing a budget and thinking before spending money, are relatively simple but go unnoticed because they're so easy to ignore. Maybe if we hadn't been so involved with our "busy and important" lives, and had stopped and paid more attention to the simple basics, we'd have seen the common mistakes we were making. And avoided a lot of heartache and sleepless nights.

I made a vow to myself — and to my girls – that I'd do my best to make sure we managed our finances in a more positive and intelligent fashion. I'd make my daughters aware of finances in a proactive and informative way, and try to make it a rewarding learning experience — not a dreaded task. (And definitely not a "punishment" as my Mom's budget had been for Black. Although I had to laugh again about breaking that news to her.)

6

This Isn't Headline News, But What Do We Tell The Public?

☎ Got a minute? I need your help again. Nick and I went to pick Natasha up from school today, and some of the moms were looking at Nick. I could tell they were wondering why he was there. I panicked because I was afraid they were going to ask why he was at the school and I wouldn't know how to answer.

📱 You need help all right. You panicked about something that might happen, but did not happen, and would not matter if it did happen.

☎ But it could have. And it does matter. It would have been very embarrassing.

📱 If someone you barely know is bold enough to ask why Nick is at the school, then tell them he came home at lunch for a "nooner" and it took longer than expected.

☎ A "nooner"?

📱 A lunchtime quickie. Or, if you want to be polite, you could say a brief midday sexual encounter. You really have been sheltered.

☎ That was probably something I could have lived my entire life without knowing. You're being no help!

📱 And you are being no fun. For the moment, you do not need to tell anyone anything. Especially mere acquaintances, such as the moms at school. There are many reasons Nick could have been home on a Friday. And if they did ask, I am sure it would have been an innocent question. It is doubtful they were looking for any dirt or gossip, although the "nooner" comment might have made their day more interesting.

☎ Cute, but at some point I'm going to have to start telling people the truth. The problem is that I'm too embarrassed to tell anyone that my husband was fired, but I don't want to lie either. What do I do?

📱 Sounds like you have a dilemma. This is one of those questions without a straight-forward answer. You know — the kind I hate.

☎ Yes, but that never stops you from telling me what to do.

📱 Well, you are going to hate my answer. Talk to Nick and figure out what he wants to tell people. This is about him. Not you. And before you start telling me it affects you too, I know. But Nick needs to establish the "party line," not you.

☎ Well, since that means no one will ever know, I suppose I'll have to maintain our "dirty little secret" forever.

📱 Forever is a very long time. We need to talk about this, but not tonight.

I could see Black's point about letting Nick decide what we would tell the general public. But should we have a different version for family and close friends? And how would we maintain multiple versions of the same story? When I initially called Black, I was feeling embarrassed. Now I was feeling frustrated.

You Are Not Alone

The thought of not being able to tell anyone except Black was a daunting thought. I knew I could rely on her for help, but I also wanted a support group.

E-mail From: Red
Subject: Don't Know What to Tell People
Sent: Thursday, February 5

I know you're at dinner. This is another one of those e-mails where I vent because I don't know what else to do. Please do NOT respond with smart-ass comments. If you have nothing useful to say, then just let me vent.

Intellectually, I know that Nick isn't the first person to be fired (in fact, there might be a few more from his department that are going to be fired), but that doesn't stop me from feeling embarrassed and ashamed that people will think Nick did something wrong or was incompetent. I know I shouldn't care what other people think, but I do. And that makes me feel like a wimp. I worry about the girls because if it gets out that their dad was fired, some kids might tease them. I'm concerned about Nick because he's apparently in denial. He has not said or done anything proactive. I'm trying to let him work things out in his own way, but that doesn't stop me from worrying.

And on top of all that, you want me to keep the truth a secret! That means you're the only person I can confide in. Now I feel like I'm being a burden to you. And that doesn't even go into any of the financial issues I have been dealing with!

At our age we should be coasting to retirement, but instead we've been thrown into turmoil. We had no advance warning. We're totally unprepared. It doesn't matter if no one's going to understand or sympathize, because I can't tell them anyway.

E-mail From: Black
Subject: Trivia Question
Sent: Thursday, February 5

You need to give Nick a little time to decide what he wants to tell people. His hand will be forced when he talks to friends and business acquaintances, and especially when he tries to find work. I am only telling you that it is his decision, although you definitely have the right to tell him how it affects you. And potentially the girls.

I know you said "no smart-ass remarks"... how do you feel about trivia questions? When you first told me Nick was fired, I researched the statistics. Any idea how many people get fired?

E-mail From: Red
Subject: Trivia Question
Sent: Thursday, February 5

No clue on the numbers. But I could give you a specific name.

E-mail From: Black
Subject: Trivia Question
Sent: Thursday, February 5

Gee, only one? What about the over 5 million other names? And more than half of them did NOT receive advance notice.

I hate to break the news to him, but Nick is NOT in a very exclusive club. However, the fact he made it to being almost 50 without being fired is very unique. Almost remarkable. More and more people are being fired, laid off, terminated, forced to resign or — my personal favorite — made redundant, than ever before. Anyway, the issue comes up in some fashion every day in *The Wall Street Journal*.

E-mail From: Red
Subject: Trivia Question
Sent: Thursday, February 5

But it's different when it's happening to you. When it's in a newspaper or a magazine, it's still only a bunch of statistics and stories. It's not real. But when your husband comes home and says, "Honey, I have been fired," trust me, it's pretty damn real! I don't expect you to understand — I'm just trying to explain.

E-mail From: Black
Subject: I understand
Sent: Thursday, February 5

I do understand. And you are not alone.

E-mail From: Red
Subject: I understand
Sent: Thursday, February 5

I know you understand theoretically. I meant literally.

Black had been fired. Not once, but twice? I found that incomprehensible. I certainly couldn't wait to hear more. Meanwhile, it made me realize that we weren't alone. And in a small way, this made me feel better. Not happier. But better.

IM You are online early. Again. I guess you like these new early morning hours.

IM Not really. I like the quiet. I just wish it came later in the day.

IM Enjoy it while you can. I will leave you to your solitude.

IM No, don't go. I have been thinking about last night's conversation. It made me think about people who I suspected had been fired.

IM Yes. There are a lot more people out there like you than you realize.

IM I know this is going to sound like a tangent, but go with me for a minute. It's like my miscarriages. I thought I was the rare woman who had gone through this and I really didn't want to talk about it. But nearly everyone we eventually told had either gone through a miscarriage or knew someone that had. It's like this big secret that no one ever talks about.

IM Really? I did not realize it was so common. Remember, my greatest concern has always been NOT to get pregnant! Anyway, I do remember when it happened to you. I was not sure what I was supposed to say or do, other than express my sadness. I did not press the issue because you did not seem to want to talk about it and I had no words of wisdom.

IM I know. Now don't get me wrong — I'm not equating having a miscarriage with getting fired — but I'm confused as to why both seem to be "taboo" subjects that no one wants to talk about. It makes it so much more difficult to get through the crisis. You feel so alone.

IM If it is so common, I would think there would be support groups out there. There seems to be one for everything else.

IM True, but I was living in England at the time. Saying they are much more reserved than Americans is an understatement. They do not talk about anything personal. To anyone.

IM Even so, I think it is human nature not to want to talk about very personal things, as it takes a lot of trust and self-confidence to expose your feelings and especially your disappointments. What makes it so sad is that by keeping things to yourself you overlook one of the strongest assets you have to work through the situation — the love and support of your friends and family.

IM You sound like Mommy — do as I say, don't do as I do. I never knew you were fired.

IM And neither did Mom and Daddy. All of you lived thousands of miles away and would have worried too much. Mom would have driven me crazy with questions and suggestions, and you would have been constantly calling to make sure I was OK. All very nice sentiments, but I would have spent a significant time comforting all of you, which would have meant less time for me to get on with my life. However, Diana and John knew.

IM Sorry. Sorry that you were fired. And sorry that I didn't know and couldn't help you.

IM No apology necessary. Things happen for a reason, and everything worked out well.

Now I felt guilty about burdening her with my problems because I felt like it was a one-way street. It would have been nice to think that one day my warm and fuzzy way of looking at life might be of use to Black. But I doubted it.

Getting Past The Stigma Of Being Fired

Even if we had told anyone that Nick was fired, I'm not sure I could have talked about my feelings. I felt it was a stigma, a huge "black mark." And I wasn't sure how, or even if, Nick would ever want to talk about it. Nick gets excited about every business venture and assignment, and in an ideal world he'd keep every conversation positive and upbeat. And would never admit any shortcomings or negative thoughts.

I know you are curious about me being fired. The first time was a function of being in the oil and gas industry during the downturn. The second time was related to corporate politics. I am concerned you have a very idealistic impression of Corporate America, and you need to understand the reality — the days of working for one company and retiring with a gold watch are long gone.

Times have changed. The entire business environment and marketplace have changed. And so has the concept of being fired. It seems almost every day *The Wall Street Journal* has a story about executives being fired for cause ... embezzlement, misleading investors, sleeping around with subordinates, cooking the books. So to be fired merely because they did not need your services any longer is not very newsworthy.

I understand this does not help your personal issues, but you need to understand being fired does not carry the stigma it once did.

Really? I knew the business world had changed over the years, but it was never something I took notice of as I was focused on "my job" as a mom. My vision was old-fashioned and went back to my childhood. It was the business world that my parents had talked about. And that I saw portrayed in the Hollywood movies from the 30's and 40's — if you were a hard worker and accomplished what was expected of you, you would be guaranteed job security and success. And live happily ever after. The End.

I understand that business practices have changed over the years, but being fired is being fired. I know this is probably naïve, but I grew up believing that if you got fired, it's because you've done something wrong or dishonest.

Once upon a time that was probably true. Once upon a time is also how fairy tales begin. And today's workplace is no fairy tale. Nick is of the old school, where loyalty, integrity and hard work meant something. Unfortunately, today those values are not nearly so important or valuable, as they cannot be measured or quantified and therefore do not help financial statements or stock prices. Now is not the time to discuss the changing corporate environment, but believe me when I say "happily ever after" is not a concept in Corporate America.

E-mail From: Red
Subject: It's a new century!
Sent: Friday, February 6

So you're trying to tell me that there's no longer a stigma attached to being fired?! I find that very hard to believe.

E-mail From: Black
Subject: (Hopefully) Last Business Lesson of the Day
Sent: Friday, February 6

Times have changed. Drastically. But even back when I was fired the first time, I figured it was obvious it was a function of the downturn of the industry. It did not have anything to do with me personally. In fact, I used most of my severance package to buy a Mercedes convertible, as I had no problem explaining where my "windfall" came from.

You need to understand there are many reasons people get fired. During my corporate life I had to fire many people — often it had nothing to do with them personally or their job performance. Sometimes a company may be downsizing or even going out of business. Even healthy companies fire people if they are heading in a new direction, or changing their corporate structure, or if there is new management who want to "clean the slate" or fill key positions with their own people. The bottom line is that there are many reasons why people get fired.

But any stigma that Nick or you feel is due to your generation and your sheltered environment. Today the stigma, if any, is if you did something corrupt or illegal. And that is not your case. Now can we stop talking about this?

I found this comforting. I really did. Before, I thought that everyone would think badly of Nick and, by association, me, if they knew that he had been fired. And although I didn't want to admit it, I sometimes thought badly of Nick. Not that he had done anything wrong, but that he could have prevented it. That somehow he should have seen it coming. But after my conversation with Black, I realized that in all likelihood there probably wasn't much Nick could have done.

What Do You Tell The World?

I was starting to feel better about our situation as I was slowly coming to grips with the fact that we weren't horrible people, and that we were going through something that a lot of people have had to deal with. And unfortunately, that a lot more people would probably have to face in the future. But that didn't change the fact that at some point we'd have to face the world with our situation. And it didn't answer the question — how and what were we going to tell people?

☎ Just checking in. How are you doing?

☎ OK. Nick is busy working on some project proposals. There's interest from a company that he used to work closely with while at the Company. They really like him, so hopefully something will come of that.

☎ Is he looking at consulting work vs. finding another full-time job?

☎ Yes. For several years he wanted to go out on his own, but it was never the right time. I guess he figures this is a chance to find out if consultancy work is right for him.

☎ Things happen for a reason. I grant you that he did not choose the timing, but the good thing is that at least he can now decide if this is what he wants to do. Or if he prefers the corporate world. But I can guarantee you that if he hadn't been forced into this, he probably never would have found the right time to do it and would have found himself at the end of his life playing the "what if" game.

☎ That's an interesting way of looking at this, but it still doesn't help me explain it to people. Can I say he decided to pursue some consulting opportunities?

☎ I told you, you need to ask Nick what he wants to tell people. Hopefully, he isn't telling people he wants to "explore other opportunities" or "spend more time with his family" because those are standard phrases used by most executives when they are fired.

☎ It seems like the truth would be easier, although I understand why Nick wouldn't want to do that. I know I don't.

☎ I have no idea why you care so much about what other people think. Anyway, the only thing that is important is you and Nick need to have consistent stories. If Nick thinks the consultancy angle is the best spin, then there is no reason why you can not tell people this version. It is not a lie. And I am not surprised he has wanted to go out as a consultant. That is representative of the dramatic changes in Corporate America — people are starting to look for personal fulfillment, and even careers in new fields, now that there is no longer any job security. Just out of curiosity, did the two of you have a conversation about this? Or has the consultancy story just evolved?

☎ Yes and no. I understand Nick well enough to know what motivates him, and I know that he has wanted to try consulting for some time. So it isn't difficult to support this decision because I know it's important to him.

☎ Aren't you the perfect wife?

Not really. The truth was, with the exception of a few close friends and Black, I didn't want to tell anyone the truth. Even though I knew I shouldn't feel like there was a stigma attached to Nick being fired, I did. I knew Nick certainly didn't want to tell his colleagues the truth because there was his professional reputation to consider.

And I was happy to let him take the lead on this, because by keeping the truth a secret, it allowed me to keep my feelings about it a secret too. And, at least on this one issue, I could return to being an ostrich.

What Do You Tell Your Family?

Although Nick and I hadn't specifically talked about who would know the truth, he had to have known I had told Black. How else could you explain my newfound knowledge about financial issues? Not to mention the constant phone calls and hours on e-mails and IM. But the rest of the family — that was far more complicated.

IM Online in the middle of the day. That is unusual.

IM I'm not sure how to talk to Nick about the "party line" on him being fired, so I thought I would send him an e-mail instead of confronting him. This approach worked well when I needed financial information, so I thought I'd try it again.

IM Good idea. What, if anything, have you told Mom?

IM You must be kidding! Nothing. For all she knows, he's going to work every day. And if I had my way, she'd never know anything different.

IM And the girls? Nick has been home for almost two weeks. How have you explained that?

This was going to be hard to explain to a woman without children. Kids are intuitive and can sense when something is wrong. I have tried to remain upbeat around them and not let them see my emotions. When I felt overwhelmed or sad or angry, I said I had to run a few errands — and then I would get in the car, park around the corner and cry. Since Nick was still in denial, his demeanor hadn't changed one bit.

IM Sawyer is too young to need any explanation. Natasha seems to be OK. Although she hasn't asked any questions, I know that at some point I'll have to explain things to her. I thought I might tell them that Daddy decided to work from home so he could spend more time with them.

IM What happens if Nick decides that he does not want to do consulting work and goes back to corporate life? Your idea could backfire if the girls think it is an either/or situation — either work or family. Plus, Nick is going to have to spend a lot of time getting his consulting practice up and running, which may not leave as much time for the girls as they would like. Especially if they think he is not going into the office so that he has more time for them.

IM I never thought about all of that. I just thought it sounded like a nice way to explain Daddy being home.

IM Think about it and then discuss it with Nick and get his thoughts. Or send him another e-mail. Remember, they are only small children. They do not need to know all the details. They need to feel like nothing is wrong. And what is happening has nothing to do with anything they have done. Explain that the daily routine has changed, but that the one thing that will NEVER change is that you and Nick love them and always will.

For a woman without children, Black had great advice about dealing with kids. But then I realized she was simply doing what she does best — pointing out the obvious. She just has a distinct advantage over me in that emotions do not cloud her judgment.

Nick and I decided to keep it simple and said that Daddy had decided to switch jobs and that he wasn't sure if he was going to work from home or go to a different office. This allowed us to handle a variety of issues, such as Nick needing time alone in his office, while also letting them know that the pattern of the house would continue to change.

And Why You Need To Tell Your True Friends

E-mail From: Red
Subject: **Apology**
Sent: Friday, February 6

I have learned my lesson and know not to send you "thank you" e-mails because all I get in return is flippant comments. So instead, I'm going to send you an apology.

I'm sorry I'm burdening you with all this, but you're the only person I can turn to for help. The fact I can talk to you and get advice and guidance, and not worry about you passing judgment or lecturing me, gives me more emotional support than you'll ever know. Or ever acknowledge.

So all I have to say is, "I'm sorry. You get to pick your friends, but you're stuck with your family."

E-mail From: Black
Subject: **Apology**
Sent: Friday, February 6

I love when you acknowledge I am the smarter, more worldly, older sister. I think it is a role I was born to play!

However, there will come a time when you should trust your friends. First of all, I bet that your closest friends already suspect the truth. Second, if they are truly friends, they will stick by you no matter what. And will want to help. You should let them. And if they turn out not to be true friends ... then the quicker you find that out and get rid of them, the better off you will be.

E-mail From: Red
Subject: Apology
Sent: Friday, February 6

I know you're right. I'm just not ready yet. And neither is Nick. Maybe when I feel more in control of the rest of my life. The good news is my longtime friends don't live in Texas, so I can pick when I tell them the news.

E-mail From: Black
Subject: Unemployed Anonymous?
Sent: Friday, February 6

What about a support group? There must be something out there similar to Alcoholics Anonymous for people who have been fired, or at least are unemployed.

E-mail From: Red
Subject: Unemployed Anonymous?
Sent: Friday, February 6

If we aren't going to tell our friends, you want us to tell total strangers?

E-mail From: Black
Subject: Philosophy Friday: Friends
Sent: Friday, February 6

Think about the success of Alcoholics Anonymous. The program is based on getting help from people (strangers) who are experiencing the same issues as you. And how is it different than Weight Watchers where you let others know your weight? You have told me many times how much listening to everyone else's experiences helps you.

This is not a debate. The decision is completely yours and Nick's, but until you decide to include other people, you will be fighting this without any support group. Either emotionally or in terms of possible business contacts. So be prepared to feel alone and isolated. And be careful, because those feelings will destroy your emotional well-being. Without going into details, I have seen the effects of this emptiness and loneliness, and it is not pretty.

P.S. — How did we get back to philosophical issues? I hate them.

E-mail From: Red
Subject: Philosophy Friday: Friends
Sent: Friday, February 6

So you experienced feelings of emptiness and loneliness when you were fired?

E-mail From: Black
Subject: Philosophy Friday: Friends
Sent: Friday, February 6

No. As you know, I have a handful of very close, longtime friends, and I was able to turn to them for emotional support. I knew I was not alone because over the years we built relationships based on honesty and trust. They might not always agree with me, but they always try to understand me. And I know my friends always have my best interest at heart.

Of course she cared. And her advice was excellent. I think that no matter how much I knew our closest friends would be there, it was still Nick's decision to make as to what to tell people. And when.

....

....

....

....

....

....

....

....

....

....

....

....

....

....

7

My Husband Gets In Hot Water — I Want To Make Soup!

📞 Just checking in. How are you?

📱 Don't ask.

📞 Too late, I just did.

📱 I'm on my way to Weight Watchers. And then a quick run to the grocery store before I rush home for Natasha's swim lesson. Then I have to make lunch and take care of the girls. And this afternoon, while Nick's watching golf or football or whatever is on TV while he's napping, I can try and work on house-hunting plans. Assuming, of course, the girls will play quietly and give me some time alone in my work room. Otherwise, I'll have to entertain them until it's time to start dinner.

📞 You forgot to add devising a plan for world peace and curing cancer.

📱 Might as well. I'm already doing everything else for everyone else.

📞 I am almost afraid to ask, but what put you in such a pissy mood this morning?

📱 Nick. I was getting dressed to go to Weight Watchers, and he made his usual snide comment, which he thinks is very amusing, about me going for my "public flogging." Rather than getting annoyed, I decided to use his comment as an opportunity to ask him what he wants to tell people about his being fired.

📞 So you blind-sided him. I am sure that went well.

📱 Last night I sent him an e-mail on the subject, so it wasn't totally from nowhere. But no, it didn't go well. He started doing his usual thing where he avoids any uncomfortable or difficult issue by talking in circles. Instead of telling me his "party line," he tried to accuse me of questioning his business judgment. I tried, unsuccessfully I might add, to get back to the real issue, but he clearly didn't want to discuss it.

📞 I am not surprised he wanted to avoid the topic.

📱 I understand, but let's not forget that I'm supposed to be the ostrich of the family. Nick should realize if I have the nerve to initiate a difficult conversation, the topic must be important.

☎ Nick is having a difficult time facing the fact he was fired. It is a blow to his ego, and the thought of telling anyone else, especially when he is still struggling with it himself, is overwhelming. His defense mode is working overtime.

📱 I know that, and I sympathize with him completely. Maybe I didn't make myself clear. I'm not angry about the topic, per se, but the fact that I can't have a real conversation with this man. No matter what I say, unless it's something totally mundane like what's for lunch, he jumps down my throat.

☎ You are both upset and scared and hypersensitive. It is understandable, but it does make for a volatile situation.

📱 Gee, you think? Thanks for this morning's statement of the obvious. But you really don't understand what I'm dealing with. Nick's in his own little world. I know he's going through a rough time, but here's a news flash — so am I!

☎ I am sure he knows that.

📱 I'm not so sure. All I know is that I have my own wounds to lick. Need I remind you of how I feel about taking on all the financial issues? I wouldn't mind some sympathy and understanding instead of aggravation and moodiness.

☎ I bet Nick is thinking the exact same thing.

📱 What's with your sympathy for Nick? It's really starting to piss me off.

☎ Fine. Quick question before I hang up. What is that line you overheard years ago about being pissed off to the limit or something? The one that always makes you laugh.

📱 "I have reached the highest level of my pissitivity!" Yeah, that pretty much sums up the morning.

Once again Black managed to bring me back down to earth. It's safe to say that I wasn't looking for a lesson in relationships from Black. In fact, I figured this would be one of those topics she'd try to avoid. I was looking for someone to tell me that I was right, someone that would support my "woe is me" attitude. I should have realized that would be the last thing Black would do. But she did manage to remind me that I wasn't the only one suffering and that I wasn't alone in my marriage.

Testing The Relationship Between Husbands And Wives

There was a time before the girls were born, when Nick and I were living in Shanghai, that I seriously thought about leaving him. I had even gone so far as to fly back to the States intending to meet with an attorney, but first met with Black. I was expecting guidance on how to end the marriage, and instead, she turned into a relationship advisor. The funny thing is that she didn't really give any advice, she just asked questions. Pointed questions. She made me identify the strengths of my marriage and compare them with what I perceived as the shortcomings. And then she forced me to honestly and pragmatically decide what I wanted most in life, and what I was willing to do to achieve those things.

Since then, our life together had, for the most part, been good. In other words, there were no major problems or fundamental issues. I use the word "good" (vs. great) because I'm not sure that anyone's marriage is ever really great. At the risk of sounding like my husband, who as an Englishmen definitely leans towards understatement, I prefer to leave the words "great marriage" to something in the movies. In that regard, at least, I wasn't living in a fantasy world.

IM What are you doing online during the afternoon? And how is your pissitivity level?

IM Better. For the moment. When I came home, Nick was going through cookbooks looking for something to make for dinner. Now he and the girls are watching TV.

IM Good. I am glad to hear you are back to being one big happy family.

IM Not really. Nothing has changed since this morning except that he's trying to get on my good side by making dinner.

IM And did you say "thank you?" Or did you just ignore his attempt at a peace offering?

IM You don't understand. It's very easy for you to sit in your ivy tower and pass judgment, but I'm tired and irritable and it'll take more than a dinner to put me in a good mood.

IM Is it ivy tower? Or ivory tower? Anyway, I understand. And I do not think Nick assumes a home-cooked meal will solve your problems, but it is his way of trying to show you that he cares. And that he is a part of the family. You two managed to work through some serious issues in Shanghai, and I know that by working together you can get through this too.

IM But our marriage hasn't been tested since then. What if it can't weather another storm? It isn't as if we have much experience working through problems.

IM Obviously, when "life is good" it is much easier to have a good marriage. But I am confused. Are you saying you wished you had more bad times so that you could have built a stronger marriage?

IM No! Why are you twisting my words? I'm saying I'm not sure Nick remembers how difficult it was for us to get through those hard times and, given his recent actions, I'm not sure he can deal with everything that's now going on.

IM Not sure Nick can deal with it? Or you can deal with it? You seem to be the one that is getting mad at Nick for being Nick.

IM I don't know why you keep coming to his defense. I'm the one that's having to figure out the finances. I'm the one who's worrying about our future. I'm the one who can't talk to my husband and has to turn to my sister.

IM Stop! You are also the one that decided to help your husband and now you are getting mad at him for letting you help? What were you hoping he was going to do? Thank you for the offer and then say, "No, it's OK, I have everything worked out" and then magically work everything out and you would live happily ever after?

IM You still there?

IM Yes. I'm thinking. I'm not sure how to respond. I don't really know what I was expecting.

IM Therein lies some, if not most, of the problem. Neither one of you knows what the future holds, and that is scaring both of you. But think about how looking back at history, whether it was your childhood or your spending habits, made looking forward easier. Now is the time you need to look back at your relationship. And the strong foundation you have built together.

IM No problem! The view looking back is prettier than the one looking forward.

IM Yeah, yeah. And you know what they say about dogsled teams: If you are not the lead dog the view is all the same.

IM That's a visual I could have done without. And it doesn't help the situation.

IM You need to lighten up. I have always said that I thought Nick and you were a good match. Nick wanted to be the traditional husband who went off to work and came home to a wife who was happy to create a comfortable domestic environment, like a 1960s sitcom marriage.

IM So now you're saying BOTH Nick and I live in a fantasy world?

IM No. I am saying you both wanted the same things.

IM But for different reasons. For me, the priority was to have children and be a stay-at-home mom. For Nick, it was a lifestyle and a certain social status that he was accustomed to.

IM But the fact remains, regardless of the underlying motives, your priorities were in sync. Has any of that changed?

IM I don't think so, but everything else has!

IM Think back to the last morning Nick went off to work. If I had called you and asked if you loved Nick, and if you loved your life, what would have been your response?

IM Black, have you been drinking?

IM OK. If a total stranger had called and asked, what would you have said?

IM I wouldn't have talked to a stranger about such personal matters.

IM Stop avoiding the answer.

IM But I hate when you point out the obvious. Of course, I'd have said that I loved Nick. And my life. I know I'm looking at what's wrong with our lives right now. It's not that I'm forgetting what's good, I sometimes just have a hard time being an eternal optimist like you.

IM Which is why it is my job to keep reminding you to focus on what you have, not on what you are afraid you might not have.

IM You mean that half-full vs. half-empty glass you love to talk about?

IM Exactly. And do not be like Mom and wonder if someone has spit in the glass. Or worry what happens if the glass gets a crack.

IM That's funny! And, I am afraid to say, true. The glass analogy really is a great way to describe people.

IM I know. I am married to a true engineer. Larry thinks the glass was not designed properly.

When Nick and I got married, I had visions of a wonderful life together. Black made me see that the foundation of our marriage had not changed — it was our circumstances that had changed. I knew that bad times test the strength of a marriage and maybe that's what was scaring me so much. But I was trying to look at things with a little more hope and a lot less fear.

Marriage Means Teamwork, Emphasis On Work

Having said all that, I was still scared. But it wasn't only a question of our marriage. I was also questioning whether I was strong enough because I was rapidly discovering that I really was an ostrich, not only about financial matters, but also personal ones.

E-mail From: Black
Subject: **Relationship Decision Tree**
Sent: Saturday, February 7

WARNING: I am not a relationship expert, although given how many years I spent dating combined with the variety of men I knew, I have a large "relationship" database. I think it might help if you look at things logically and in a businesslike fashion. No one goes to the office every day with the specific plan to do nothing, yet expect that somehow it will lead to success. Marriage, like a successful career, takes work and dedication.

1. First and foremost, take the issue of Nick being fired out of the equation. Assume that he was still working. All the financial issues would still be there, but at least you would have a steady income with which you could address them.

2. Think back to all the underlying reasons you and Nick initially got, and ultimately stayed married. Ask yourself if any of that has changed.

    a. If the answer is NO: You need to focus on all the reasons you got married. Proceed to Step 5.

    b. If the answer is YES: Proceed to Step 3.

3. Do these changes affect the fundamental things that are important to either you or Nick?

    a. If the answer is NO: You need to focus on the things that are truly important and try to ignore the little stuff that is merely annoying. Proceed to Step 5.

    b. If the answer is YES: Proceed to Step 4.

4. You have identified issues that need to be addressed. Since you are not alone in the marriage, you need to discuss them with Nick and not make any unilateral decisions. For most issues there are compromises or other workable solutions. Proceed to Step 5.

5. SUCK IT UP AND WORK AT IT!

6. GET THE HELL OUT!

E-mail From: Red
Subject: Relationship Decision Tree
Sent: Saturday, February 7

Interesting decision tree. Everything leads to step 5. Are you trying to tell me something?

E-mail From: Black
Subject: Relationship Decision Tree
Sent: Saturday, February 7

Now who has an uncanny knack for the obvious?

E-mail From: Red
Subject: Relationship Decision Tree
Sent: Saturday, February 7

And what about Step 6?

E-mail From: Black
Subject: Relationship Decision Tree
Sent: Saturday, February 7

As far as I am concerned, some things are totally unacceptable, like child abuse or beating your wife. In those cases, I would immediately go to step 6: Get the hell out! But other things, like infidelity, are issues that might be surmountable. But since none of that applies to either of us, we can skip that step.

E-mail From: Red
Subject: Relationship Decision Tree
Sent: Saturday, February 7

You said, "either of us." Does that mean you've actually used this decision tree? Your marriage seems perfect.

E-mail From: Black
Subject: Perception vs. Reality
Sent: Saturday, February 7

Yes, it does. From the outside. But it is like cars ... do you really know if the person owns it or whether they are upside down in their car note? Public perception and personal reality are not always related. In fact, they can be totally different.

E-mail From: Red
Subject: Perception vs. Reality
Sent: Saturday, February 7

That doesn't answer my question! Are you and Larry having issues? Is there trouble in paradise?

E-mail From: Black
Subject: Perception vs. Reality
Sent: Saturday, February 7

Not really, or at least nothing that I know of. But our marriage is not paradise. I went into it knowing I had made trade-offs and compromises. And that is OK. I had no false expectations. But at times I have to stop and ask myself if either of us has changed or whether I have merely forgotten to adjust my thinking for changing circumstances. I always thought Larry and I had the potential to be great together. Not because we were a perfect couple, but because we were an imperfect couple that appreciated our differences.

But when it comes to you and Nick ... the two of you need to face reality. Together. As a team.

By the way, how is your house-hunting going? That is a perfect place to start working together. And a lot more productive than wasting the afternoon online with me!

I found Black's comment about having a great marriage very interesting since I didn't think it existed in real life. However, her comment got me thinking that maybe my expectations of marriage needed to be adjusted to be more realistic. I guess I was thinking a great or even really good marriage was one where two people were perfect for one another. One where there were never any major issues that tested the relationship. One where problems had obvious and easy answers. One that ran on automatic and didn't require any special effort. OK, so I was living in a fantasy world. Nothing new there!

☎ Quick update while Nick is out for a few minutes. I thanked him for making dinner and asked what I could do to help him. He said he had it all under control and that he just needed to run out and get some fresh herbs. So, do I get a gold star, Miss Relationship Advisor?

☎ Good girl! The important thing to remember is that you are both on the same side and that as a team you have the strength to fight this together.

☎ So why do I feel like we're not doing this together? Why do I feel like Nick wants me to do the fighting while he gets to enjoy the doing nothing?

☎ I find that very interesting. You are usually the one that avoids confrontation at any cost and Nick is the more argumentative one. You might want to consider the fact Nick might not have known this side of you existed and he may be unsure of what to do with it. Then again, it might be something as simple as he is happy to have your help. You must admit that in the past you have depended on Nick to make most of the important decisions.

☎ And look where that got us!

☎ Yes, look at where you are. You are in a marriage that up until this point has provided you not only with an easy and comfortable life, but also two wonderful children. Until recently, you had no serious problems or worries. Stop complaining that your life is no longer perfect. Shut up, suck it up and work at it.

☎ Thanks for the sugar coating! And for the record, I don't mind the work. What I mind is that I feel like I'm the only one working.

☎ That is because you are doing more than you are used to doing and you do not think Nick is doing anything extra.

☎ True. And I don't think it's fair!

☎ Yes, it is. It all averages out. The first few years I was racing the Ferrari, my crew did not have to do much to the car on race weekends. Basically "nut and bolt" her, fill her with fuel and clean the windshield. The car was new, I kept my nose clean and stayed out of accidents and away from the walls. Then late one afternoon I had a minor "sharing of paint" with someone, and they needed to stay late and work on the car. I apologized to the crew. My crew chief, Scott, explained that was their job. The fact that it had been easy up until then was fine, but they were always prepared to do whatever it took to keep my car racing. A marriage is no different.

☎ I don't think you can compare racing a Ferrari to a marriage. One is an expensive hobby, and one is your life!

☎ Really? Scott is in charge of making sure my race car is ready to be driven to its limit on a racetrack at speeds in excess of 150 miles per hour. If something goes wrong at that speed, things can get very ugly. And I have to be secure in knowing that the car is 100% race-ready. You cannot have doubts in your mind. I would say my relationship with Scott is as serious as a marriage, because every time I put my car on the track, I am trusting Scott with my life.

☎ I never would have thought of it that way. So do you trust Larry with your life?

☎ Trust in a marriage is different. The point you need to understand is sometimes a marriage is a 50-50 partnership, and sometimes it requires one party to increase their usual workload to get through challenges. At the moment, you may feel like it is skewed, but even if it is 90-10, the important thing is you have to work together. That might mean that you have to bear a bit more of the "work" right now.

☎ So I'm supposed to accept the fact I'm carrying more than my share of the work and let him get a free ride?

☎ In a word, yes.

I knew that in order to make it through this crisis, Nick and I had to recognize what the other person needed and was capable of doing. Although it went against my character, I needed to fight and vent. Nick, on the other hand, needed to retreat into himself, take off his easy-go-lucky public face and lick his wounds in peace. But together maybe, just maybe, we could make this work. But it would take work.

Teamwork 101: Building New "Work" Habits

I started to go into the kitchen, but stopped myself in the hallway as I heard laughter and the sounds of pots and pans, combined with the wonderful aroma of a chicken roasting in the oven. Nick apparently had decided on one of his elaborate dinners and was having Natasha and Sawyer help. I had witnessed this before and sometimes even participated, although I usually stayed off to the corner, slicing and dicing, so as not to get in the way of the "crazy professor" disguised as a "master chef." (Or was it the other way around?) Sawyer would be relegated to some safe task, like tearing lettuce for the salad, but she always took such pride in her work, it made me smile. And watching Natasha, you would think she was born in a kitchen. I wouldn't be surprised if it was the career path she ultimately chose.

IM Glad you are online. Nick is cooking and the girls are "helping" and I decided not to spoil their fun. It got me wondering — other than getting into arguments and then having him do little things as a peace offering, how do I get Nick to do more of the teamwork? Obviously it isn't something we can discuss, as our attempts at important conversations are part of what is frustrating me.

IM Communication is a significant issue which cannot be resolved in a matter of a few minutes, but as far as working together, how about starting with some easy things? I am sure there are plenty of things either around the house or with the girls that he could do and which would genuinely help you.

IM True. My "To Do" list — which is no longer a beautiful list, but rather a jumble of things floating in my brain as well as scraps of paper and Post-it Notes scattered on my desk — has plenty of mindless tasks that I'm sure Nick's more than capable of handling.

IM I am impressed by your faith in Nick to handle the mundane. But I would not present it to him quite like that. Write down a few tasks and ask Nick if he could do them for you. Tell him it would help you out and that you would really appreciate it. I suspect he will jump at the opportunity.

IM I guess I can do that. And it makes sense. I'm sure he would be happy to help.

IM A "honey-do" list of items, although initially groaned at, is actually a big help. They do not have to think about what you want them to do, and they can just get on with the job at hand. And remember to thank him. Both before and after.

IM Maybe I should just pat him on the head and give him a doggy treat?

IM No, but I am certain he would not turn down a "thank you" treat in the bedroom.

IM It would take more than a few "honey-dos" to earn that reward. Too bad I can't give him a list of what I want to discuss. And what I need emotionally.

IM Part of me wants to address your comment about "earning" bedroom treats, but that is a very different topic. All I will say is that from my experiences with men, and that is significantly more than yours, being rejected — or even ignored — in the bedroom creates more problems than you can imagine. And it is closely related to you wanting Nick to address your emotional needs.

IM Obviously, I'm not qualified to participate in this discussion, other than to say I don't see what's wrong with wanting Nick to address my emotional needs.

IM You want him to address your emotional needs, but yet you do not want to address his physical needs? I think we should go back to the general topic of working together. Think of this as Teamwork 101. Start with the easy "honey-dos." Initially you are trying to get into good work habits. Over time you can add more advanced tasks and topics. And rewards!

IM Did you train Larry this way too?

IM Prior wife did most of the work, so I just fine-tuned it. (Thank you, Kim!) And in a way we trained each other. There is a spot in the bar where I leave Larry's mail and any other papers I need him to handle. At times I will leave him notes of things I need him to do. Once he has done it, he will actually put a big check mark on the note to let me know it has been done and then leaves the note in my pile. Almost like a little kid proudly declaring he ate all his vegetables. I use the note as a reminder to thank him.

IM For two very high-powered business types, it seems like a very simplistic way to deal with things.

IM Why does it have to be complicated? It is the old K.I.S.S. strategy. "Keep it simple, stupid."

I realized that the only way Nick was going to know what I needed or wanted was to tell him. But, I wasn't sure I'd always be able to keep it as simple as a "honey-do" note.

Talking And Thinking Do Not Always Go Hand-In-Hand

Now we were going to have the challenge of working on how we communicated with each other in the midst of everything else! This should be interesting.

E-mail From: Red
Subject: So much for being nice!
Sent: Saturday, February 7

I feel like our Saturday nights are becoming very predictable. You go to a nice dinner with Larry at Tony's, while I stay at home and get annoyed with Nick. Then I get to ruin your evening by venting via e-mail.

I don't know what I did wrong tonight, but somehow we ended up in a huge fight. I decided to make a conscious effort to not only start working with Nick, but to let him know I was there for him. After dinner I made a point of thanking him for making dinner as well as complimenting him on the delicious meal. While we were in the kitchen cleaning up, I thought I would bring up a non-confrontational subject to let him know I was on his side.

I told him that I thought it was totally unfair and despicable how the Company had treated him. That I felt like he had given them his life for over 20 years, and they thank him by firing him? But I barely got the words out of my mouth before Nick started telling me I had no idea how hard he worked for them and all the sacrifices he made. I tried to explain I was not mad at him, but that I was mad at the Company. He didn't want to hear any part of it. He started slamming cabinet doors, and so I walked out of the kitchen.

To make matters worse, not only are we not speaking, but I never got the chance to tell him that although I hate the situation, I have every intention of standing beside him and supporting him. I'm not sure we're going to be able to work through this. Whatever I say or do seems to makes things worse — not better.

What did I do wrong? All I wanted to do was let him know I'm on his side.

E-mail From: Black
Subject: So much for being nice!
Sent: Saturday, February 7

You were having a nice evening, and he was probably enjoying the escape from all the stress of your daily issues. When you brought up the Company, it caught him off guard and brought him back to reality. What you did was not wrong. It is important for Nick to know you stand by him. However, you have to keep in mind that your form of communication might not be Nick's preference. And that just because you have thought about something and are ready to talk, it does not mean that he is ready.

E-mail From: Red
Subject: So much for being nice!
Sent: Saturday, February 7

Why is it that every time you point out the obvious, I feel so stupid? Tonight was just a repeat of my failed attempt this morning to have a serious conversation. Why couldn't I see that?

E-mail From: Black
Subject: So much for being nice ... try again!
Sent: Saturday, February 7

It does not take a rocket scientist to see the obvious. Remember these are very emotional issues. Looking at things pragmatically becomes even more difficult. Especially for people like you.

The important thing is to try again. Soon. Having a conversation, or at least an impromptu one, does not seem to be the answer. You have used e-mails to address other important issues with him, so clearly he is better with the written word than the spoken word. Since this is such a personal issue why not write him a "love letter" to express your feelings?

E-mail From: Red
Subject: So much for being nice ... try again!
Sent: Saturday, February 7

I don't understand why we can't have a normal conversation. Why do I have to write a letter? And a love letter at that! He should be writing me love letters!

E-mail From: Black
Subject: So much for being nice ... try again ... his way!
Sent: Saturday, February 7

Why should Nick be writing you love letters? You are the one who wants to tell him something. You can either do it in a way he will understand what you are trying to tell him or you can insist on doing it your way and get nowhere! Your choice.

E-mail From: Red
Subject: So much for being nice ... try again ... his way!
Sent: Saturday, February 7

That was rather blunt.

E-mail From: Black
Subject: So much for being nice ... I am too tired to be nice
Sent: Saturday, February 7

It is late, I am tired and I am NOT warm and fuzzy. Tomorrow we can waste more time doing philosophical discussions about relationships, blah-blah-blah, but right now I want to go to bed. End of conversation.

Sometimes I wish I could be more like Black in that she seems to get away with being blunt, almost to the point of being rude, and yet she can pull it off because it is totally "in character" for her. There's a consistency and sense of predictability in how she handles things. And maybe that was part of Nick's and my problem right now. We were acting out of character. I wanted to fight and talk about things while Nick wanted to "retreat." And we really didn't know how to deal with the changes. Which made communication even more important. And challenging!

IM Good morning.

IM Is it? Does that mean the love letter worked? Wink-wink.

IM Haven't written it yet, but I plan to.

IM Good. Remember when you came back to the States ready to divorce Nick? You were complaining that Nick did not communicate.

IM Yes. I think I know where this is going, but I hope I'm wrong.

IM Sounds like you remember the talking stuffed animals.

IM They didn't talk much, they wrote me letters.

IM Same difference. Nick communicated his feelings to you through letters "written" by stuffed animals. I remember specifically asking you if you really thought the animals had written to you.

IM Back then I thought it was cute and amusing, now it would piss me off because I want Nick, and not the stuffed animals, to talk to me.

IM As I explained then, and it is still relevant, it does not matter how you two actually communicate as long as you communicate. Letters from stuffed animals, e-mails, conversations ... whatever works!

IM OK. I had forgotten how that conversation ended up being a turning point. It helped me understand how we could work together. Maybe I should prop up one of the stuffed animals with the Real Estate section of today's paper and a note "I don't want to live on the street!"

IM I might change the note to "I need a new home!" But otherwise ... whatever works!

I never had intended to tell Black about the letters from the stuffed animals, as I thought she would find it childish and immature. It just slipped out. Looking back, I understood they were the best way for Nick to express himself, yet maintain his "proper" appearance. I forgot the important role those letters played. It was as if I now needed to take a step backwards and remember things that helped in the past, before I made decisions about how to move forward.

IM You online again? I thought you would be out house-hunting.

IM Not today, but we went through the Real Estate section of the Sunday paper and then I put together a checklist of our preferences.

IM I am impressed.

IM Don't be. It's only a Microsoft Word document, not an elaborate spreadsheet.

IM I was referring to your "WE went through" and "OUR preferences." Sounds like you and Nick are making progress.

IM Why would I argue with the man who will be sitting next to me on a porch swing at our retirement ranch as we grow old watching the grass grow?

IM Excuse me while I throw up.

IM I thought that would get you. But yes, things are a little better. I took your advice and put a Post-it Note on the Real Estate section of the paper, asking Nick to let me know when he had a few minutes to discuss how we should attack house-hunting this week. Later, while we were going through the paper, we noticed a few pictures of ranches and we started talking about our dream of one day having some land.

IM So you two are still dreaming about that ranch?

IM Yes, but I think it will probably always remain a dream since right now we'll be lucky to get a house. All the same, it's nice to have a dream to talk about.

IM I am envious.

IM Of a ranch? Then write a check and buy a few thousand acres.

IM Not of the ranch, but of talking about your dreams.

IM Larry and you must have your dreams, too. After all, you've been designing the Arizona house for years, and now you're working on the high-rise here.

IM It seems more like a business plan than dreams of the future. He tells me what he wants, and I execute the plan. But I guess that is what you get when you marry an engineer. However, it would make some of my decisions easier if I knew WHY he wanted these things.

IM You're very clever. You mean you haven't been able to work that into one of your conversations?

IM I have tried. Countless times over the years. On countless topics. But I never got relevant answers. I have resigned myself to the fact that Larry keeps his hopes and dreams, not to mention his fears and disappointments, to himself.

IM As blunt as you can be, why haven't you just flat-out asked him?

IM Because any questions that cannot be answered with very concise factual statements are interpreted as interrogations — not questions. No matter how carefully I position them or phrase them. Larry keeps almost all his feelings bottled up inside, and any attempt to get close to them (him) causes him to get defensive and mad. And it has gotten worse over the years. We are now at the point where sometimes even "How was your day?" sets him off.

IM I'm sorry. I knew he was quiet, but I never knew the extent of it. You are so "out there" and "in your face" that his refusal to open up must drive you crazy.

IM Sometimes, but I had a good idea of what I was marrying. In fact, I figured we were a perfect example of how opposites attract, but it also meant that I had to determine the best way to communicate with him. Larry, like Daddy, is a man of few words, so I listen closely to whatever he says because I know it must be important. Since I am very talkative, I tell him what I am thinking or doing. And why. If he does not ask any questions or disagree, then I proceed as if he is in agreement.

IM Sounds risky. Wouldn't it be better if he would tell you straight-out what he is thinking and why?

IM Yes, but that is not a reasonable expectation. This approach has worked so far, so no reason to change things. And remember, talking is not always communicating. Nick can talk in circles and tell you nothing. But the fact he was able to respond to your Post-it Note and it even developed into a discussion of your dreams means you found a way to communicate. And that is the key. Finding what works for you.

I found it sad that Black had married a man who was so non-communicative, although she seemed to have come to terms with the situation and even figured out what worked for them. And I needed to do the same.

Expect Reality — Not Perfection

Black and I were so different, especially in terms of relationships. If you had asked me if I could learn from Black's relationships, my initial response probably would have been — yeah, I could learn what NOT to do. But I would have been wrong. Very wrong!

E-mail From: Black
Subject: **Slaying the Dragon**
Sent: Sunday, February 8

I really do not want to get into a philosophical conversation, but I want you to make sure your expectations of Nick are reasonable. As usual, this will come with a disclaimer that I am NOT a relationship expert, and Larry and I are far from perfect examples. In fact, I think we have reversed the Venus and Mars roles, but that is not important to this discussion. What is important is I have thought about our roles and have tried to understand them. If you find any of the following helpful — great. If not, just hit the delete button.

I have told you I think you and Nick both wanted a 1960s television sitcom marriage where the husband went off to work and the wife stayed home. And there is nothing wrong with that. But keep in mind that in those scenarios they had no serious "issues" and all the problems were easily solved. In fact, they rarely went to bed mad at each other, except maybe Ricky Ricardo because of his temper, but he eventually forgave Lucy of whatever silly thing she did. Can you remember any serious discussions about relationships? Or hopes and dreams? Or fears and disappointments? No. Just daily life.

At this point you are probably thinking you know all this and that you realize a real marriage is nothing like the ones on television or in the movies. But now think about what historically has been a "good husband." All he had to do was be a breadwinner and not have any major flaws. It was acceptable for him to work all day, come home to a martini, expect a home-cooked meal and then watch television before going to bed. Basically as long as he did not cheat on his wife or beat his children, he was considered a good husband and father.

But as our roles have changed, so too have our definitions of a "good husband." As we do more, which is our decision, we sometimes expect men to do more, too. Again, our decision. But is this really fair? Is it fair to expect our husbands to also be our friends, our confidantes, our soul-mates? I am not saying it cannot be accomplished, but I am questioning whether it is fair to expect that of them without them even getting to vote? It is one thing if both sides agree to change the rules of the game, but it is totally different to have one-sided rule changes. And keeping the changes a secret is against all the rules!

Now take this a step further. If Nick was willing to try to be your best friend, would he know what was expected of him? You assume he knows what you want and need, but remember you do not come with an instruction manual. In fact, even if you were to write one for yourself, it would probably need a translation guide. And that is part of the reason men do well with "honey-do" lists. They like to know what is expected of them. If you could create a bullet point step-by-step guide for men on how to be friends with their wife, you could make a fortune.

But here is the caveat. Your expectations must be realistic. Keep in mind you have always wanted Nick to be a successful executive. Many of the skills necessary to do that require him to be the antithesis of a caring, emotionally intimate partner. Do not expect him to slay the dragon and then come home and want to discuss how he feels about it.

E-mail From: Red
Subject: **Slaying the Dragon**
Sent: Sunday, February 8

Wow. As much as I hate to admit it, with the exception of the Venus/Mars comment, the rest of your e-mail certainly applies to me. For the record, though, I'm surprised that you would have based your thinking on a 1960s sitcom marriage.

E-mail From: Black
Subject: Slaying the Dragon and Venus and Mars
Sent: Sunday, February 8

Remember, when Larry and I got married, I basically had retired from the corporate world. Because he was used to — and liked — a stay-at-home wife, I had to take that into consideration before I agreed to marry him. That was part of the trade-off I was making ... giving up my independence for the security of our marriage.

Curiosity Question: Why do you think Venus/Mars does not apply to you and Nick?

E-mail From: Red
Subject: Slaying the Dragon and Venus and Mars
Sent: Sunday, February 8

Because I have no idea what you're talking about when you say that Larry and you have reversed the Venus and Mars roles.

E-mail From: Black
Subject: Book Review: *Men Are from Mars, Women Are from Venus*
Sent: Sunday, February 8

The book. You must have been living somewhere very remote when it was released because it was a huge bestseller about relationships. The basic premise is that men are from Mars and women are from Venus, and although they come from different planets, they somehow met and fell in love. Everything was wonderful until they came to Earth and amnesia set in. They forgot why they were different and so they no longer respected, or even accepted, their differences. The book addresses how to deal with differences and make relationships work vs. trying to change differences.

E-mail From: Red
Subject: Book Review: Men Are from Mars, Women Are from Venus
Sent: Sunday, February 8

Sounds like something I would read ... not you!

E-mail From: Black
Subject: I am a Martian!
Sent: Sunday, February 8

Agree. I only read it because Larry mentioned he had read it during his previous marriage. Larry is a true engineer. He will study a problem, do his homework and learn from his mistakes. Unfortunately, he modified his behavior so that he could get along with the typical Venusian, or whatever you would call someone from Venus, and then he married a woman who is a Martian!

E-mail From: Red
Subject: I am a Martian!
Sent: Sunday, February 8

That's funny!

E-mail From: Black
Subject: I am a Martian!
Sent: Sunday, February 8

Not sure Larry would agree. The book oversimplified the differences between men and women, so it is not surprising that the stereotypes used do not apply to everyone. But in our case, we seem to have the roles reversed. Problem is, I do not think Larry would appreciate being told he acts more like a woman from Venus than a man from Mars!

E-mail From: Red
Subject: I am a Martian!
Sent: Sunday, February 8

No kidding! But why do you think he changed? I didn't think people changed.

E-mail From: Black
Subject: I am a Martian!
Sent: Sunday, February 8

Larry did not change who he is — he merely modified his behavior. And the "new and improved" version probably would have been a great husband to his ex-wife. However he failed to take into consideration that I am very different from his ex-wife.

E-mail From: Red
Subject: I am a Martian!
Sent: Sunday, February 8

Talk about stating the obvious! You're very different from most women. From most people. Claiming to be a Martian may even be an understatement.

Even without reading the book, I could see why it was a best-seller. I was beginning to see that Nick and I had fundamental differences, which initially we were able to overcome in our lives together. Somehow, as time went on, we either forgot or got pre-occupied with other things. I guess we forgot we came from different planets, although it was obvious to me that Nick came from another country. And another culture.

IM Glad you're online. I was thinking about your Venus/Mars theory.

IM Please tell me you have more important things to do.

IM Remember the times Mom would complain to us about Daddy, and you would ask, "Are we talking about Daddy, Nick, Larry or men in general?" At first I thought you were just being a smart-ass. Until you started in on one of your monologues about men. I remember thinking at the time how funny it was, and then afterwards how true it was.

IM So?

IM So, if men are all the same and the only difference is the packaging, I'd like to trade in Nick — who is currently napping in front of the TV with his head back, snoring loudly and looking distinctly unattractive — for George Clooney.

IM Not me.

IM Liar!

IM Am not. I do not want to be married to George. Not sure I would even want to have sex with him. But I would do about anything to be friends with him. He seems like he would be a lot of fun to be with! We could sit on the balcony of his Italian villa and smoke cigars, drink wine and talk. And laugh.

IM Maybe you are a Martian! You are probably the only woman who fantasizes about George as a "friend."

IM No, I am probably the only person you know that has pragmatic fantasies. Which I guess is a contradiction in terms. But as far as a trade-in for Larry, I have already told him his competition is no one.

IM How sweet. Now it's my turn to throw up.

IM Read my words carefully. I did not say he had no competition. I said his competition is "no one." Those are two very different things. If I ever decided I did not want to be married to Larry, it would be because I did not want to be married. To anyone.

IM Got it. I must admit there are times, like right now, that the idea of not having someone around to cause me aggravation and give me more "work" sounds very appealing.

IM But that would mean you would have to get a job to support yourself and the girls. And you would not be able to be at home for them. Are you sure you want to be a single Mom? Is that trade-off worth it?

IM I was talking about a few hours at a time. Not all the time!

IM It does not work that way. You need to make sure your expectations are reasonable and obtainable; otherwise, you will be setting yourself up for failure or disappointment. But the reality is you and Nick are compatible - you share the same dreams, you both appreciate the value of you being a stay-at-home wife, and you both are committed to your children.

At first, I started to tell Black that I agreed that Nick and I were very compatible — he's happy to wait until I ask/tell him to do something rather than being proactive and offering to help with something. He's happy to sit back and watch M*A*S*H reruns all afternoon while I am busy with a thousand and one things. He's happy for me to talk while he doesn't listen to a word I say. But then I realized those were the points she was trying to make with her initial "Dragon" e-mail and then with the reference to the Venus and Mars book.

Instead I decided to think about our dream of the ranch. For me, I saw the ranch as an escape and a way for the family to reconnect on weekends. I suspected Nick saw the ranch as bragging rights and returning to the life of his youth since he grew up in a large house with land in England. And then I thought about what Black had said, and I realized the specific reasons or motives behind what we both wanted didn't have to be the same. The important thing was that our dreams and goals were compatible. Maybe not every little thing. But the things that really mattered.

Different Is Different Than Right Vs. Wrong

E-mail From: Red
Subject: **Another Argument**
Sent: Sunday, February 8

I tried calling but you must still be at dinner. I have a feeling I may have overreacted tonight and I need to figure out the best way to undo something I said.

After dinner I mentioned to Nick I needed to get all the financials updated so that we could complete the pre-approval process of getting a mortgage. I was basically giving him an overview of everything I had already done since I was proud of the fact I was starting to understand our financials. I wasn't looking for him to do anything, although I told him I'd need him to review it when I was done to let me know if I left anything out. Then I told him that I thought there were certain financial things we could do differently in the future. And before I knew it, we were arguing.

He starting telling me that he takes "exception to this" and "exception to that" and then accused me of always thinking and taking the position that I'm always right. That I could never admit that I was to blame. That it was always his fault or someone else's fault. Not mine. I was so mad at that point that I told him that it's not that I'm always right — it's just that I'm never wrong.

E-mail From: Black
Subject: **Another Argument**
Sent: Sunday, February 8

Sounds like "Happily Ever After" did not last long.

You cannot take back something you said, but you can apologize. How about telling Nick you are sorry that you are always right and that you understand it can be an annoying trait to have to live with on a daily basis.

E-mail From: Red
Subject: **Another Argument**
Sent: Sunday, February 8

I'm not going to apologize! Not even sarcastically! I didn't do anything wrong! And how do I deal with the fact that lately I feel like Nick's wrong most of the time and I'm right.

E-mail From: Black
Subject: A STUPID Argument
Sent: Sunday, February 8

There are two separate issues. The first goes back to Venus and Mars. It sounds like your conversation started out with you wanting to talk and Nick wanting to fix, which meant you two were not having the same conversation. This then escalated into a pointless argument with each of you determined to "win." At that point, the only thing that was guaranteed was that no one would be the winner.

And as far as you being right and Nick being wrong, are you sure there is a right and wrong? Or are you just determined to make Nick see things your way and interpret things in the same way you do? That seems more like a debate than a conversation.

E-mail From: Red
Subject: A STUPID Argument
Sent: Sunday, February 8

Not sure. I have never really thought about it before. But now that you mention it, there are times I feel like I'm standing next to myself, listening to my conversations with Nick, and I think to myself that I know that I'm not right, but I just keep on talking as if that's going to persuade him.

E-mail From: Black
Subject: A STUPID Argument
Sent: Sunday, February 8

Or wear him down. And I bet it never works. It probably just pisses him off, not to mention it actually makes your point weaker. The strongest way to make a point is to state it clearly and succinctly and then shut up. But neither one of us knows how to shut up.

What I find most interesting is that for someone who hates confrontation, you not only disagree with Nick, but you continue to do so even after you realize you might be wrong. It is possible to win a debate without believing your side because a debate uses facts, logic and persuasive skills to convince your opponent you are right. And it becomes a test of abilities. Lawyers do it all the time. But in a marriage, arguments should not be a duel to the bitter end. At some point you need to agree that you disagree. Or at least let go of the argument.

E-mail From: Red
Subject: A STUPID Argument
Sent: Sunday, February 8

Easier said then done. Nick would never concede an argument, and if I do, then I'm basically admitting I'm wrong.

E-mail From: Black
Subject: A STUPID Argument
Sent: Sunday, February 8

You have to get off the idea that there is a right and a wrong. I bet if, when you initially started "arguing," you had been able to keep to the original topic, you could have agreed that you were looking at it differently. Instead, you both started expanding the argument to include other topics, and each of you was relentless in your determination not to back down. At least you now know you are stronger than you previously had thought. The fact you avoid confrontation does not mean you are not capable of holding your own in a fight. Even a stupid one!

E-mail From: Red
Subject: A STUPID Argument
Sent: Sunday, February 8

Gee, thanks, but that doesn't make me feel any better. Now what do I do?

E-mail From: Black
Subject: Do ... nothing
Sent: Sunday, February 8

Let it go. There is nothing — repeat nothing — that can be gained from continuing this argument. But learn from it. Learn that Nick and you will not always see eye-to-eye on everything. Learn that sounding like a broken record will not help things. Learn there will be a time when one of you needs to be the first to shut up.

E-mail From: Red
Subject: Do ... nothing
Sent: Sunday, February 8

Whew! I was afraid you were going to tell me to apologize.

E-mail From: Black
Subject: Do ... nothing
Sent: Sunday, February 8

That would not hurt as long as you simply apologize and do not bring up something that would continue the argument. But given how Nick apologizes, it might not be necessary to say anything. You might be able to show him you are not still mad.

E-mail From: Red
Subject: Do ... nothing
Sent: Sunday, February 8

What are you talking about? Nick NEVER apologizes.

E-mail From: Black
Subject: Actions Speak Louder Than Words
Sent: Sunday, February 8

How quickly you forget. Think all the way back to … yesterday. When you and Nick argued in the morning and you came home to him looking at cookbooks, and then he, with Natasha and Sawyer as his "helpers," made dinner. He realized he overreacted and that was his way of apologizing. And before you ask why he can't utter the words "I'm sorry," think about the purpose of words … to communicate.

Larry will say "I'm sorry" for everything and anything. Saying it and meaning it are two different things, and since it is his programmed response to any issue, it makes them empty words. Nick will not say the words "I am sorry." However, if you know he is being extra nice or doing something to please you, that's his way of apologizing. Remember, if you can communicate the same concept via actions as you can with words, then you need to accept the apology in whatever form it is offered.

E-mail From: Red
Subject: Actions Speak Louder Than Words
Sent: Sunday, February 8

That all makes sense. At least in terms of Nick and me. But I'm not sure I understand Larry's position. I know you said Larry doesn't trust you with his feelings, and I find that hard to believe. And even harder to imagine living with.

E-mail From: Black
Subject: Enough Already!
Sent: Sunday, February 8

It is. Now quit complaining and count your blessings. I am going to bed and suggest you do the same.

Black might have gone to bed, but I stayed up thinking about what she had said. I remembered Nick's Dad telling me years ago when we got engaged, "Nick has to be right, even when he's wrong." I have always felt that was a really good summarization of Nick. But now I might have to admit that it could be said of me as well. And I didn't find it an attractive trait in either of us. But at least I came to the realization I did have the strength to fight, although I would prefer to save my strength for important battles instead of pointless arguments. And to fight along side Nick — not against him.

As you know, I hate these philosophical topics. But I also know you are going to bug me about the fact Larry does not trust me with his feelings, and so I will try to explain the situation. Keep in mind this is a one-sided analysis as I have been unable to get Larry to discuss this with me — which is not only the problem, but more importantly the only way past the problem. And just like my "Dragon" e-mail ... if any of this has any value — great; otherwise, hit the delete button.

You need to count your blessings because you and Nick seem to trust and respect one another, and that is the foundation for a strong marriage. You and I both have a few very close friends that have been in our lives for decades, and if you look at those friendships, I think you will see the secret to successful marriages. The relationships are held together not by mutual interests but by mutual trust. Our true friends love and accept (respect) us as we are. And that makes us feel safe. Marriage should strive to accomplish exactly the same thing.

Even in business, the strongest relationships are based on trust and respect. For example, financial advisors and lawyers. They have a responsibility to focus on the long-term business interests of their clients. They establish reliability and a track record of coming through for their client. They do not make promises they do not intend to keep. And even though their experience and expertise may result in them having a different point of view than their client, they remember to value the uniqueness of their client and give him the respect he deserves. In my mind, a marriage should include all those same qualities, but instead of fulfilling business needs, they should fulfill emotional needs.

Unfortunately, Larry is able to trust me with his money but not his emotions. I have proven my abilities and reliability on the financial front, but not on the emotional front. I know you cannot force someone to trust you, you can only demonstrate trustworthy characteristics. I try, through my actions, to show that I have not only his best interests at heart, but those of his children and parents as well. And I can only hope that over time he will come to trust me with his feelings.

I know you are wondering why he does not. And that I cannot answer, but I can guess. First keep in mind Larry is an engineer and therefore prefers things that can be proven. Trust and respect cannot be quantified or proven, only disproved. So with that as a constraint, I am paying the price for the actions of others. Larry has said very little about his first marriage, and from what little he told me about the second marriage, I believe she betrayed his trust. Whether she actually did something wrong or he just thought she had is not important. The fact still remains the trust was destroyed. And Larry does not want to be vulnerable to that pain again. It is a very protective and rational response. I do not take it as him thinking I will do the same thing, but more that he is not willing to take the risk. For him, the potential reward is not worth the risk. Very analytical. Very logical. Very sad.

You and Nick are both fortunate in that you did not bring "baggage" from prior marriages. Hell, you did not even bring any relationship experience to the table! And I am not sure being engaged to me gave Nick any valuable experience either. I can only hope some of his other relationships were more useful. So if there is anything you can learn from Larry and me, it should be that you need to make sure you do not do anything to undermine the foundation of trust that exists in your marriage. And respect each other. Not only as individuals but as part of a team. Remember that you cannot demand that someone trust or respect you — you have to earn it.

For someone who did not want to discuss philosophical issues she did an amazing job of analyzing her situation. And I was grateful she shared it with me. Not only did it make me understand her situation better, but it made me realize the importance of trust and respect. Not that I didn't already know it, but more that I needed to make sure I didn't take it for granted. But I guess I would expect nothing less from Black. At times she appears to live life by the seat of her pants, but I think that is because she processes data so quickly, not because she doesn't think things through.

IM Good morning. I got your e-mail. I read it twice. It's very sad. But it does make me count my blessings.

IM Great. And as long as you are in a counting mind-set, can we get back to some of your financial issues? PLEASE !!

IM Fine! Give me an hour.

The weekend started out with Nick being in hot water and me wanting to make soup, and somehow ended with me working on a recipe for a successful marriage. I'm not exactly sure how Black managed that, but I was smart enough to count my blessings —on all fronts. Not just my relationship with Nick, but also the one with Black. And although I knew I wanted to thank her for all she had done this past weekend, I also knew I'd be better off keeping my mouth shut.

8

It's Time To Take Charge Of The Charge Cards

IM I'm back.

IM Back to finance, I hope.

IM Unfortunately, yes. I know we need to work on credit cards, but I really don't want to tackle this project. I HATE our credit card debt!

IM You hated the number when you first totaled up your assets and liabilities, so I would not expect it to look any better today. Good news is at least you know what you are facing.

IM I'm not sure I do. I just went through Saturday's mail and was greeted by yet another credit card statement. This is getting ridiculous. They keep coming. Will it ever end?

IM Not until you have no credit card debt. Otherwise, you will continue to get one statement per card per month.

IM No credit card debt? Talk about living in a fantasy world! Anyway, what I meant was getting statements for cards I didn't know even existed. I thought Nick had told me about all the credit cards, but he seems to have forgotten a few. Maybe I need to go through the stack of mail on Nick's desk to see if there are any more surprises.

IM How about just asking him? Via e-mail, of course. He already knows you are trying to complete mortgage-related paperwork, so this would be a logical request.

IM I agree, but since things are relatively calm this morning, I'd rather not risk starting another argument. It's just easier to look myself.

IM So much for trust and respect in the marriage. I can hardly wait to see the fireworks if you get caught going through his papers.

IM I am only looking for credit card statements. I open all the bills now, so I'm going to find out everything over the course of the next few weeks anyway. I'm merely trying to speed up the process.

IM OK, Sherlock Hopeless, what do you plan to do until the appointed hour of transgression?

IM I have a feeling "nothing" isn't an acceptable answer, so I guess I need to focus on the credit cards I already know about. Mine aren't too bad, but Nick's are outrageous.

IM I am impressed you have your own credit cards and not everything is a joint account. Where did you learn that?

IM What are you talking about? My credit cards are basically the ones I had from before I was married to Nick. They are accounts I opened after I graduated and was living at home. Once Nick and I got married, he never offered to add me to any of his accounts, and so we still have separate accounts. Is there something wrong with having our own accounts?

IM No, quite the opposite. It allows you to establish your own credit and build a credit history. Texas happens to be a community property state, so any joint accounts would hold both parties equally responsible; but as I understand it, separate accounts are the sole responsibility of the cardholder. But that is not important. Getting the debt worked off is.

IM So, I did the right thing without even knowing. That's pure dumb luck. Anyway, given how much debt Nick has run up, I'm not sure he can go cold turkey and not incur more. Maybe for a few days or weeks, but I doubt he can stop altogether. When I first showed him the total, he mumbled something about getting it all paid off eventually, but I doubt it. We're drowning in debt. I feel like we need a life preserver. No, make that a lifeboat.

IM Sounds like Nick may need Debtor's Anonymous.

IM Very funny.

IM I was not trying to be funny. Nick may be a compulsive spender. Debtor's Anonymous has a debt quiz that helps you determine if you have a serious problem. They also have a list of warning signs. Just like alcoholics, the first step on the road to recovery is admitting you have a problem.

IM Well, I admit we have a problem. A huge problem, but there's no way that Nick's ever going to admit that.

IM Well, numbers do not lie. And since you have now made me aware of the magnitude of your debt, I have no problem being the "bad" guy! I will e-mail the quiz and warning signs to you and Nick.

IM Gee, thanks. I can hardly wait. However, I'm not sure admitting we have a problem will do anything to help pay off the debt.

IM The fact you are trying not to incur any more credit card debt is a huge step. And I can help you develop a plan of attack to start paying off your credit cards one-by-one.

IM How do we pick the order in which they'll get paid off? Alphabetical? Or just toss the monthly statements into the air, and once they land start at the top and make payments until I run out of money?

IM You could play favorites, which is what I did. When I was within several months of being totally broke, I only made payments to my favorite stores and ignored all my other credit cards. Logic told me I should make payments based on APRs, but I let store loyalty get in the way of better judgment.

IM What are APRs?

IM Annual Percentage Rates. Charge cards, like American Express, require the balance to be paid off every month. However, credit cards do not. So unless you pay them in full every month, you are borrowing money from banks and stores. Hence why they are called "credit" cards. APRs are the interest rate they charge you for the use of their money. It is part of the agreement you accept when you open an account. The APRs appear somewhere on your monthly statement and, although I am certain you are not going to like the numbers, you need to look at them.

IM Why do I have a feeling our credit card statements just got even uglier?

I hadn't even thought about the fact we were being charged interest on all the money we had spent on credit cards. But first things first. I had to understand credit cards better. Not what they are and how to use them — Nick and I had an advanced degree in that. I had to understand how to use them properly and when.

The History Of Credit Cards — How Convenient!

☎ Quick call. I think it be might be helpful for you to understand the history of credit cards.

☎ What ever happened to "Hello?" I'm trying to come to grips with our own personal credit card history, and even that's more than I want to know. I don't think knowing the history of credit cards is going to help me deal with our personal dilemma. I'm not sure anything will help.

☎ I know you feel overwhelmed, and I have no desire to continually look backwards, but sometimes understanding history helps you. It did when we looked at the history of your spending habits.

☎ It doesn't sound like you're going to drop this, so can you at least make it quick?

☎ First, there were gas charge cards, which eventually lead to general purpose charge cards, like American Express. Keep in mind these were charge cards, which meant they had to be paid in full every month. They were created as an alternative to having to go to a local Western Union office to wire for money, which is what people did instead of carrying large amounts of cash or trying to cash out-of-state checks. Then in the late 1950s Bank of America issued the first "credit" card — meaning they were extending credit to the cardholder — and initially promoted it to people traveling, in particular salesmen, who could not easily access their home banks.

☎ That makes sense. I remember Mommy telling me how when she and Daddy traveled out West in the 1950s for three months, they had to use Western Union to cable Grandma and Grandpa for money on a regular basis. Now this is all very interesting and will be useful if I find myself on a game show, but what, pray tell, does this history lesson have to do with my credit card debt?

☎ Patience, grasshopper! The point is credit cards were started as a business tool to save time and provide convenience. Credit cards were NOT initially designed as consumer debt or financial aid.

☎ That may not have been the initial plan, but times have changed. Nick and I, and our mountain of credit card debt, are proof of that!

☎ True. But if you returned to the original purpose of what credit cards were meant to be — a convenience so that you did not have to write lots of checks or have cash available all the time — you might find that you use your credit cards differently. Rather than looking at them as a line of credit or endless funds to buy things, you would start to view them as simply a convenience tool, nothing more.

☎ You mean actually pay off what you spend each month? All the time? Do people do that? It's an interesting concept, though perhaps not very realistic, and an entirely new way of looking at credit cards.

☎ Actually, it's a very old way. The original way. And that is the point I am trying to make. Think about it. Mom and Daddy always paid their credit cards off every month, and even today, Mom only carries about four credit cards, if that many. I think it is important to remember the history — and true purpose — of credit cards.

It was extremely annoying when Black was always right. Especially when I thought I finally had the better of her, and then, she proved me wrong. Understanding that credit cards weren't originally intended to be used as long-term debt makes a huge difference.

Wish I Could Earn 18% On My Money!

When I was working on assets and liabilities, I had put together a handwritten list of all our credit cards, which included our credit line, outstanding balance, minimum amount due (which was also the amount I was paying) and payment due date. I did it the old-fashioned way: I used a lined notepad and pencil and simply erased the old numbers and added new ones when the next statement came in. Every so often I would take out my calculator and update the total amount we owed on all our credit cards. And gasp in horror.

But this morning, besides hating the numbers, I didn't even like how the list looked. I went back to Black's "Where Is Your Money Going?" e-mail that included an Excel spreadsheet and decided to try creating my own credit card spreadsheet. I transferred all my data to a spreadsheet and then added an APR column. I was shocked at the interest rates for new purchases — most were 18%, and a few were even higher. And they charged an even higher interest rate for cash advances. It was bad enough owing all that money, but to see the interest rates we were paying made it even more painful.

IM I'm sitting here at my desk, staring at my credit card spreadsheet. On the one hand, it feels great to have put all this information on the computer. On the other hand, now that I have listed the APRs, all I can say is — Yuck!

IM Not a technical term, but I understand. What I do not understand is "my credit card spreadsheet."

IM Oh, that. It's just your basic Microsoft Excel spreadsheet listing all the relevant information for each credit card. I did it this morning. Need me to do one for you?

IM Who are you? Either tell me the name of our childhood pet or I am calling the police.

IM A poodle named Yenta. I have one question though. I figured out how to set up columns with data, but I don't know how to make the program calculate totals. Having said that, since I already know the total is horrendous, I'm not sure I'm in any rush to see the updated amount.

IM OK, it really is you. I can teach you how to do totals, but for now you have everything you need to identify what you have to tackle and in what order. The first thing I would look at is the APR column. Focus on the cards with the highest APRs. That is your most expensive debt. To reduce your interest charges, you need to lower the APRs.

IM I'll just wave my magic wand!

IM Wave all you want, but the quickest and easiest way to reduce your interest charges is to transfer balances to cards with lower APRs. All you need to do is to pull out that Ziploc bag with the credit card offers that I told you to start saving. They typically have promotional offers that include low APRs for balance transfers.

IM Easy enough. And that would explain the third category on the finance charge schedule. I was wondering what the balance transfer rate referred to since they were usually lower than the other rates. I'll start combing through the offers. And I assume I should then cancel the original credit cards after I have transferred the balance to the new cards?

IM NO! You are getting ahead of yourself. First you need to review the offers and add them to your spreadsheet. Pay particular attention to the details. The low APR is typically only good for the balance transfer, which means it does not apply to new purchases. And sometimes the APR is until the balance is paid off, and sometimes it is just for a set period of time and then the APR increases significantly. In addition, you need to see if there are any annual fees or balance transfer fees. You need to read and compare the offers very carefully.

IM If credit cards have different interest rates for different type uses, how am I ever going to be able to compare them? I already noticed some are better for new purchases than others, and some have lower cash advance rates than others. And now you want me to add new cards? You must be kidding!

IM I wish I was. And keep in mind when you pay your monthly bill, unless you pay it in full every month, your payment is usually applied against the lowest APR balance first. Everything is disclosed on the back of the monthly statement. Your job is to read it, understand it and be very careful how you use your credit cards.

IM Why do they make this so confusing? You have to be a finance major to figure this out.

IM The "why" is easy. Credit card companies are trying to maximize their profits. The easier they make it for you to spend money on their credit cards, the more you will spend and the more money they will make. The slower you pay off your balances, the more money they make. The higher the interest rate, the more money they make. Notice a common theme? The law requires full disclosure of all the rates and terms, but the law cannot force you to read it. Or understand it.

As far as being a finance major, that would help. There was an article in The Wall Street Journal about a study that indicated more than half of all students graduating from college lack the ability to handle complex, real-life tasks, such as understanding credit card offers. If you want to get really confused, we can add credit cards offering cash-rebates and other reward programs into the matrix. And store credit card incentives.

IM Thanks, but no thanks. APRs are confusing enough!

I wished that Nick and I could stop using credit cards altogether or at least use them as if they were charge cards, but I knew that wasn't realistic. At least, not yet. So the next best thing I could do was get as many credit cards as I could down from the 18% (or higher!) APRs that we were paying. When a statement says 1.5% a month (or a mere 0.049315% a day), it seems like a tolerable "service charge," but once I realized that it was mathematically the same as 18% a year, it completely changed my attitude. And so I was on a mission.

E-mail From: Red
Subject: I found lower APRs!
Sent: Monday, February 9

I'm so excited. You were right. In my Ziploc bag of offers, I found cards with significantly lower rates than the cards we're currently using. I have attached my Excel spreadsheet so you can see what I found. I'm ready to start transferring balances!

P.S. — I assume I should use them to pay off the cards with the highest APRs. Yes?

E-mail From: Black
Subject: I found lower APRs!
Sent: Monday, February 9

No. Do not transfer any balances yet.

I looked at your list and sorted the cards based on APRs and also added totals to the appropriate columns. (I have attached the revised file and can walk you through how to sort columns some other time.) Almost all your debt is on bank credit cards vs. store cards. Before you transfer any balances, call the banks and ask if they would consider lowering your APRs in light of your good credit history. Mention you are considering several offers from other banks to transfer the balance to a lower APR credit card. And as long as you have them on the phone, find out if they have any balance transfer promotions.

P.S. — You did a great job setting up the spreadsheet.

E-mail From: Red
Subject: I found lower APRs!
Sent: Monday, February 9

I didn't know you could negotiate with banks.

E-mail From: Black
Subject: Retire the high APRs!
Sent: Monday, February 9

You can and you should. They may not lower it as low as the "promotional" offers you received, but it may affect which balances you are going to transfer. The key is to get the total amount of interest you are paying as low as possible. Once you can get rid of the high APR balances, you need to "retire" the credit card to somewhere safe so that you will not inadvertently use it.

E-mail From: Red
Subject: Retire the high APRs!
Sent: Monday, February 9

I plan to do one better. I plan to close down the accounts and destroy the cards.

E-mail From: Black
Subject: Retire the high APRs!
Sent: Monday, February 9

No. Put the cards in a safety deposit box or somewhere out of reach. Depending on what the future holds, it may not be easy to get new credit cards. And you will probably need to make a few small — very small — charges every six months or so to keep the account "active." Older accounts show your credit history, which is very important to getting and keeping a good credit score.

E-mail From: Red
Subject: Retire the high APRs!
Sent: Monday, February 9

Credit score?

E-mail From: Black
Subject: Credit scores ... soon enough
Sent: Monday, February 9

Credit score is a number that represents your credit worthiness and is based on credit report information. It is something you should review periodically, but I did not mention it before now because you were in the process of applying for a mortgage; they will pull your credit report and scores, and we can review them then. For now, you need to focus on your APRs.

Once that is done, we can look at all your options and analyze everything in more detail. For example, the first thing I would do is find out if you can reduce the down payment on the house (that will be the cheapest money you will be able to borrow) and instead use that money to pay off expensive credit card debt. If not, you may want to consider a debt consolidation loan. Or you may decide to pay off your high APR credit cards altogether. Depending on how much you have in savings and investment accounts, and if you feel comfortable giving up some of your safety cushion, it might be a wise use of money. I do not have to look at any of your financial statements to know you are not earning double-digit interest on any of your money, let alone 18%! However, if you do not want to take anything out of savings, that is also understandable.

At the very least, if you are "saving" some of the money from your new and improved shopping habits, you should use it to make bigger payments on the higher APR cards. Plus, keep in mind that by lowering some of the APRs, you will be paying less in interest, which means even if you keep the monthly payments the same, more can be applied against the outstanding balance.

Bottom line: Sometimes you should not save money — sometimes you need to pay off debt.

E-mail From: Red
Subject: Credit scores ... soon enough
Sent: Monday, February 9

All that makes sense. Nick and I are about to go house-hunting, or at least narrow down the neighborhoods. We are going to drive by some of the houses we flagged in yesterday's Real Estate section, as well as some recommendations we got from our Realtor. As soon as we get back, I'll start calling the credit card companies. Wish me luck on all fronts.

E-mail From: Black
Subject: Luck!
Sent: Monday, February 9

See "subject line" above.

I was amazed by Black's e-mail as I thought she would have said to save as much money as I could. But what she said made sense — if I could stop the pain of 18% APR credit cards by using some savings that wasn't urgently needed, then in the long run I was doing myself a big favor. But all that would have to wait until we figured out what was happening in terms of a house and a mortgage. At the very least, this new spreadsheet would show me the minimum that I had to include in our monthly budget for paying off credit card debt. At the same time, I now knew my goal was to figure out how to maximize the amount I applied to expensive debt.

Credit Limits Have Nothing To Do With Your Ability To Pay

I can remember when I graduated from college and received an avalanche of credit card offers in the mail. It was exciting, and I took it as proof that I was now an adult. I thought these companies were offering me credit cards because they were impressed with my college education and were confident I'd find a great job, make good money and live a financially responsible life. Boy, was I naïve! Little did I realize they were betting on the fact I'd want to live the good life, whether or not I could afford to pay for it.

E-mail From: Red
Subject: **News Flash: This E-mail is Not to Vent!**
Sent: Monday, February 9

I know you're still at dinner, but I wanted to give you an update. We narrowed down the neighborhoods we are interested in (and can afford), and since there are only a few houses in our price range, I think the selection process will be fairly easy. The key will be getting approved by the mortgage company.

Tomorrow I plan to start calling the credit companies and so I added phone numbers to the spreadsheet. I couldn't help but notice you ran a grand total of the amount of credit available to Nick and me. It's a ridiculously large amount. Who would be stupid enough to offer us this much money?

E-mail From: Black
Subject: **News Flash: Credit Cards are BIG Business**
Sent: Monday, February 9

A business that wants to make money. A business that realizes millions of people are willing to borrow more in order to have more. A business that does NOT promote the fact it gets paid from both sides — charging the merchants a small percentage for each transaction and then charging the consumer high interest rates on unpaid balances.

And much of that applies to mortgage companies, too. And more. Do you want to get into how numbers can be crunched so that between the down payment and the value of the house the mortgage company can "approve" you? And then how the mortgages are packaged together and sold off to other financial institutions. The mortgage business is fascinating.

Want me to continue?

E-mail From: Red
Subject: News Flash: Credit Cards are BIG Business
Sent: Monday, February 9

NO!!! I wasn't asking a literal question. It was more the idea that the total amount of credit available to us is a ridiculous number. I don't understand it. Of course, the fact that we've accepted these offers is crazy, but that's another issue entirely.

E-mail From: Black
Subject: News Flash: Credit Cards are BIG Business
Sent: Monday, February 9

Since we are focusing on your credit card debt, I will leave my thoughts on mortgages for another time. My issue has always been with the fact that unless you fully understand financial matters, credit card companies make it very easy to get in debt over your head. If you only had one or two credit cards, the total amount you could borrow might be manageable. But multiply that by ten or twenty, and you can drown in the debt.

Accepting the offers, which in reality is only establishing credit lines (albeit expensive ones), is not necessarily stupid. In an emergency — repeat EMERGENCY, and a shoe sale is NOT an emergency — it is a quicker way to access money than trying to get a bank loan, especially since it is not a function of your ability to pay it off.

E-mail From: Red
Subject: News Flash: Credit Cards are BIG Business
Sent: Monday, February 9

No kidding! Based on how much money we can access via credit cards, it's obvious that it isn't based on our ability to pay it off. I always thought it strange that as we charged more, although we never paid off the balance, they'd keep increasing our credit limits without even asking us to update our financial information. Now I understand — the credit card companies are helping us go bankrupt. How charitable.

E-mail From: Black
Subject: Don't Blame the Credit Card Companies
Sent: Monday, February 9

The credit card companies are only tempting you to overspend, but you are the one making the purchases. Mom and Daddy would save first and spend later. They never even had a car note. Our generation is determined to live as well as, or even better than, our parents and is willing to get into debt to do so. We not only do not save before we spend, we often do not even think before we spend. Which would explain why a million people filed personal bankruptcy last year.

E-mail From: Red
Subject: Don't Blame the Credit Card Companies
Sent: Monday, February 9

I don't want to be one in a million!

E-mail From: Black
Subject: Don't Blame the Credit Card Companies
Sent: Monday, February 9

I am not suggesting you file bankruptcy. But remember at the point-of-sale you are the only one who can decide whether you are using the credit card as a convenience or as a loan. And if you know that you cannot afford to pay in full at the end of the month, only you can decide whether it is a smart use of your credit.

E-mail From: Red
Subject: Don't Blame the Credit Card Companies
Sent: Monday, February 9

That's easy for you to say because you can afford to pay off all your credit cards. But if you're telling me to never use credit cards unless we can pay in full every month, then that's not realistic! Now who has lost touch with reality?

E-mail From: Black
Subject: Do As I Say ... Not As I ... Did
Sent: Monday, February 9

FYI, I do not always pay my credit cards in full every month, but there is a method to my madness.

However, I disagree with your comment about me losing touch with reality. I can still remember what it was like to be in debt over my head. I already admitted I was almost broke. In fact, I was within weeks of being totally out of money. It was after I was fired the first time. I lived off my severance package until it was gone, and then liquidated my retirement account. Ultimately I maxed out several credit cards and was using cash advances off of other cards to survive. Eventually I sold my beloved Mercedes to get some cash, and then leased a less expensive car.

E-mail From: Red
Subject: Do As I Say ... Not As I ... Did
Sent: Monday, February 9

WHAT? You never told me all this. I probably should go to bed, but this is fascinating. How did it get that bad? And then what did you do?

E-mail From: Black
Subject: Do As I Say ... Not As I ... Did
Sent: Monday, February 9

Remember *Gone With the Wind*? I guess I was a modern-day Scarlett O'Hara. At one point in the movie, she refuses to face reality and announces, "I can't think about that right now. If I do, I'll go crazy. I'll think about it tomorrow." And that is what I did. Until I ran out of "tomorrows" and had to suck it up and deal with the situation. I focused on getting a job and then, although it took me a while, I managed to work my way out of debt and actually started saving money. But I learned my lesson and I knew I would never do that again! Kind of like when Scarlett declares, "As God is my witness, I'm going to live through this, and when it's over, I'll never be hungry again." Or something like that.

E-mail From: Red
Subject: Do As I Say ... Not As I ... Did
Sent: Monday, February 9

Interesting story, Scarlett. And now that you've married Larry, you really will never be hungry again!

E-mail From: Black
Subject: Do As I Say ... Not As I ... Did
Sent: Monday, February 9

True, but Larry is no Rhett Butler! The significance of this story is I understand how easy it is to get in debt and how difficult it is to get out. If you continue to think credit card debt is a necessary evil, then you will never rid yourself of the burden. If you start to work yourself out of debt, then you have a chance of getting to the point of totally eliminating it.

E-mail From: Red
Subject: Do As I Say ... Not As I ... Did
Sent: Monday, February 9

If that's true, then explain why you don't always pay off all your credit cards every month.

E-mail From: Black
Subject: OPM is different
Sent: Monday, February 9

There are times I do not want to raise any red flags and admit to Larry how much I may have spent in any given month. Sometimes if I have an overzealous month at Neiman Marcus or Tootsies, or if I decide to buy a new watch, I might put it on a credit card instead of American Express, so I do not have to "confess" to the purchase. It is worth the interest expense for a month or two to hide my big purchases and smooth out my spending level. But when I do this, I cut back for the next few months to make sure I pay off the outstanding balances quickly. In other words, I use the credit as a short-term loan. And since I am using OPM, the APRs are not important.

E-mail From: Red
Subject: OPM is different
Sent: Monday, February 9

OPM? Is that like APRs?

E-mail From: Black
Subject: OPM is different
Sent: Monday, February 9

Better. OPM stands for "Other People's Money." I told you I shop from boredom. I know I can pay off the total every month, and I have no incentive to save. Would I shop at these same levels if it meant getting into debt or me having to dip into my "separate property" savings to pay the bill? HELL NO!

E-mail From: Red
Subject: OPM is different
Sent: Monday, February 9

Boy, talk about a double standard! Does Larry know any of this?

E-mail From: Black
Subject: OPM is different
Sent: Monday, February 9

I would tell him if he ever asked, but he does not seem to care, so I figure it is on a need-to-know basis. And he does not need to know. Night-night.

I found Black's double standard interesting and her *Gone with the Wind* quotes extremely amusing, but the underlying logic and lessons were important. I was amazed by how much I'd learned about credit cards in a single day. I wished I could make amends equally fast.

The Hardest Lesson To Learn — Control Yourself!

Habits become ingrained over time, and it's so easy to pay with a credit card, even when you know you shouldn't. I needed to focus on the long-term effect of credit card purchases instead of the short-term gratification. Intellectually, I understood the concept, but once I grasped the full impact of the numbers, it became instantly obvious.

E-mail From: Red
Subject: OPM – What about us?
Sent: Monday, February 9

I have not been able to go to sleep thinking about everything you said about credit cards. Tomorrow I'd like you to pretend you were me and spending our money. Tell me how you would handle our credit cards and debt. And skip the sarcasm. And the movie quotes!

E-mail From: Black
Subject: OPM – What about us?
Sent: Tuesday, February 10

No movie quotes? Or sarcasm? Boy, that takes all the fun out of it!

First, I would admit it is probably unrealistic to have no debt. You will probably always have a mortgage and a car note. But having no credit card debt is a reasonable goal. I would also admit that although you should pay off all credit cards before spending money on anything that is not essential, in reality that probably will not happen.

Ideally, you should not use debt for anything that does not have an associated "asset value" like a house or car. That would mean you would not use borrowed money to buy consumption items, like food and clothing. A $200 pair of jeans is OK if it is within your budget, and the only decision is whether to write a check or charge it and pay it off when the bill arrives. But the purchase does not seem very intelligent if you are going to have to carry the debt at 18% interest.

Using the jeans as an example — if you put the $200 on a credit card that charged 18% interest and only required you to pay 5% of your balance every month, after five years you would still owe almost $25 on the jeans AND you would have paid approximately $75 in interest. All of a sudden the $200 jeans are now $275, and you better still like them in five years because you still have not paid them off.

Over time I would try and take my thinking to the next level. Assuming the $200 jeans were in my budget, I would ask myself if I was spending the money because I would enjoy the jeans or because I had the money in the budget. There might be some months where I might get more enjoyment, or at least satisfaction, from applying the $200 to a credit card balance.

I might not always save before I spend, but I can always think before I spend.

E-mail From: Red
Subject: OPM – What about us?
Sent: Tuesday, February 10

As usual, this all makes sense, except maybe your example. $200 for a pair of jeans? You really do live in la-la land!

I had to laugh at her $200 jean example. I don't think I ever spent more than $50 on a pair of jeans, so the thought of spending $600 was hysterical — talk about someone with no grasp of reality. And I bet they were the jeans that were frayed and had holes. The ones Natasha said were "broken." The only logic I saw in her purchase was that she didn't use ridiculously expensive debt to buy ridiculously expensive jeans.

The balance of that day, as well as during the next few days, I spent hours on the phone trying to negotiate new APRs with our existing credit card issuers and updating the APRs on my spreadsheet. I juggled the credit card calls and number crunching with house-hunting efforts and mortgage-related tasks. Before long I started feeling exhausted by all this financial maneuvering and I decided I needed a break. The logical thing would have been to take the girls to the park or to go to a movie, but instead I returned to a prior escape mechanism. And got busted!

 Got a minute?

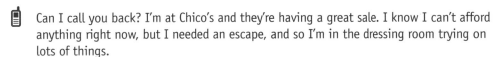 Can I call you back? I'm at Chico's and they're having a great sale. I know I can't afford anything right now, but I needed an escape, and so I'm in the dressing room trying on lots of things.

☎ I know you love Chico's. And sales are a great way to stretch your budget.

▯ Not to mention I feel like I earned a reward for all my hard work. I hadn't really budgeted clothing for me, but I did find a credit card that is only 5.9% for transfers as well as new purchases.

☎ So much for the idea of using American Express so you would be forced to pay it in full every month. Well, at least you are only offsetting the sale price by 5.9% instead of 18%.

▯ Subtle, aren't you? I think I'll put everything back and leave the store.

☎ Or maybe choose one or two things that you really want and maybe even need and can pay for in full this month. Or at least pay off in the next few months.

I was so glad that Black called me; otherwise, I'd have bought out of habit and the excitement of a sale. After all, I didn't need anything. I had a closet full of clothes. Once I was physically removed from the store, along with one carefully chosen pair of pants, I stopped and thought about it and was both happy and relieved. At first, I was pleased that I didn't spend a lot of money and that I could pay for my single purchase at the end of the month. That was indeed a small triumph over past behavior and spending patterns.

But the more I thought about it, the more I realized that although I knew buying clothing was not a priority in my life, bad habits plus credit cards can easily equal mistakes. At least today's mistake was smaller than usual — not perfect, but progress.

☎ Thanks for calling earlier while I was at Chico's. You have no idea how important a phone call that was.

☎ Really? I thought I was being a wet blanket.

☎ You were! But that is exactly what I needed. To make a long story short, it made me realize that if I'm going to achieve what I want in life, I need to start having more control over my buying habits. And especially what I buy on credit!

☎ If you get in the habit of seriously thinking about a purchase before you hand over your credit card, that will make a big difference. That is why I suggested using American Express as much as possible, since it will make you think about whether you can afford to pay for the purchase when the bill arrives. Plus, it totally eliminates the issue of interest expense.

☎ I understand and agree. In fact, it was your comment about the interest expense reducing the amount I was actually saving by it being on sale that really hit home.

☎ It is easy to forget about the effect of interest when you are making a purchase. I used to write the APR on each credit card with a Sharpie. On more than one occasion, I changed my mind at the cash register when I pulled out the credit card.

☎ That's a great idea! And a more timely and less painful reminder than when the monthly statement arrives.

☎ It may not help with all the charges, but it will help with the mind-set of interest costs. And remember, sometimes by the time you pull out your credit card, the damage has already been done. Like at the end of a meal or the end of a vacation.

☎ Oops. I think I just figured out how one of our credit card balances got so large.

I had noticed that one of Nick's credit cards had a huge balance, but based on the limited activity of the prior months I wasn't able to figure out how it had gotten that large. I could have gone back to try and figure it out, but since recent activity was more reasonable I didn't waste the time. However Black's comment about vacations brought back fond memories of a wonderful California vacation that I realized we were still paying off. In fact, even though we'd only take a vacation every year or two, we were probably still paying off several vacations. The memories were still fond, but they were also very expensive!

Monthly Credit Card Review: Look At Everything!

I knew if I worked diligently, I could get our average APR down significantly. This, along with increased payments on the higher APR accounts, would make a sizeable difference in the amount of interest we were paying every month. Reducing overall spending and lowering interest charges would mean I could apply more money to paying off balances vs. just staying current. I felt good. I had never missed a credit card payment and almost always paid my bills on time. Or at worse within a few days of the due date, which I never thought was much of an issue. Wrong again.

☎ I'm absolutely livid and I have to vent. I just got off the phone with one of our credit card companies. They jumped a 3.9% balance transfer APR to over 14%.

☎ Why? Was there an expiration date on the promotion that you did not realize?

☎ No. They said it was because our payment was late.

☎ You triggered a "promotion turn-off event." Sneaky little concept that appears somewhere in the tiny print listing all the terms and conditions and is forgotten unless you happen to trigger it. Which you did.

☎ Whose side are you on? Yes — we were late. But only by about a week. I got busy doing other things and forgot to pay the bill. But it wasn't a month late, and we haven't been a delinquent customer in the past. From what I can tell, we have a perfect credit history with this card.

☎ Not any more. Remember they are a business. And the promotional offer was an enticement to get you to transfer balances and start using their card instead of one from a competitor. Obviously, they would much rather earn 14% than 3.9%, and so the terms provided a way to increase your rate. But they could not do it unless you gave them the opportunity, which you did by not paying on time. You could try calling them back and asking to speak to a supervisor to see if they will re-consider, but I am not optimistic about the outcome. You need to make sure that you follow all the rules.

No kidding! But it was a valuable lesson to learn, and made me realize that even after I spent lots of time making sure all our credit cards were in acceptable APR ranges, my work wasn't done. I had to make sure that I paid everything on time, that they received the payment timely, and that I didn't do anything that might trigger an increase in my APRs.

IM Sorry about earlier today. I know you were trying to explain to me why they raised the APR. I wasn't in a good mood.

IM I noticed.

IM I think what really pissed me off was that it was a careless error that caused the APRs to increase. Something that could have been totally avoided.

IM If the balance on the account is large, you may want to transfer the balance. If not, adjust your payment schedule for the increased APR on this card. The good news is that you caught it early. It could have easily gone on for a few months or longer.

IM True. I noticed it when I looked at my monthly statement. I usually don't review it that closely, but I was double-checking the statement APRs against my spreadsheet.

IM I am afraid to ask … do you mean you typically do not look at the APR rate every month? Or that you do not review your entire statement line by line?

IM Do you want the right answer or the real answer?

IM Bad answer. You should review your statements line by line for several reasons. The most obvious is to make sure that all the charges are correct. Over the past several months I have found at least one incorrect charge, and a few that I was not sure about and needed additional detail. Things can get double-billed. Credits may not appear. I even had a $1,000 payment get entered as $100. The systems are good but not perfect. And keep in mind you have to identify and report fraudulent credit card activity in a timely manner.

IM I usually just skim the charges. I figure if something is wrong or fraudulent, it will be significant enough that I'll catch it.

IM Sounds rather careless. Especially given how hard you are working to try and get your credit card debt under control. I thought you were going to input all the charges into Microsoft Money so you could track them. Why would you get lazy at this point?

IM I am doing that with the American Express charges because that's the primary card we're now using. Most of the other credit cards have no activity except payments, but a few of the lower APR ones have a little activity. All-in-all, with the exception of American Express, there's not much to review. And please — no lectures about spending on credit.

IM It is your money, so you decide how to spend it.

IM Thanks.

IM For what? Not lecturing? It is obvious you know what you are doing with your credit cards. I know I have said it before, but it is worth repeating, you are my best student!

IM And I'll repeat myself by reminding you I'm your only student. But I'll start reviewing all my statements line by line every month, just in case.

I did feel like I was a good student. In the past, even though it was only my personal credit cards that I paid from my "secret" account, I'd get the bill, write the check, and then file the statement. Now I'd carefully review each statement, not only to make sure the charges and APRs are correct, but to remind myself of how we're spending money.

9

I'm Too Busy To Make A List Of All The Things On My "To Do" List

IM Good morning.

IM Not really. Do you know that we're still paying for vacations we enjoyed years ago?!

IM Look on the bright side — I would rather be paying off a wonderful vacation than something frivolous like ...

IM You still there? Like what?

IM Give me a minute. I am trying to think of something I would consider frivolous.

IM How about expensive groceries, clothing you don't need, dinners out that you didn't even enjoy (or want), stacks of magazines that never get read. Do you want me to continue? Because I can.

IM You and your lists.

IM That wasn't a list! Those are just things that immediately came to mind. But since you mentioned lists — I do miss my nice neat computerized lists.

IM If you haven't been making lists, how have you been doing everything related to credit cards? And house-hunting? And the mortgage?

IM For the credit cards I have been writing notes on my Microsoft Excel spreadsheet. House-hunting is a file folder, with newspaper clippings, flyers from houses we have seen and a handwritten list of "things to do" stapled inside the cover. Luckily the mortgage paperwork, which is extensive and would have scared me to death a month ago, has been organized by our banker. Rachel is wonderful and has provided me a checklist, so she basically did most of the work. Or at least the organizing.

IM How have you organized everything else ... correspondence, phone calls, mail, things you need to do or buy, etc.?

IM I haven't! Everything is scattered everywhere! Either somewhere on my desk or in one of the stacks on the floor. It's a nightmare.

IM Even the important things? How do they not get lost in the mix?

IM I try to remember them. And if it's really important, I put a Post-it Note on my computer screen. Otherwise everything is filed chronologically.

IM Filed chronologically?

IM Yeah. The pile closest to the computer has the most recent stuff on top, and the further down in the pile you go, the older the stuff. The pile just to the right of that file is older, and the one to the right of that even older. The piles on the floor are very old. When the new stack gets too tall, I just shift everything to the right and start a new pile.

IM Sounds more like filed chron-ILLogically!

IM It's your fault. You're the one that told me a few weeks ago to ignore all the unimportant stuff, including my list-making, and focus on what needed to be done immediately. So everything's piling up, and I mean that literally!

IM True, I am the one to blame. At the time, you were seriously freaking out about your financial situation and I thought you had more important things to do than spend time making sure your lists were nice and pretty. Sorry. I should have let you work on your lists (and piles) instead of focusing on your finances and trying to find a home and getting a mortgage. Not to mention working on your marriage. We should have added all those items to your lists and gotten to them ... whenever. My fault. Entirely.

IM I was only following instructions.

IM Fine. Then follow these instructions: Start working on your lists again.

IM Really? Thanks! It would be wonderful to have one big list of everything that I need to do, although I dread going through all these piles!

IM I said lists — with an "s." If you think you are going to get everything done by making one big list, you are dreaming! Again.

Organized Chaos Relieves Stress

In the past, my life was simpler and so were my "To Do" lists, which made them much easier to keep under control. And although my system for keeping things organized and updated might not have been perfect, it fit my needs and worked well for me.

IM If one big list isn't the answer, what is? And where do I start? And what about everything that's lost somewhere in these mountains of paper? There's no way I can go through all these piles and organize everything into lists. It would take forever!

IM Chill! Those mountains are causing you stress due to their mere presence. Those piles of paper represent unmade decisions and incomplete tasks. And as they grow, so does your stress level.

IM No kidding!

IM And if you let them keep growing, you will get to a point where you will have ignored everything for so long that trying to figure out what you really need to do will be such a major project that you will feel totally overwhelmed.

IM Too late, I'm already there. Any chance I can wave a magic wand and make it all disappear? And start from a clean slate? And a clean desk? And clean floors?

IM You and your magic wands! You have been watching too much Disney. If you want to start clean — throw everything away and start over.

IM That's not an option! I know some things in these piles can continue to be ignored, but I also know there are things hiding in there that are important.

IM If you can not throw the piles away you have no other option than to go through them. The good news is it is more important to know what you are ignoring than it is to actually deal with everything in the piles. Make it a two-prong attack.

IM You have not seen these piles. Two-prong? Try twelve-prong.

IM That is one of the things I hate about IM. You can keep interrupting me.

Remember when we were doing your expenses and you sorted things into "required" vs. "discretionary?" Well, you are going to do something very similar with these piles. Take a handful off the top and start sorting it into piles based on priority — immediate, this week, next week, next month, next lifetime. If your piles are similar to mine, there will be plenty of non-essential things, such as filing, reading (miscellaneous magazine or newspaper articles) and general correspondence (things with no deadlines). I would start separate piles for those.

Once you get that done, keep only the most important piles on your desk. Move every thing else to the floor. Then you can focus on what is on your desk and start to put together your "To Do" list based on the priority of these papers. Obviously, if you have items that need to be done immediately, you may have to stop your sorting and handle them, but otherwise keep working.

If it makes you feel any better, I bet most of your piles will end up being things you can continue to ignore, or at least that are not important enough to earn a place on one of your beloved lists. In fact, I am sure that most of it will not even make it to your desk! Getting started is the hardest part, but it is something you can easily work on in 15-or 30-minute increments and make slow, but steady, progress. So get off IM and start.

IM Are you done? Can I say something?

IM Yes.

IM Bye.

I didn't want to tackle the piles because I knew it would be such a huge job. Plus, it never seemed as important as other things I had to do. Unfortunately, the mountains of paper on my desk and floor weren't going to disappear just because I didn't have the time, or the inclination, to deal with them. They were going to continue growing. And I was going to continue to get more and more stressed out about it.

So after I took Natasha to school, I came home immediately, went directly upstairs and took a deep breath. I sat down on the floor and grabbed a handful of papers and started making new piles based on importance. To my amazement, in less than 30 minutes I could see the lowest priority piles were piling up the fastest. I found that a great relief, and it provided the motivation for me to keep going.

I started to input the information into Franklin Planner, a computerized time management system that Black had introduced me to years ago. Although the system had many features, I only used the daily planning pages and the calendar. Now my workload seemed to be too much for the system. I wasn't exactly sure why, or what my other options were, but I knew who to ask.

E-mail From: Red
Subject: **HELP! What do I do about my "To Do" lists?**
Sent: Thursday, February 12

I have good news and bad news. The good news is that I'm staring at lots of hills, rather than mountains. I even managed to send a lot of paper to the recycle bin. Funny how what seems important to save becomes totally unimportant if you ignore it long enough. Anyway, it took only two hours, even though Sawyer was in the room with me. (I "cheated" and put on her favorite videos so that I could work uninterrupted.)

The bad news is I need to find a new system to get me organized. Before Nick got fired, I was very organized and my lists were always beautiful and up-to-date. Now it's obvious, based on the hills on my desk and floor, that I have a lot more things to do. I took your advice and focused on only the highest priority pile on my desk. I started to input those tasks, but quickly realized there were so many line items that the list itself would be completely overwhelming. And that would be after the tedious and time-consuming job of inputting everything!

I hate to say this, because I love Franklin Planner, but I don't think it works for me anymore. Is there a better planning program? My feeling of accomplishment in sorting everything is quickly turning into panic as there's no way I can organize all these piles. I'm starting to feel overwhelmed. Again! You juggle lots of balls — handling all your financial stuff, Larry and his girls, house plans, racing, Make-A-Wish. How do you do it? And how am I ever going to get a handle on everything? PLEASE HELP!

Subject: HELP! What do I do about my "To Do" lists?
Sent: Thursday, February 12

Calm down. You are overreacting. Again. And this time, unlike a few weeks ago, it is not warranted. You have already attacked the most critical items. (You figured out how to organize everything related to the house-hunting and mortgage, as well as your credit cards. And your important financial papers are no longer lost in the piles.) Now you are facing an administrative challenge, not a major life decision.

First of all, not everything has to be on Franklin Planner, which is why I started the morning by warning you not to have a single list. I will go through the other computer programs that I use, but you need to understand that I still use Franklin Planner as my planning bible.

• **_Microsoft Project:_** I taught myself Project when we started the house in Arizona because the builder uses it. It is designed to manage projects efficiently and effectively and integrates tasks, schedules and finances. It is great for large projects and probably could be used if you defined "My Life" as a project, but that would definitely be overkill — even for someone like me who has taken being organized to a level that might be considered a sickness.

• **_Microsoft Excel:_** I find certain things work best on Excel spreadsheets. For example, travel arrangements (dates, hotels, flights) and my race-related checklists. I like the fact I can easily sort and analyze the columns of data like we did with your credit card spread-sheet. Plus Excel is great for financial applications because you can enter formulas (totals, etc.) and it automatically recalculates everything if you change the numbers.

• **_Microsoft Word:_** Occasionally I use Word, and although it is a very versatile program (you can easily cut and paste and manipulate the appearance) it still is only a word processing program. Keep in mind Mom still uses either blank paper or a typewriter for her lists. (I am afraid to imagine the lists she would generate if she wanted to learn to use a computer.) In my opinion, if you are going to take the time to input information into Word, you would be better off using another program.

• **_Microsoft Outlook:_** I also use Outlook. It can be used to manage time and information because it integrates communications (e-mails) with calendars and tasks. I do not use it for tasks, but I use the calendar for activities related to the girls. And I am dependent on it to manage all my e-mails because it allows me to organize them and flag ones that require follow-up.

• **_Old-Fashioned Paper:_** I find paper files are still the best way to handle certain things. Often it is easier and more efficient to file miscellaneous pieces of paper by priority or deadline and go through the file on a routine basis, than it is to try and list every specific task on a computerized list.

• **_Franklin Planner:_** This is my primary planning program, not to mention the keeper of my calendar. I not only use it on the computer, but the printed lists and calendars have become such a way of life for me that I cannot imagine keeping track of things any other way. Although I sometimes need to include a task on Franklin Planner that refers back to one of my Excel spreadsheets, an e-mail on Outlook or a file folder, it is still the primary program I use for organizing everything.

I am sure all of this is overwhelming and you are wondering why one program and system will not work for everything. All I can say is a basic black dress will serve many purposes, but depending on the occasion you need different accessories. Think of Franklin Planner as the basic black dress and all the other programs as the accessories.

E-mail From: Red
Subject: I Need Help With My "To Do" Lists
Sent: Thursday, February 12

You're right about one thing. That WAS overwhelming. And as clear as mud.

Let me make sure I understand. Basically you said two computer programs really won't work for my list-making (Microsoft Project and Microsoft Word), so I can rule those two out. One (Microsoft Outlook) will help me organize e-mails and might be an option as a computerized calendar. That leaves me with a spreadsheet system (Microsoft Excel) and Franklin Planner, which I have already said isn't going to work for me.

You mentioned paper files, which seems like a step backwards, but it may be my only option. Maybe I just need a VERY large notebook and lots of big, fat, sharp pencils. Not to mention lots of erasers.

E-mail From: Black
Subject: Franklin Planner is still your answer
Sent: Thursday, February 12

Take a break and go make yourself a cup of tea or something. Right now, you are focused on making a list vs. deciding what you need to do and then making lists. I think Franklin Planner is still your answer. Between "Daily Task" and "Master Task" lists you should be able to categorize and prioritize everything so that it is manageable and accomplishable.

Maybe if you can visualize how you would organize your "very large notebook," I can help you put it on the computer. Remember — anything you can do with a pencil and paper, you can also do with a computer.

E-mail From: Red
Subject: Franklin Planner is still your answer
Sent: Thursday, February 12

Don't you have that backwards?

P.S. — What are Master Task lists?

E-mail From: Black
Subject: Franklin Planner is still your answer
Sent: Thursday, February 12

Question 1: No.

Question 2: Now I understand why you are struggling with Franklin Planner. Think of Master Tasks as a specific elephant and Daily Tasks as the pieces of the elephant you intend to eat on any given day.

If you are not using Master Tasks, then one of two problems occur. You are either listing an entire project (elephant) on a given day, which means it is such a huge task that it will probably never get done or maybe not even get started. Or you have broken a project down into smaller bite-size pieces and then you have more tasks than anyone could realistically allocate to specific days. Either way, you are setting yourself up for failure from the very start.

E-mail From: Red
Subject: Franklin Planner is still your answer
Sent: Thursday, February 12

I'm impressed! How did you picture my mess without actually seeing it? Wish I could visualize your system.

E-mail From: Black
Subject: I will show you mine ... not sure I want to see yours!
Sent: Thursday, February 12

That is an excellent idea. It would be much easier to show you how I organize everything rather than try to explain it. We need to find a day where you have the time to come by the house.

E-mail From: Red
Subject: I will show you mine ... not sure I want to see yours!
Sent: Thursday, February 12

How about one evening? Anytime after 8:00 p.m. works for me.

E-mail From: Black
Subject: I will show you mine ... not sure I want to see yours!
Sent: Thursday, February 12

How about tonight? Be here at 8:01. And I think I will bring some wine home from the restaurant ... I have a feeling I am going to need it!

It sounded like a great idea, but I was a little apprehensive. Larry is an engineer, and I have heard him remark on more than one occasion that he's organized, but nothing compared to Black. What was I in for?

From Pencils To PC's. Or Vice Versa?

I knew the lessons I was about to learn would be more than I could absorb all at once so I reverted to my studious student days and took copious notes. The following is a summary of that night's "class."

1. Paper Lists

Handwritten note:

1. Paper Lists
- Focus on the thought not the system
- Pretty printouts are pretty; not necessarily productive
- Do not confuse perception with reality
- Anything that can be done with paper and pencil can be done on the computer. NOT vice versa!

Black showed me how she organizes things, emphasizing it was the thought process that was important. She kept telling me (almost to the point of being irritating) that sometimes it was better to start off doing things with paper and pencil so that you're forced to think things through and focus on getting organized vs. getting fixated on the physical appearance of the lists. Attractive, typed lists that are constantly updated might look better than hand-written ones with items checked off or crossed out, but that didn't mean they functioned better.

2. Franklin Planner (FP)

Handwritten note:

2. Franklin Planner
- DISCLAIMER: Black does not use exactly as designed
- Suggests I should use as designed
- Program is easy to use
- Black uses older version
  - more straight-forward
  - easier to modify
- Paper system also available
- Driving vs. racing analogy
- Cell phone analogy

Black started with a disclaimer stating she didn't use Franklin Planner as designed, although the system was easy to use and very well thought-out. She had modified it slightly to meet her specific planning quirks, but strongly suggested I learn to drive before I start to race. Black explained she preferred an older version because it was more straight-forward and compared it to cell phones, saying that sometimes you don't want or need all the fancy features, sometimes you just want it to make calls.

Daily Task Lists (1st Pass)

☹ • My daily lists ... Horrible!
• Garbage in = Garbage out!!!
• Do NOT just list things
• Be realistic
• Ask yourself ...
  – can it get done?
  – can it even get started?
• My list's not as bad as she initially thought
• 1/2 my list was marked high priority
• Few items were critical
• Need to learn to prioritize
• These are NOT wish lists

FP: Daily Task Lists (1st Pass)

Black started with my old Franklin Planner Daily Task lists to try to better understand my thought process. I'll always remember her look of horror when she saw them. I was piling up individual tasks on the daily pages. On the day Nick was fired (the last day I had updated my list), I had over 50 tasks on the Daily Task list, and about 40 had been forwarded from prior days. Most tasks were not getting done; they were merely being moved from day to day. The snowball effect had become an avalanche heading my way.

I knew Black's Daily Task lists would be nice, neat and well-organized, so I asked to see hers. Of course, she had already printed out a few. The most obvious thing was she didn't use all the allotted lines, whereas mine had not only filled all the lines but often overflowed onto a second page.

Master Task Lists

• Think of as specific elephants
• Black's categories are very general
  – Art
  – Girls
  – Shopping
  – Telephone Calls
  – Wine
  – Miscellaneous

Paper version = separate pieces of paper for each category

FP: Master Task Lists

Black then showed me a printout of her Master Task lists. She said to think of them as individual elephants and the Daily Tasks as the pieces to be "eaten" on any given day. Black had about a dozen categories and printed each one separately. It was very obvious that even if I didn't have Franklin Planner, it would have been very easy to set up lists using separate sheets of paper in a notebook or on a notepad.

We went back and looked at my "list of 50" line items so that I could identify how best to categorize them and ultimately move them into separate Master Task lists. I was thrilled to see a way to shrink my Daily Task lists, until Black reminded me that the tasks wouldn't go away, they would merely be on a different list.

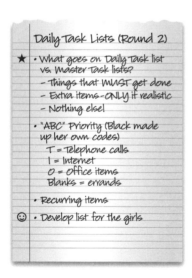

FP: Example of a Master Task

Many of my tasks were phone calls, so I asked Black to walk me through her "Phone Calls" Master Task list. She did, and then she had me set up my first Master Task list. First, we moved the phone calls that were on my "list of 50" to this new list. I mentioned that I try to call Mom every Monday, Wednesday and Friday, and Black muttered something about me being the "good daughter" and then explained that instead of placing them on this list, we would set it up as a recurring task when we went back to working on the Daily Task lists.

Next, I pulled out my Ziploc bag of "high priority" papers and started going through it. Every time I came across a phone call, I added it to the Master Task list and then, with great joy, ripped up another piece of paper. I was now excited and motivated, and asked Black if we could move on. Black took a gulp of her wine and we proceeded.

FP: Daily Task Lists (Round 2)

We returned to Daily Task lists, and Black showed me how to set up my recurring Monday/Wednesday/Friday phone calls to Mom. She explained that she had tasks that were daily, such as "review priority file folder," but warned me against putting down routine things like "brush my teeth." (She was being sarcastic, as usual, but I made a note to teach the girls how to create practical lists, and "brush my teeth" would be a perfect line item for them.) I noticed Black's recurring tasks were highlighted in yellow, and she said Franklin Planner automatically highlights them, but not to worry if I only had a black-and-white printer as they'd appear as slightly shaded.

Black explained the "ABC" column was used to assign priorities. All the "As" (highest priority) automatically appear at the top of the list, which makes it easier to focus on the important things. Followed by the "Bs" and then the "Cs." Black said that items without any priority appear at the very top of the page. She admitted she did not use the "ABCs" and had made up her own codes, and used the column to designate the type of task, rather than its priority. However, Black strongly suggested I use the system as designed. I could see where I'd use the "A" and "B" codes for priority, but I wanted to use the "C" to designate phone calls.

Calendars

- Standard calendars with appointments
- Set up "recurring" appts.
  - example: Weight Watchers
- Black's printed calendar included handwritten notes
  - more efficient
  - updates computer when time allows
  - NOT every time something changes

FP: Calendars

Although I hadn't been using the lists on Franklin Planner properly, I was happy to find out I had been using the calendar and appointment features correctly. The system not only prints nice, neat calendars, but when you print the Daily Task lists, it automatically includes the day's calendar and appointments.

When I told Black how I loved having beautiful, clean calendars, she rolled her eyes and showed me her current month's calendar. I was shocked to see it was such a mess. There were lots of handwritten appointments and changes. Obviously, it was more efficient to make changes on the printed calendar than to continually update it on the computer; otherwise Black wouldn't be doing it this way!

I was beginning to see that sometimes it wasn't more efficient to do everything on the computer. Although I now understood that the amount of detail that Franklin Planner could manage was amazing, and the lists and calendars looked great when kept up-to-date, I also knew I didn't want to spend my days tied to the computer. So I asked Black if she had any suggestions. (Careful what you ask for, you just might get it!)

3. Planning Bible

- Blue leather binder: "Circa" from Levenger
→ - Get three ring binder

Black's Contents
- Daily lists - for next 3 days
- Key lists
  - select Master Task lists
  - select Excel spreadsheets
- Calendars - for next 3 months
  - yellow (FP)
  - pink (Microsoft Outlook)
- Race schedule & details
  - color coded by car
- Personal items

3. Planning Bible, aka "Blue Book"

I then had the honor of looking at Black's "Blue Book," which is how she refers to her planning bible. Hers has a blue leather cover, hence the name, but instead of having three rings, it is held together by eleven discs, with the thickness determined by the amount of paper contained between its covers. She said she found these "Circa" binders years ago in a Levenger catalog and is now addicted to them and uses them for many different applications. (You have to wonder about someone who is "addicted" to binders!) She showed me a few that used translucent plastic covers, but proudly stated she felt her "Blue Book" deserved special treatment because she relied upon it to keep her life organized. Plus she usually took it wherever she went. (I think the real reason it has a blue leather cover is that it often sits in the passenger seat of her blue Ferrari.)

I envied the book – for its appearance, for its versatility, for its contents, even for the printed dividers. It was an organized assortment of Franklin Planner lists, Excel lists, e-mails and other documents. (And I quietly smiled to myself when I saw it included several items I would consider warm and fuzzy: a drawing from Natasha, Make-A-Wish articles and a few personal e-mails that she quickly skipped over.) I noticed there were two different types of calendars printed on different colored paper. Black said the yellow ones were her calendars while the pink ones were calendars for her stepdaughters. She explained the times they had possession of the girls were on both calendars, but the "pink" ones she gave to the girls, and so they included things like school activities, vacations, etc. that affected their schedule.

Although the contents of the "Blue Book" seemed like a hodgepodge of formats, the finished product was a thing of beauty and functionality. I promised myself that I'd make one as soon as possible, although I knew mine wouldn't be a fancy leather one. Probably a basic black vinyl three-ring binder. Or maybe I could find a fabric photo album or scrapbook. But no matter how it looked, my "Book" would serve the same purpose as Black's – to be a versatile and portable way to keep myself organized and up-to-date.

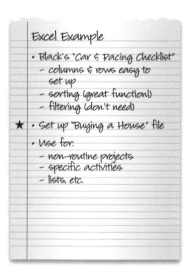

4. Microsoft Excel

Since I had created my credit card spreadsheet using Microsoft Excel, I was already familiar with this program. It's basically the computer equivalent of old-fashioned ledger sheets consisting of a grid of columns and rows. Black explained that many people think Excel is only for financial or other number-related applications because it makes number manipulation easy by automatically recalculating totals or other formulas. (At this point she used my credit card spreadsheet to teach me how to do totals and other basic calculations.)

She then explained how Excel is also designed to be used for data management because of its ability to store, organize and sort huge amounts of data. She started to babble about rows, worksheets, linking files, etc. All I can repeat from that part of the conversation was that Excel could handle millions, maybe billions of "cells" of data. Obviously, it could handle more information than I could, so I asked if she could just show me a simple — emphasis on simple — example.

5. Example of Excel

Black opened her "Car and Racing Checklist" file and I was surprised to find how straight-forward and easy to understand it was. She used the column where it listed the car (I laughed to myself that I would never have to keep track of multiple cars, let alone three race cars) to show me how to sort the data. She then showed me how to filter the information so that I could look at only tasks related to a specific car. I was content to learn how to sort, because the ability to organize lists based on a particular column added great flexibility. The fact I could "filter" a column seemed like a nice option, but since it wasn't very important to me, I didn't pay too much attention.

Suffice it to say, Excel can do more than I can understand. Black suggested I use Excel to manage all the tasks and different people associated with buying a house, and before I knew it, she had me constructing a new worksheet in Excel. And sorting columns!

I wondered out loud how I would remember to do things that were on an Excel spreadsheet without having to look at every list on a daily basis. Black explained that most of her Excel lists were things that didn't need to be handled daily, and if routine review was required, she'd set it up as a recurring task on Franklin Planner. (For example, her grocery list was on Excel; but since she'd fax the order to the grocery store on Fridays, she'd have a recurring Thursday task of updating and generating the grocery list and a recurring Friday task of faxing the list.) Other lists might have a weekly or monthly review set up as a recurring task. Obviously, any important ongoing projects, like buying a house, wouldn't require reminders.

5. Microsoft Outlook
- Setting up new e-mail folders
- Other e-mail functions (maybe later)
  - flag for follow-up
  - setting up automatic rules
- Time management applications (not now)
- Calendar (vs. Franklin Planner)
  - integrates with other programs; multi-tasking
  - prefers stand alone system
  - not relevant for me

5. Microsoft Outlook

At this point I needed a quick bathroom break, and when I returned, I found Black doing e-mails. She used Outlook, like I did, but she had a long list of file folders, whereas I only had the ones that came set up with the program. Until now, I hadn't given my e-mails any thought. There were a lot of them and they all sat in my in-box until I had the time or the inclination to deal with them. Jokes were lumped in with important e-mails, and greetings from friends were mixed in with junk e-mail.

Then Black showed me how to create different folders so that I'd be able to file and organize my e-mails — both incoming and outgoing. And like the physical piles of paper I had recently dealt with, it was obvious if I could sort the e-mails into smaller piles; I could then focus on only the most critical ones and not be overwhelmed by the sheer magnitude of my in-box.

Black explained the time management and calendar applications of Outlook, and I asked why she used Franklin Planner if Outlook came pre-loaded on her computer. Black started to talk about applications in a corporate environment and having a system that integrates with other programs. I was about to hit computer overload so I interrupted her and asked if we were finished. If not, could we please move on? She said that we would finish where we started — with good, old-fashioned paper.

6. Paper Files

6. Paper Files

a. Today Folder (bright yellow)
- *review every a.m.*

b. "WOO" Folders
- *WOO = Waiting on Others*
- *High Priority (yellow) review every a.m.*
- *Low Priority (orange) review 1-2 times/month*

c. 1-31 (Accordion Folder)
- *you can buy or make your own*
- *current month papers*
- *file by date*
- *examples: birthday cards, invitations, maps*

I had hoped — incorrectly, I might add — that by putting everything on the computer I could eliminate the need for paper files. Boy, was I wrong!

Black told me that she still used traditional paper files and opened her desk drawers as proof. It looked like an Office Depot catalog on LSD — a rainbow of colored file folders! I decided she'd taken organization to a new, perhaps insane, level and that she might have gone a teensy bit overboard. And I figured (hoped?) I could skip most of this. But once I started looking at the files and labels, I realized there were many important lessons I could learn and that maybe there was some method to her colorful madness:

a. "Today" File: This bright yellow file sits on Black's desk next to her computer and contains things of the highest priority. She tries to go through it first thing every morning, and although everything in it may not get done that day, by putting something in this file it doesn't get forgotten or misplaced.

b. "WOO" Files: These are the first files in her desk drawer. I couldn't wait to find out what "WOO" stood for, but it turned out the truth ("Waiting On Others") wasn't as amusing as my imagination. Anything that was sent or delegated to others and was waiting on a response or action was filed in either the WOO — High Priority folder (yellow) or WOO – Low Priority folder (orange).

c. "1-31" File: Black has an accordion-type folder with dividers labeled 1-31 and uses it to file things that need to be done during the month on specific dates. For example, greeting cards to be mailed, invitations to social or business events, or maps for an appointment.

```
d. Days of the Week
  • Black labeled colored folders
  • holds papers needed that day
  • keep next day or 2 on desk
  • others filed in "1-31" folder

e. Monthly
  • you can buy or make
    your own
  • easy way to file future tasks
  • file "perfect" greeting cards
    – also include recurring task
      to review file AND calendar
```

d. Days Of The Week: Black uses seven different colored file folders which she labeled for each day of the week. They don't have to be different colors, but she said it makes things easier if she is using more than one folder at a time. They hold papers or notes needed on that particular day. For example, if she needs to make a bank deposit, the deposit slip and associated checks would be in that day's folder. Once there was something in the folder, it either goes next to her computer or in her carry-bag. Folders for later in the week are filed in the "1-31" file.

e. Monthly: Black has plain folders for each month of the year which allows her to file future tasks quickly. As an example, we went through her folder for next month. It included a map for a doctor's appointment and she explained that after the last appointment she had put a Post-it Note on it, indicating when she needed to follow-up, and then filed it in the appropriate monthly file. I also noticed birthday cards, and she explained that when she is card-shopping she often finds "perfect" cards for people. So she buys them and files them in the appropriate month. Black then told me she has a recurring task which appears on the 25th of each month, reminding her to review the next month's folder, as well as the calendar to check for birthdays, anniversaries and special occasions.

```
f. Others (assorted files)
  • develop as necessary
  • by function:
    – bills, phone calls, internet,
      copying, etc.
  • by person
    – Mom, girls, Nick, tax
      accountant, etc.
  • general files
    – Insurance, Wills, etc.
  • color coded (not necessary)

➤ Check The Container Store
```

f. Others: There's also a large assortment of files that Black uses to accumulate tasks – either by function or by person, as well as general files. She said that as I went though my papers, it would become obvious what files I needed to create. I asked why all her folders were different colors, and she explained that was how she differentiated between personal responsibilities, her consulting business and Larry's projects, including each of the houses. At least I could get away with using plain manila folders , although I already knew I'd probably use different colored labels.

I was surprised that Black had not found a filing system "off the shelf" to use, but when I questioned her about it, she said she had been doing this for years and so it had evolved over time and she had never thought to look. She said that The Container Store would probably have something in case I didn't want to start from scratch.

That evening was, without a doubt, one of the most productive in my life. Yes, it was at times an overload of organizational information, but it also gave me the key to finally organizing all my paper in an efficient manner. Before I headed home, I grabbed some file folders and labels from Black's supply closet (it was like her own personal Office Depot) and took one last look at her "Blue Book" and file drawers for inspiration. I left Black's house excited and eager to start the next day. I was finally going to be able to organize all my tasks into a system that not only made a lot more sense, but also that was actually manageable.

Controlling Your Life With A List

IM Glad you're still up. I have a quick question.

IM Sorry, you used up your quota for the night.

IM Driving home, I was wondering — why do you think we're so dependent on lists?

IM Because we want to be like Mom?

IM That's not funny. I was looking for a real answer.

IM a. Because we have awful memories
b. Because we dream of being time management gurus
c. Because we are control freaks
d. All of the above

IM Be serious.

IM I am. And I pick "c." I admit I am a control freak.

IM I don't think I am.

IM Maybe. Maybe not. But well-developed and thought-out lists give you more control over your life. If your desk or work area is covered with paper that needs to be handled and you have Post-it Notes and other reminders scattered all over the place, how are you supposed to feel confident all the important things are being handled? You are going to feel out of control, right?

IM Yes, like this morning when I felt desperate because I had no idea what I was facing — except a mountain of paper.

IM Exactly. Did you feel better after sorting through everything ... even though you didn't actually do any of the tasks?

IM Absolutely! But I still felt anxious because I didn't know the best way to deal with all the paper, especially the higher priority piles.

IM And what about now?

IM After tonight I feel more in control of the situation. Or will be tomorrow, once I finish organizing all the important tasks into manageable lists. And please note the "s!"

IM I rest my case. The key is taking control of the situation and staying in control. And if things start to get out of control again ... take a deep breath and get back on track.

IM Whoa. What do you mean — If things start to get out of control again?

IM There are times when I get busy — maybe working on house designs or focused on a Make-A-Wish project — and I neglect not only keeping my lists up-to-date, but sometimes, I do not even take the time to look at my lists. Before long, I start feeling anxious. But if I can force myself to take the time to get re-organized (or maybe re-prioritized is a better way to describe it), even if I am not actively checking things off my list, I feel more in control and less stressed.

IM Hold on. You mean this feeling of being in control when you're organized is something that's always around? Not just when there's a disruption in life?

IM Only for people who have a life.

IM Cute. I had a life before Nick was fired — it was just simpler. Much simpler.

IM And you had lists — albeit simpler lists — which meant you felt more in control and therefore less stressed. Nick getting fired added things to your list quicker than you could keep track of them. It was only reasonable that you felt out of control. Now that you are getting organized, you will feel better. I promise.

IM It's like the cartoon Daddy used to have in his office — "When you're up to your ass in alligators is not the time to remember you forgot to drain the swamp."

IM True, but you were thrown into the swamp without any advance warning. No time to plan ahead. Time management allows you to be more productive and efficient, but it cannot prevent unplanned events or create more hours in the day. Or the night. And right now, the best use of my time is to go to sleep. Later, gator.

I thought about it and realized Black was right. And it wasn't a matter of using Franklin Planner or Microsoft Outlook, but more a matter of getting organized. It could be as simple as grabbing a notepad and a bunch of Ziploc bags (one of my favorite organizing supplies since everything stays nice, neat and visible, and there's even a box to label the contents) or big envelopes or file folders. The key was finding a way to get started.

Time Management Includes Self-Management

IM I cannot believe you are up already.

IM Yup! I was so excited about working on my lists that I got up at an insane hour. It's safe to say that I have rekindled my love for Franklin Planner, now that I understand how to use it. Thank you so much!

IM It is too early in the morning for your enthusiasm, Little Miss Sunshine! Can we, at least, wait until sunrise?

IM Why do you always want to rain on my parade?

IM Not intentional. It just happens. And I am sure there are things on your lists that are more important than IMing me, so go spread your sunshine somewhere else.

IM I do have one question. What exactly did you mean by time management? I understand there's a limited amount of time in the day, but unless I give up sleeping altogether, I'm not sure how to find the time to do everything on my lists. I'm already getting up at 5:00 a.m. (and this morning even earlier!) so that I have some quiet time before I start the "mom" thing. Any suggestions? And just this once, skip the smart-ass comments!

IM If I could tell you how to create more time in your day, I could make a fortune. There are countless books on time management, but I doubt you will find the time to read one, so I will tell you what works best for me.

IM Type faster. What's the secret?

IM There is no secret. The best you can hope for is to balance the demands of your "To Do" lists against the reality of how much time you have.

IM Great. Another "clear as mud" comment.

IM Not really. More like another "statement of the obvious" comment. First, I look at my calendar to see where I have appointments or non-negotiable demands on my time. This allows me to visualize where I have open blocks of time. I then review my high-priority tasks to determine what absolutely has to happen — whether on a specific day or sometime in the immediate future — and I get that planned. At that point, I have a pretty good feel for how much unclaimed time there is for me to try to tackle other things on my lists.

IM Makes sense. In the past, I best-guessed different tasks for different days, often just randomly assigning them. I definitely didn't plan my time, but that might have been because I didn't have as much that needed to get done. It sounds like I need to start thinking about what I have to do in light of what each day holds. Or at least as best as I can predict it.

IM Yes. Think before you spend. Think before you schedule. See a trend?

IM Yes. A trend of you making smart-ass comments! What about having a Master Task called "This Week" for all those tasks that need to happen some time during any given week, but where the exact day isn't important?

IM Whatever works. I need to go offline, so if you want to continue this conversation, call me on the house line in about five minutes.

In reality, this answered enough of my questions to allow me to go back to working on my lists and organizing my time, but I was curious why Black wanted me to switch to a phone line. And I hoped it wasn't so that she could make more flippant comments.

☎ Hi. What's up with logging off so early?

☎ I have a lot of appointments today, and I wanted to get my cardio workout done before Robert gets here at 7:00 a.m. for weight training. If I start to sound out of breath, it is because I am on the elliptical machine, not because this subject excites me.

☎ Very funny. But you bring up an interesting topic. Multi-tasking.

☎ What about it?

☎ How do you plan it?

☎ Not sure you really do. It just happens. Like right now.

☎ Or phone calls while driving.

☎ Which is not a good habit, but that is where the Ferrari helps build good habits. The engine is too loud to be able to talk on the phone while driving.

☎ I try not to be on the phone while I'm driving, especially if the girls are in the car, but I know I can safely make calls while waiting in the carpool line or while watching the girls at the playground. I guess I could keep some of my low-priority reading in the car in case I have any free time.

☎ And you can wash windows while the laundry is in the washing machine and the chicken is cooking in the oven.

☎ What excellent suggestions, you are such a big help! And, pray tell, when have you done any of those things, yet alone all three at once?

☎ The point I was trying to make is multi-tasking with mundane tasks is easy, but try not to overdo the concept of multi-tasking. FYI, many successful CEOs say they accomplish so much because they do not multi-task. They try to concentrate intensely on one thing at a time.

☎ I bet these CEOs are men who have never run a household! It'd be nice to have enough time in my day so that I didn't feel the need to multi-task, but at the moment

I don't feel I have that luxury. And where do they find the quiet time to concentrate on only one thing? I'd love to know how to earmark time for those projects or tasks that require time without any interruptions. I don't mean a quick phone call that I can slot in somewhere or paying the bills once the girls go to sleep. I mean things where I need a few hours of time to really make a difference.

☎ And that goes back to my CEO comment. If you need a few hours to get a specific task done, then you have to plan for it. Look at your calendar and find a block of time to dedicate to the project. Since Sawyer does not go to school yet, that means you will have to earmark either early morning or after bedtime to focus on bigger, more complicated tasks. During the time she is up, you probably can only do things which can be interrupted since that is what she does best. Obviously, if she is quietly watching television, you may have a few more options.

☎ Great. So, in other words, until Sawyer goes to school, my only hope of getting a block of time to focus on things is to set the alarm for 4:00 a.m.?

☎ Or find someone to take Sawyer off your hands for a few hours while Natasha is at school. Maybe, since you have taken on so many new responsibilities that were formerly Nick's, he would be willing to take her out of the house for a few hours once or twice a week, which would give you a block of quiet time. Think of it as your "dedicated" time when you can give some concentrated effort to a single task.

☎ In other words, don't use it to answer e-mails or talk on the phone.

☎ Exactly. And on that comment I will hang up. I want to switch to the rower, and I can not hold the phone and row simultaneously. My multi-tasking capabilities do have their limitations.

Ever since Nick was fired, I was using the time that he could watch Sawyer for appointments, as well as tackling my errands list, because these are easier and quicker to do alone. I rarely stayed in to do paperwork or home projects on those days. But I thought about what Black had said, and it dawned on me that if I stayed home, that would give me a block of uninterrupted time.

📱 I'm so excited. I just had to call you.

☎ And what has you so excited? A pretty new list?

📱 Better. A list with items crossed off. Nick was free today, so I asked if he could take Sawyer out of the house for a few hours. He not only did that, but also picked up Natasha from school and took them both to the playground for a while, so I was able to focus on my mortgage and house-hunting tasks. I'm flabbergasted at how much I was able to accomplish.

☎ So if you have quiet time, why are you wasting it talking to me?

📱 I'm not. That was earlier today. Now I'm running a few quick errands.

☎ Sounds like a productive day.

📱 It was an experiment, and it worked great. I knew errands were much quicker without Sawyer in tow, but I never realized how much I can get done at home without her underfoot.

☎ Or Nick underfoot.

📱 True, but he was a big help today. I'm never quite sure what he's working on, but he's on his computer a lot. I can only assume it's related to finding work, but right now I'm not going to ask for details. All I know is, he said since he didn't have much to do, he wouldn't mind taking Sawyer out. Personally, I think it gave him a legitimate reason to leave his "office."

☎ Then I am not sure who should thank whom.

📱 I feel like I should thank you. By suggesting that I use some daytime, non-Sawyer hours at home, rather than running errands, I feel like you've given me extra hours in the day.

☎ No problem, you can "owe" me some hours. And remember, over time, as you catch up on higher priority-projects, you will have created a system where you can work on lower-priority projects.

📱 A system?

☎ Yes, a system. I will explain it to you later.

In actual fact, I gave myself the extra hours in the day by planning my time better. I was amazed by how much I could get done in a short period of time, and couldn't help but wonder what I ever did with all my free time before I had children.

E-mail From: Black
Subject: A "System"
Sent: Friday, February 13

Congratulations! Today you learned the obvious. A system is merely a logical approach to getting something done. You got a lot done because you logically used your time, and not only thought about how much time you had available, but also what would fit best.

You always need to take into consideration "fit" when you allocate tasks. Today you did it as an experiment, but when you are looking at your tasks and trying to figure out how and when to move things from a Master Task list to a Daily Task list, you need to apply the same thought process.

Lesson 1: Today you had several hours of quiet time during the day which allowed you to focus on high-priority projects (house and mortgage) that required you to contact people during working hours. Obviously, when you are sitting in the carpool line, you can make quick phone calls, but long detailed conversations that might require you to reference files or other papers would not be a good fit.

Lesson 2: Today you could have taken your "alone" time and run a few hours worth of errands, but instead you did them at the end of the day once you finished everything else. On some days it might make sense to schedule your errands around outside appointments. Which, by the way, is how I plan my errands. I know if I have an appointment downtown, then I can also plan to do some of the downtown errands. Or ones located on the way to and from downtown. There are days I may have more than one appointment out of the house and not have enough time between them to come home, but not have any errands that I really need to do. Instead of killing time shopping in between appointments, I might make phone calls from the car or stop for coffee and do e-mails.

Lesson 3: You may also find the time of day influences your scheduling. I know I am mentally most alert in the mornings, so that is when I try to schedule "thinking" tasks. Whereas afternoons I save for no-brainer type tasks, like filing or local errands. The downside is this sometimes causes scheduling conflicts as I also like to run errands in the morning when there is less traffic and parking lots are not as crowded. My solution is that some weeks I may trade off a morning of "thinking" time at home for a block of time to take care of errands.

Lesson 4: On the weekends we have the girls, I know there will be a chance to catch up on some of the smaller "interruptible" paperwork projects. So if you know you are going to be home with the girls, you may find small chunks of time when they are watching television or playing quietly. If you find yourself with a "free" 15 minutes, keep in mind it is usually more efficient to work on a task that can be completed in that amount of time (or less) than it is to start (and stop) a larger task.

Lesson 5: Some weeks, especially if I am at the track or out of town for a few days, it is obvious I will have very little time to do anything except for appointments and what is of the highest priority. In fact, on those weeks I might print out my entire week of Daily Task lists so that I spend less time on the computer, since once I get on I often get sidetracked and waste time. I may even go to the extent of scheduling "exercise appointments" to make sure I earmark time in my day to exercise because it is a high priority for me.

Time management is a juggling act and requires thinking. But the better the fit of the tasks with the available time in your schedule, the more productive you can be. I know this sounds like a complex system, but in reality it is a simple system that works. As long as you keep it simple.

E-mail From: Red
Subject: A "System"
Sent: Friday, February 13

Wow. I may have to read that a few times before it all sinks in (I printed a hard copy and put it in my version of your "Blue Book"), but it makes perfect sense. Except the comment about you making phone calls between appointments instead of shopping. I hope you don't expect me to believe that!

E-mail From: Black
Subject: A "System"
Sent: Friday, February 13

I bet time management will become a habit before you know it. And FYI, the "instead of shopping" part of the e-mail was one of those "do as I say, not as I do" comments. EOM

E-mail From: Red
Subject: A "System"
Sent: Friday, February 13

More alphabet soup? EOM? I figure the "M" stands for money, but I can't figure out the "EO."

E-mail From: Black
Subject: A "System"
Sent: Friday, February 13

EOM = End of message. Internet slang so that e-mails or IMs do not go on needlessly. If used properly, they can increase productivity so you do not continue to babble back and forth. In fact, if it is used in the subject line, it means the message does not even have to be opened; i.e., there is no message other than the subject line.

E-mail From: Red
Subject: A "System"
Sent: Friday, February 13

Makes sense. There are days when I go online to check e-mails, and 45 minutes later I'm still doing e-mails or surfing the internet and none of it's important. I can waste so much time online. And this is a perfect example! I got online to quickly check e-mails before starting dinner, and here I'm still "talking" with you.

E-mail From: Black
Subject: A "System"
Sent: Friday, February 13

My point exactly. EOM

First Priority: Prioritize

IM Considering what time you got up this morning, I am surprised you are still awake.

IM Barely. You just caught me. I'm feeling frustrated and I'm about to quit and go to bed.

IM Why do you feel frustrated? You made great progress organizing your lists this morning, and only a few hours ago you told me how much you had accomplished on the house and mortgage this afternoon.

IM Yes, but this evening I noticed there was still an assortment of other tasks that didn't get crossed off today's list. Which means it all moves to next week, since I rarely get anything done on the weekends. And then, when I went to forward all of today's uncompleted tasks to Monday, I noticed Natasha is off from school that day!!!

IM I am confused. If you are focusing on high-priority tasks and they are getting done, what exactly is not getting done? Low-priority things? Big deal.

IM Medium-priority things. Not critical, not urgent. But things, nevertheless, that I want and need to get done.

IM OK. The fact you can differentiate between high- and medium-priority is a HUGE step in the right direction. From there you have two choices. Either list only the high-priority items on your Daily Task list and refer to a "Medium-Priority list" if you have spare time; or include the medium-priority items on your list and acknowledge they may not get done.

IM That seems too easy.

IM Easy and realistic. Right now it sounds like your lists are still not totally realistic, which means you are setting yourself up for failure instead of using them as an opportunity for success.

IM Sounds like business babble. Maybe I'm tired, but what are you talking about?

IM If you know you have a crazy week, then only put down absolutely critical items, even if it means listing only a handful of tasks each day. That way, when you do cross them off, you will feel like you have really accomplished something — both in terms of completed tasks as well as good planning.

IM Makes sense. But you must admit, it feels so good to cross things off a list.

IM If all it takes to make you happy is to cross off tasks, add "brush my teeth," "wash my face" and "go to bed" to your list. And then cross them off immediately! EOM

I loved that idea. Not the suggestion to list mundane tasks, but the idea of setting myself up for success rather than failure. What a novel concept. But it wasn't brain surgery. Or even difficult. It just meant thinking about things a little more and then making adjustments when necessary.

IM Good morning. Happy Valentine's Day!

IM Same same.

IM Busy? If so, I will leave you alone.

IM Not really. I'm working on today's "To Do" list. Besides the grocery store on the way home from Weight Watchers, I really don't have any errands to run. And I only have one or two small items that absolutely have to get done at home. I'm sure there will be some blocks of time when the girls are watching TV or playing, and I'll try and get some of my medium-priority tasks done then.

IM How about doing one or two of them right now? EOM

Now that I was using the Master Task lists properly, combined with the fact my week-days were so hectic, I decided to experiment and only list high-priority items on my Daily Task lists. I created a new Master Task called "This Week" for those tasks that had to get done during the week, but it didn't matter on which specific day. Originally, I was going to include medium-priority tasks on "This Week," but decided it made more sense to create another new Master Task category called "Medium Priority."

As Black kept pointing out, the key was not only differentiating between the priorities, but also making sure there was a good fit. I printed my "This Week" list and stapled it to my Daily Task lists and added "Review This Week list" as a daily recurring task. I liked this approach and decided that instead of continually transferring non-critical phone calls or small home office projects from a Master Task or forwarding them from prior days, I'd print my Master Task lists of "Phone Calls" and "Home" and put them in my "Blue Book" which I now gave a place of prominence on my desk.

I saw that my "Home" list included an assortment of tasks I needed to do either in my workroom or around the house, so I knew I had a good chance of accomplishing some of them this weekend. What a great Valentine's Day gift to myself — better-looking lists that actually had a chance of having items crossed off. Almost as good as chocolate!

☎ Got a minute?

📱 Yup, I'm just leaving the grocery store.

☎ One more high-priority thought. You need to make sure you include things on your Daily Lists that are important, as well as urgent.

📱 What's the difference?

☎ Urgent things have deadlines, like paying a bill or filing your taxes. But important things are ... things that are important to you. For example, it might be things like making sure that you spend time with Natasha working on her reading or coloring with Sawyer. And since today is Valentine's Day, maybe even "romance" time for Nick.

📱 You must be joking! I haven't been putting personal stuff on my "To Do" list, just specific tasks.

☎ I am not saying to put personal things on your list every day. I just thought it might make sense since you mentioned this morning that you have "unclaimed" time today.

📱 OK, now I see what you mean. I guess that's not a bad idea.

☎ It is no different than when things get hectic for me and I schedule my 5-mile runs like I would any other appointment.

📱 Knowing you, you probably schedule sex with Larry.

☎ Sure you want to know?

📱 I'm sure I do NOT want to know. Does EOM work on phone calls?

☎ It does now. Bye.

Black had a good point. I could use Franklin Planner as a reminder system for personal things that I didn't want to fall through the cracks. I also realized if I used it to schedule some select personal things, like playing with the girls or exercise time, it could help me start and maintain good habits.

I even dropped a note in my April file folder to start a Master Task list called "Summer Projects" and included a few ideas on different things to do with the girls. It will be slightly different from other lists in that it isn't tasks that must be accomplished, but rather a menu of options so that when summer arrives, I'm prepared.

And Then Categorize

IM Online? On a Saturday afternoon? Who do you think you are? Me?

IM Nick and the girls are going to surprise me with Valentine's Day cookies, so I am "hiding" in my workroom. I figured I'd use the time to organize my shopping list.

IM You went grocery shopping this morning. What are you organizing? Your list by aisle?

IM No, my "shopping list" is anything that I have to do outside of the house — and it seems to be endless. The fact almost everything is low-priority doesn't make the list any shorter.

IM It sounds more like one big list of miscellaneous errands.

IM Yes. But renaming the list "Errands" won't change the length of the list. I thought I was making progress because I managed to take all those annoying scraps of paper and Post-it Notes and create a single list on the computer. Why isn't this working?

IM Because your list is too long.

IM You're no help. I'm trying to figure this out, and you're pointing out the obvious.

IM When am I not? Consolidating all your errands is a good first step. However, if the list is too long, break it down further.

IM How? Separate shopping from errands? Or do you mean different lists depending on priority?

IM Neither, really. I was thinking geographically. To make my out-of-the-house lists more useful, I break them down into locations. I have a separate Master Task list for my neighborhood and one for the Galleria-area, because those are the two areas where I do most of my errands and shopping. Then I have a third list which is for any general shopping items.

IM The geographic lists make a lot of sense, but I'm not sure I understand the general shopping one.

IM If I need mascara, it would go on the Galleria list because I buy it at Neiman Marcus. However, if I need protein bars, it would go on the "Shopping List" because there are several stores that sell them and I could either buy them locally or when I am in the Galleria area. The "Shopping List" also includes any clothing or accessory items I am looking for, but do not have a specific store (or even city) in mind.

IM So how do you know when to actually do these tasks?

IM I only move an item off the Master Task list onto my Daily Task list when I either have to do it that day (based on its priority) or it stands a reasonable chance of getting done because I know that I will be in that part of town. The rest of the time, I just keep a printout of the most recent version of each of the three lists in my "Blue Book." If I find myself with some spare time, or unexpectedly in a different part of town, I can get a few extra things done. Or, if I end up in an "I am bored and going shopping" mood, I at least have some goal in mind.

IM Excluding the last comment, that's basically what I intend to do with my "Phone Calls" and "Home" lists. This really isn't anything new — just a few more pieces of paper. But helpful. Thanks. And EOM. (P.S. — I love that phrase.)

IM One more thing. I use these printed lists to write down new tasks, as I often think of things when I am away from the computer and find paper works as well, if not better, for jotting down notes and reminders. I tried using a handheld computer system, but the type was too small for my baby-boomer eyes. Bottom line: pen and paper worked better! Now ... EOM

That all made perfect sense. I had mistakenly thought that by creating a category, in this case "Shopping," I was automatically solving the problem. I forgot that sometimes a category can be too general, and then the list becomes so long, it's virtually useless.

The Lowdown On Low Priority

I was excited because I had organized everything on my "To Do" lists. However, I realized there were many tasks that would probably never get done. These were the low-priority ones without deadlines or due dates. These tasks or projects were different from the low-priority items that would eventually move up in priority as time went by, such as plans for the girls' birthdays or putting together teacher gifts for the end of the school year.

IM You there?

IM Yes, but why are you?

IM Reviewing my new, beautiful organized lists while the girls are watching the video of Brittney and Chelsea in Mexico swimming with the dolphins. That's their favorite video. And Nick's on a mission — making me a special Valentine's Day dinner.

IM How sweet. Excuse me while I throw up.

IM You're excused. But when you return, I have a question. I can see how all my high-priority tasks will happen. And most of the smaller, individual tasks — like phone calls, correspondence and errands — will get done in a reasonable time frame. But I can also see where there will be low-priority projects that will never get done. In fact, many of them are sitting in piles in the corner of my workroom — taunting me.

IM Then the next time you are in The Container Store, buy some storage boxes and hide the piles. Or, if they are things that will never be important enough to get done, throw them away.

IM It's not that they aren't important. They're big projects that are important to me; however, they'll never be urgent. And I'm afraid that not only will they never get done — they won't even get started.

IM Sounds like a personal problem.

IM Thanks for your help.

IM You said the piles were taunting you, so I gave you two suggestions — hide the piles or throw them away. If you want more specific help, you have to give me more specific information.

IM If I do, you'll laugh.

IM Hahaha … Happy now? Either give me an example or give me an "EOM." Your choice.

IM OK. One of the things that has been on my list forever is working on the girls' scrapbooks.

IM Scrapbooking? It is a big business and nothing to laugh at. But since I am not a scrapbooker (not sure that is even a real word), could you give me a little more detail?

IM When each of the girls was born, I started a scrapbook and included cards, pictures and other mementos. I haven't kept up with it, and now I have boxes of stuff. And still adding more.

IM It is no different than the initial mountains of paper in your workroom. Once you broke them down into smaller, more manageable piles, you were able to make progress. Can you start by sorting the stuff into Natasha vs. Sawyer piles? And then maybe grab a bunch of Ziploc bags and start dividing those two piles into months or holidays?

IM The boxes are probably close to being in reverse chronological order so it might be easier to sort them into months first, and then separate them into piles for each girl.

IM Whatever! The point I was making was if you break it down into more manageable pieces, it will not be so overwhelming. It is just another elephant. Plus, it sounds like it might be something you could do with the girls, although not as quickly as if you did it yourself. But it would allow you to spend time with them AND work on this task. Another good fit. An elephant picnic!

IM You and that stupid elephant analogy. I hate it when you make everything seem so obvious.

IM And I love it when you hate it! Obviously, it is Saturday night, and Valentine's Day no less. So obviously, Larry and I are going to Tony's for dinner. So obviously, I need to go get ready. EOM

In reality I love the elephant analogy. It's such a wonderful visual! And a great reminder on how it's possible to tackle and complete something that initially seems insurmountable. Take one bite at a time. And try not to put too much on my plate. Corny, yes. But also incredibly helpful!

I Need A List Of All My Lists!

I began to worry that all the hours I was spending — first creating my lists and then planning my time — was taking up a lot of valuable time that I could be using to actually accomplish tasks on the list.

IM Good morning. You were not online last night. Does that mean you crossed "romance" off your "To Do" list?

IM No comment, but I certainly feel like my lists are multiplying by the minute. I need a list of the lists.

IM That is one of the criticisms of time management. Some people spend more time managing their lists than they do completing what is on them.

IM I know the feeling! All too well.

IM Lists, like priorities, are moving targets. They change from week to week, day to day, sometimes even from hour to hour. You should not fall into the trap of thinking that once something is on your list, prioritized a certain way, that it is etched in stone.

IM That makes sense, but constantly reviewing everything takes time. I thought the whole point of getting my lists organized properly was that I wouldn't have to invest so much time with them. I just want to start checking things off my "To Do" list.

IM I understand. Which is why you need to review your lists on a regular basis — which is not to be confused with on a constant basis. As with any activity, there is a point of diminishing returns. What are your plans for the rest of the morning?

IM It depends on what you suggest I do about my list of lists. Ideally, I would love to shut off my computer, forget everything on my lists and enjoy a leisurely Sunday.

IM Then do just that. I will send you an e-mail late this afternoon explaining how I keep track of all my lists. Meanwhile, you need to add one more task to today's list ... "Enjoy the day." And I expect you to report back tonight that you completed the task.

And that's exactly what I did. I straightened up a few things on my desk, shut down the computer and went upstairs to see what the girls were doing. We spent the day together doing nothing special. We played games. We watched Disney movies (with lots of popcorn!) and I laughed watching the girls laugh. And before you knew it, we were all in the kitchen making dinner together. And I never even thought about the piles on my desk. Or the floor. The break was wonderful!

E-mail From: Black
Subject: Sunday – Scheduling my Week
Sent: Sunday, February 15

Reviewing and updating your lists on a routine basis does not take much time, and it will keep you focused and allow you to accomplish a lot more. I schedule the time just as I would any other task and set it up as a recurring task for every Sunday. I call it "Review Lists" although "Schedule My Week" would probably be a more accurate description. I know you like checklists, so this should make you happy:

1. I try to clean up the Daily Task lists on the computer every few days, but if I miss a few days, that is the first thing I do.
2. I make sure any new tasks or appointments are input. During the week I keep track of them by either writing them down on a printed list or the Calendar. Sometimes

I may have Post-it Notes, e-mails or other pieces of paper I use as reminders, and then I either put those in the front of my "Blue Book" or in a special folder labeled "Franklin Planner."

3. I then look at my Calendar and allocate Daily Tasks for the coming week to see if, and where, I have available time to do additional things. And what would fit best in those time slots.

4. Since I have a few separate lists in my "Blue Book," I quickly review those to see if anything else needs to be done this week. Note: I do not constantly update these on the computer, but instead just use a pen to add/delete items on the printed list and then update when necessary.

5. Finally, I go through all the Master Lists to see what needs to be moved or deleted. Obviously, there are times when I have accomplished something that has been on a Master Task list (vs. a Daily Task list) and sometimes I decide a task is no longer important. And then there are times that the priority may change.

I have found Sunday evenings work best for me. Besides the fact a weekly review keeps everything current, there is comfort in knowing that nothing can get more than a week old or be totally forgotten. Plus, it allows me to start each week fresh and ready to go.

Reviewing my lists on a weekly basis, rather than the daily basis that I thought it required, sounded more manageable. And so I decided to make it part of my Sunday evening ritual. I knew that not everything would happen during the week as I planned it because life happens, but at least I knew that I could start each week on a clean slate, better organized and ready to accomplish things.

Focus On The Positive, Not The Negative

IM Got your e-mail. Thanks! I have already reviewed everything and even started a file folder called "Franklin Planner updates." I feel really good and ready to start the new week organized and focused.

IM Great, but the important question is, did you get to cross off "Enjoy the day?"

IM Yup! Spent the day with the girls. Sometimes I think I used to put so many small, easy-to-achieve tasks on my lists so that I'd get the enjoyment and fulfillment of knowing that I had accomplished something when I crossed them off. Of course, now that there's so much to do, I don't need to find things to put on my lists.

IM Whether you have two or two dozen things on your list, it still feels like an accomplishment when you cross something off. But now that you are organized and prioritized, you can focus on what is getting done vs. feeling overwhelmed by having so much to do and not even knowing what needs to be done, let alone in what order.

IM I'm just so grateful that I was using Franklin Planner before. At least it was only a matter of learning how to use it more effectively. Otherwise, I'd have been staring at a blank piece of paper with no idea where to start. It would have been a nightmare.

IM Not really. Being organized and making lists does not require computer programs. Mom has used both handwritten and typed lists for years. Larry, even with a staff of computer experts at his disposal, uses handwritten lists. You need to remember that you did the most difficult part without the help of a computer.

IM I did?

IM Someone had to prioritize, categorize and compartmentalize everything. The computer did not do it all by itself, it merely made it easier to manage the information. The bottom line is, you did the thinking.

I wasn't sure about that. I think Black may have done much of the thinking while I did most of the inputting and paper shuffling. In any event, the difference in how I felt on Thursday morning vs. Sunday evening was amazing. At the beginning, I felt like I was drowning in paper, not knowing exactly what I had to do, just knowing that there was too much to do. Now I felt organized and in control. It was still a bit overwhelming, but I also knew that I had the skills and systems in place to handle all of my new responsibilities, as well as the old ones.

I knew I'd still get stressed out. I knew I wouldn't be able to get everything on my lists done. But I was learning from Black how to best manage my time so as to maximize both its effectiveness and my feelings of success when I accomplished things. Most importantly, I realized that sometimes I'd have to invest time in order to save time.

IO

So You Think Staying At Home Isn't A Full-Time Job?

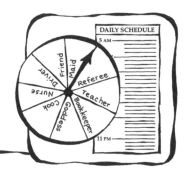

IM Another early morning?

IM Yes! Now that I did the Sunday night review, I can see how you wake up on Monday mornings ready to tackle the week. Except today is Presidents' Day and so Natasha's home from school.

IM Anything special planned?

IM Why do I have to have something special planned? In fact, why do I have to be the one who does all the planning?

IM Sorry I asked ...

IM Sorry I'm the one who's always in charge. Yesterday Mommy called hinting about me driving the girls up to The Woodlands to see her. Last night Natasha was bugging me about plans for today. And at bedtime, Nick was muttering something about looking at TVs for the new house, as if we could afford them.

IM Sounds like you have several options for the day. I do not understand the problem.

IM You wouldn't. You're not a mom, or at least not a full-time mom. It seems like everyone wants a piece of me — the kids, Nick, Mom. Sometimes I feel like I don't have a second to think, or even go to the bathroom, without someone interrupting me.

IM That's because when you said, "I do," it was short for "I do everything!"

IM You may find that amusing, but I don't. Everyone needs me to do something. And they want it done on demand.

IM Look on the bright side — at least you know you are needed.

IM That's what Mom said yesterday, but she said it looking for sympathy. The "woe is me — no one needs me" speech. I tried explaining that it wasn't the being needed — it was the being needed for every little thing.

IM So when you say it, you are NOT looking for sympathy?

IM That's different. I'm just venting. And only to you.

IM Thanks for making me feel needed. Being needed is the ultimate in job security.

IM Great. So I guess that means there's no chance I'll get fired.

IM Highly unlikely. You chose a career path with great job security but awful hours. Not to mention your job is far more difficult than anything I experienced in the corporate world. And that was before Nick was fired.

IM Thanks. I'm not sure I believe you but I appreciate the acknowledgement that being a mom is more than sitting around eating bonbons.

I have always admired Black. She had been a driven career woman determined to climb the corporate ladder. So to hear her say that she thought my "job," which was really my life, was more difficult than any of her corporate positions was pretty incredible. And right now I could use whatever encouragement I could get, so I held on to this thought. Although I did question its validity.

A 24/7 Job Without Time Off For Good Behavior

I decided that I was going to spend the day at home, and since Natasha wanted to do something special, I thought I'd take Black's suggestion and let the girls "help" me with one of my low- priority projects. I also decided that I might try to take Black to task on the topic of my mom "job." Since my getting the best of Black almost never happens, if I were successful, it would make it a very special day, at least for me.

E-mail From: Red
Subject: **Your Career Vs. My "Job"**
Sent: Monday, February 16

I have been thinking about your comment that you think my "job" as a mom is more difficult than things you've done in the real world. I find that very hard to believe, especially considering you've held senior management positions in the corporate world, and I'm just a stay-at-home mom.

FYI, I decided that I'm going to tackle sorting the girls' scrapbook stuff with them today. I figure I can make it into a game of building piles and counting. And then they can either draw pictures or practice their ABCs by labeling the Ziploc bags. Sounds like a real challenging "job," doesn't it?

Subject: "Job" Description
Sent: Monday, February 16

I stand by my statement:

1. You mention things I have done in the "real world." We both made choices as to what aspect of the real world we wanted to focus our lives on, albeit we went to the opposites sides of the work-family balancing act. One is no more real than the other, although I could argue some of the corporate objectives were unrealistic and the politics were "unreal."

2. Your claim that you are "just a stay-at-home mom" belittles the huge responsibility you accepted when you decided to have children. In fact, it was more responsibility than I was willing to accept, and so I decided not to have children.

3. You are a mom, first and foremost. No matter what time of day or night, or where you might be, you are always a mom. However, that does not allow you to ignore any other responsibilities you may have as a wife or daughter.

4. Your "office hours" are 24 hours a day, 7 days a week, 52 weeks a year.

5. Vacation time (if any) requires significant planning and, in reality, since you travel with the family it will only be a scenery change and not a true escape.

6. You live at the office, and I mean this in both a literal and figurative sense. Even when I was working my hardest, pulling late-night and crack-of-dawn patrol, I was still able to physically leave the office and escape to my home.

7. And last, but not least, quitting your job is not an option, although you may be able to semi-retire after the first 20-25 years.

E-mail From: Red
Subject: "Job" Description
Sent: Monday, February 16

Wow! I'm almost speechless. I never looked at it that way. Obviously, you've given it some serious thought. Care to expand on bullet point 2? In particular, the part as to why you decided not to have children. I have always wondered about it but never wanted to pry.

E-mail From: Black
Subject: Career Decision
Sent: Monday, February 16

You can always ask me anything. I can always choose not to answer. Or I can answer your questions with questions. Did you always want children? Were you ever torn between wanting a career and having children?

E-mail From: Red
Subject: Career Decision
Sent: Monday, February 16

You're avoiding the question. But yes, I always knew I wanted to have children. And no, I didn't mind working, but I never had a strong desire to have a career, and so it wasn't a dilemma. But it sounds like it was for you.

E-mail From: Black
Subject: Career Decision
Sent: Monday, February 16

No dilemma. I always loved working. I loved the stimulation and mental challenges, the camaraderie, the independence of making my own money. So the career decision was easy. But once I was in the corporate world, I realized that the time I would have to spend raising a family would take away from the time I had available for my career, and I was not willing to make that sacrifice. I did not feel like I could hold two full-time jobs and expect to perform at my peak at both, and I was not willing to raise children as a part-time mom. Some women can find a work-family balance, but I knew myself well enough to know I was not one of them. I tend to do everything at 100% and am not very good at compromise. So I chose career over kids. Does that answer your question?

E-mail From: Red
Subject: Career Decision
Sent: Monday, February 16

Absolutely! And thank you. But it does beg another question. In light of everything you just said, why did you quit the corporate world after you married Larry?

E-mail From: Black
Subject: Career Decision
Sent: Monday, February 16

Different time in my life and different subject entirely. The point of this conversation is to make you realize your job as a mom is every bit as important and demanding as one you would find in the corporate world. Do not undervalue yourself. Or your job.

E-mail From: Red
Subject: Career Decision
Sent: Monday, February 16

But I don't think of my life as a mom as a job. It's what I have chosen to do and I love doing it. Most of the time.

E-mail From: Black
Subject: You need to love what you do
Sent: Monday, February 16

I understand. And I loved working, although sometimes there were projects or people I did not like. Loving what you do everyday is important, but it is different when you do not ever get a break.

The CEOs of major companies work long hours and may lose sleep because of business, but they are not on call 24 hours a day, every day. A doctor in an ER works intensive shifts, sometimes 24 hours or longer, but they get to go home. People with jobs outside the home have opportunities to leave work behind, whether at night, weekends and/or vacations. You never have the luxury to totally escape. You live at your office. And now Nick does, too!

E-mail From: Red
Subject: You need to love what you do
Sent: Monday, February 16

Thanks for the reminder!

I agree it's a demanding 24/7 job. Nick has always helped with the kids and the house, but I still feel like I'm the one in charge of making sure everyone's happy and healthy, and that the house is running smoothly. I love Nick and appreciate what he does, but I don't think he truly understands that from the minute I wake up in the morning (which is now 5:00 a.m., thanks to you!) to the minute I fall into bed at night, I'm "on call." And even then I might be woken by one of the girls and have to go back to work.

E-mail From: Black
Subject: You need to love what you do
Sent: Monday, February 16

I think he is going to get a better understanding of your hours now that he has set up a home office. And vice versa. Nick may not have worked 24/7, but he still worked full-time and then came home and was a dad and a husband. Now that he is starting his own business, he will have to put in even more hours focused on work.

E-mail From: Red
Subject: You need to love what you do
Sent: Monday, February 16

Why do you always come to his defense?

E-mail From: Black
Subject: You need to love what you do
Sent: Monday, February 16

Part of MY job is playing devil's advocate. And I love my job. And remember ... you love your job. Maybe not at this very moment, but most of the time. EOM

Sometimes Black can be infuriating, but her thoughts really got me thinking about my life and my decision to be a stay-at-home mom. I have never regretted the decision and deliberately waited until Nick was established in his career to start our family because I knew that I didn't want to work after I had kids. And I have always been grateful (although I don't think I ever mentioned it to Nick) that I was fortunate enough to be able to make that choice.

"H.E.R." (Household Executive Responsibilities) Job

What I didn't realize was that I'd never work harder in my life than once I added the responsibilities of being a full-time mom to those of being a wife and a daughter. And now, as I have taken on the management of the family's finances and the work associated with moving to a new house, my workload has gotten even bigger.

☎ Just checking in. What's going on? It sounds like World War III.

☎ Let me call you back.

☎ Sorry it took me so long to call you back. We were in the middle of labeling Ziploc bags when the girls decided to start fighting over the markers. Then, as I was trying to stop them from arguing, Nick told me that he had promised to paint with the girls, but we were out of watercolors. That's when you called.

☎ Did you get it all resolved?

☎ Oh, yes. I told the girls if they didn't stop fighting, no one was going to get to use the markers, and we wouldn't go through any more of the scrapbook stuff, which they were really enjoying. They settled down immediately. I told Nick I'd add watercolors to my shopping list, but told him that I'd check to see if I had some extra paint in my secret gift stash. There was, so that emergency was handled and now things are back to being calm. For the moment.

☎ Told you so.

☎ Told me what?

☎ Your job is every bit as demanding as a corporate position and, in fact, you use many of the same skill sets.

☎ Dealing with markers and paint? You need to get out more.

☎ Me? I think it is you that needs to get out more. First, you motivated the girls to help you with the scrapbooks by making it a game. When they started to fight, you demonstrated negotiating skills. And then you dealt with Nick's emergency. So you can add "quick decision-making in an ever-changing environment" to your resume, along with your financial and time-management skills.

☎ You do know that the way you look at things is NOT normal, don't you? Not that there's anything wrong with it since it always gives me something to think about, but it's certainly different.

☎ And now you are demonstrating your communication skills. Questioning my thought process, but buffering it with a compliment.

☎ Now you're being a smart-ass.

☎ True, but I bet you praised the girls for helping you with the scrapbook project. In all seriousness, you would make a good office manager.

☎ I'm not trying to be an office manager. All those things are just part of being a mom. And they happen all the time. That's my life.

☎ A life full of business skills you are taking for granted.

Once upon a time, I lived in a very peaceful, calm home and I took all my time alone for granted. Now, two kids later, I take for granted that my life and house are in a constant state of activity. I'm not complaining, although I'll admit to longing for more peace and less drama. Black, however, sees my life in another context.

IM What are you doing online? Done scrapbooking?

IM The girls are busy painting with Nick, so I thought I'd quickly check e-mails. I wish this job came with a secretary.

IM It should since you are now a CEO, a CFO and a COO!

IM Huh?

IM A Chief Executive Officer — A Chief Financial Officer — A Chief Operating Officer

IM And don't forget Julie the Cruise Director from Love Boat!

IM I was being serious. You are the one who said you juggle a thousand and one balls ... I am merely assigning job titles.

IM Yes — it's called being a mom.

IM And that was before you decided to take on the financial responsibilities and logistics related to a new house. From my perspective (which you so kindly explained is abnormal), it is as if you are running a small business.

IM I can honestly say that in a million years I never would have compared being a mom to running a business. Does this mean I get to fire my employees if they don't perform to my expectations? That would be fun.

IM I cannot imagine you firing your kids, which leaves only one other full-time employee — Nick. And since he has already been fired once this year, I would leave him alone. Not to mention you typically would not fire anyone until you found a replacement; otherwise, you would have to do their work too.

IM Well, if I can't fire him, can I at least let him know who's the boss?

IM That is your prerogative, but I am not sure it will accomplish much. In fact, it will probably create more problems than it will solve. In corporate life I learned that "pulling rank" was never a good way to manage people. Although at times it was tempting for the sheer satisfaction of it.

IM Great. So now I'm in charge of managing people?

IM You always have been a Human Resource Manager. And that is probably the most difficult part of your job as you have the delicate role of trying to make sure that all the "employees" — you, Nick, the girls, Mom and even me — work well together. And that does not take into consideration all the contract help and consultants — like doctors, accountants, plumbers, Natasha's teacher, etc.

IM Well, I wish I could afford to hire an administrative assistant.

IM So that you could have another person to manage? I cannot help but chuckle to myself when I hear women complain about how hard it is to supervise their maids or in some cases to manage their household staff.

IM Nice problems to have.

IM True. But employee problems, nonetheless.

IM And talking of employees — Natasha, one of my biggest helpers (most of the time), just came in and wants to use my computer. Now that's a department I do NOT want to be in charge of. I know that her computer skills are going to surpass mine very soon!

IM Not sure that is saying much. Maybe you can put her in charge of IT. (FYI, IT = Information Technology, not "it.") EOM

I wondered where Black comes up with her analogies. If nothing else, they are always amusing and often helpful. I also wondered about her capacity to remember trivia. Sometimes I think her brain was better at data management than my computer.

E-mail From: Black
Subject: It's Not Just My Opinion
Sent: Monday, February 16

Our conversation reminded me of an article that I read in *The Wall Street Journal* and so I searched their website. In an article entitled "King of Their Castles," they talk about a survey commissioned by America Online. The survey shows that 41% of parents rated themselves as CEO caliber — Chief of Everything Officer — since they believe they run their homes on a variety of fronts. Although these parents are no more wealthy, professionally accomplished or well-educated than others who participated in the survey, they seemed to excel at thinking of themselves in their roles as medics, therapists, decision makers, multi-taskers and advisors.

Believe me now?

E-mail From: Red
Subject: It's Not Just My Opinion
Sent: Monday, February 16

I never said I didn't believe you. I said you look at things from a different perspective. However, I do find that study interesting. I wish I had more time to read, and I hate to admit this, but I barely have time to skim the local newspaper.

E-mail From: Black
Subject: It's Not Just My Opinion
Sent: Monday, February 16

Really? I thought you always thought of yourself as a well-read intellectual. I cannot believe you admit to only skimming the newspaper. I figured you would at least subscribe to *The New York Times* or *The Washington Post* or some other "important" paper. Not that you would have time to read them, but at least you would have a high-brow stack of unread newspapers piling up in your workroom.

E-mail From: Red
Subject: It's Not Just My Opinion
Sent: Monday, February 16

Are you finished? I'm so glad you find me so amusing.

E-mail From: Black
Subject: WSJ
Sent: Monday, February 16

I am, too. But seriously, if you do not have much time, that is all the more reason you should start reading *The Wall Street Journal*. They summarize the most important news stories of the day into two columns on the front page — one for business and finance and the other for worldwide news. My attitude is, if the news is not important enough to make the front page of *The Wall Street Journal*, then I can survive without knowing about it.

E-mail From: Red
Subject: WSJ
Sent: Monday, February 16

I'm not going to get *The Wall Street Journal* just to read the front page. Since I have no interest in the business world, the rest of the paper would go straight into the recycle bin. Unless, of course, they have a Mom Edition.

E-mail From: Black
Subject: WSJ
Sent: Monday, February 16

No Mom Edition, but I think you would be surprised at how much of it you would find interesting. They have a section called "Personal Journal," where they have articles on topics such as personal investments, insurance, travel, food and cooking, etc. And every Friday they do movie reviews.

E-mail From: Red
Subject: WSJ
Sent: Monday, February 16

That last one got my attention. Save your Friday *Wall Street Journals* for me.

So, Where's My Paycheck?

If I was a high-powered domestic executive, or at least that was what Black was trying to convince me, where was my million-dollar salary, annual bonus and retirement program?

IM While cleaning up the dishes, I decided it's totally unfair that I'm doing this "more than full-time" job that requires a whole variety of financial, organizational and management skills and I don't even get to deposit a paycheck.

IM First, who ever said life was fair? Second, if you want to complain, go find a mirror and talk to your CFO. FYI, that's Chief Financial Officer.

IM Yes, I know that now. Still, I can't help but wonder what my salary would be in the corporate world if I was paid for everything I'm currently doing.

IM Now you sound like Mom. How many years did we hear her complain about staying at home and not working? And then she would follow up by saying Daddy did not pay her enough.

IM Let's face it — you're the only person I know who is paid enough by her husband.

IM First of all, "enough" is a relative term. Secondly, I would argue that I earn every penny of it. And thirdly, the "company" can well afford to pay me well.

IM So you admit you are well paid? VERY well paid!

IM Yes, but I have no guarantee on how long I will continue to get paid and the retirement plan sucks. Anyway, this is not about me. This is about you. And the fact you want to be compensated for all you do. You already are.

IM Really? Please explain. At the very least, this should be amusing.

IM Let me give you some insight into the corporate world since we both know your perception of the business world is not exactly realistic. Typically, you would get an annual performance review, which means for most of the year you generally have no idea how you stand in the eyes of management. If you are lucky, your boss will tell you when they think you have done something wrong or could improve, but rarely will you receive any compliments or be made to feel like you are doing a great job.

IM And your point is?

IM I am getting to that. You, on the other hand, have the benefit — and pleasure — of seeing in your kids' faces when they are happy. Think about the times Natasha comes home from school and gives you a big hug or Sawyer tells you that she loves you. You get immediate feedback and a far better "paycheck" — their love and appreciation.

IM You do realize you're starting to sound warm and fuzzy.

IM No, I am answering your question.

IM Whatever. How about if I pass on the paychecks and just ask for an annual bonus?

IM What makes you think that if you do a perfect job at work, you are entitled to a bonus? It would be nice, but it often does not work that way. I can remember one year that my department exceeded the goals established in our annual plan. Everyone was excited, and some of us (myself included) were already spending our bonuses. But we got a rude awakening when the president of the company told me that although our department had done extremely well, other departments had not met their goals, and so the company as a whole did not meet target. The result — no bonuses for anyone.

IM This whole IM started with what I thought was a clever comment about getting a paycheck. I wanted to get some sympathy. My mistake. I should have known this was going to turn into more than I wanted. But you did cheer me up. Between Nick and you, I realize neither the corporate world nor a marriage provides "job security," but as a mom I know I can't be fired. I think that's a good thing ...

IM Glad I could help in some roundabout fashion. Uh, and to answer your question about the going rate for a full-time mom ... I have no idea, but I know you could not pay me enough to do it!

Black was right — although I don't receive a paycheck that I can cash at the bank, I receive instead something far more valuable. I get to have rewards every day that, as the saying goes, money can't buy. And that makes it all worthwhile. Although I wouldn't turn down the cash.

E-mail From: Black
Subject: **Salary Update**
Sent: Monday, February 16

According to a story on MSN Money ... "a full-time stay-at-home mother would earn $134,121 a year if paid for all her work, an amount similar to a top U.S. ad executive, a marketing director or a judge."

P.S. — They did not indicate where you should send the invoice.

11

A "Mind-Field" Called Insurance

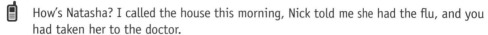

How's Natasha? I called the house this morning, Nick told me she had the flu, and you had taken her to the doctor.

She's OK, thanks. It's flu season. I took her to the doctor to play it safe, and as expected he prescribed plenty of rest and fluids. Nick told me you had called on your way to practice or test or whatever it is you do at the racetrack, but I didn't want to bother you so I didn't call you back.

How is she feeling?

Not too bad. I, on the other hand, am sick to my stomach.

Do you have the flu, too?

I wish. No, I realized when I paid the doctor that we no longer have health insurance. I'm not kidding. I actually feel queasy thinking about this.

Well, before you throw up, look at Nick's severance package. I bet you are still covered. Look for anything related to insurance. There should be some mention of COBRA.

Cobra? Like the poisonous snake?

No. Cobra, like the Shelby car.

Look, I'm stressed out that we have no insurance and you're playing word association games. I really don't know what you're talking about.

Lighten up. All you need to know right now is that the law provides for the continuation of group health coverage in certain circumstances, and getting fired is one of them. We can discuss it in more detail later, but for now go through Nick's termination papers and look for anything related to COBRA or health insurance. If you cannot find anything, call the human resources department at the Company. You have coverage ... not sure how much or for how long, but you have coverage.

Thanks, doc. If that's the case, then I'm feeling a little better.

I wasn't exaggerating. I really did feel physically ill. It wasn't only because we were financially exposed for small things, like colds and the flu, though I didn't like that. But what if there was a more serious medical condition? And when I thought about that, it also made me think of other potential catastrophes — such as if something happened to Nick. I faced the scary realization that we had lost ALL of the insurance that had been provided by the Company. I could feel myself starting to panic.

It's strange. I had never really thought about insurance, particularly health insurance, because I had always been covered, first by my parents, then by my employer, and then by Nick's employer. But now it wasn't only about me, I had the girls to think about. Once the insurance "safety blanket" was removed, I felt extremely vulnerable. In the best of times, insurance seems boring and costly. But in the worst of times, it's something that keeps you awake at night because it can be the only thing that stands between your family and financial disaster.

Question One: What Do We Have?

E-mail From: Black
Subject: COBRA
Sent: Tuesday, February 17

I do not know if you found anything in Nick's papers, but I wanted to give you a little more detail about COBRA, which stands for Consolidated Omnibus Budget Reconciliation Act of 1985. I will not bore you with all the legal details of this federal law, but since the Company had a group health plan, COBRA mandates that a terminated employee MUST be given the option to continue their health insurance for a maximum of 18 months. There are some exceptions and various qualifications, but the bottom line is Nick is eligible. However, there are certain requirements regarding notice and enrollment periods and payment deadlines, so you need to find out immediately what, if anything, Nick has done.

E-mail From: Red
Subject: COBRA
Sent: Tuesday, February 17

Thank you! That's a huge relief. So far, I wasn't able to find anything in Nick's papers, but I'm still looking. If I don't find anything, I'll ask Nick to call the Company first thing tomorrow morning. At least I have over a year to research and find other insurance. I assume that COBRA covers all the insurance that we had. I looked through Nick's employee handbook and saw that we were covered for health, dental, vision, legal, disability, life and accidental death.

E-mail From: Black
Subject: COBRA does NOT cover everything
Sent: Tuesday, February 17

NO! COBRA only covers medical benefits, so health and dental are included and possibly the vision insurance. COBRA does NOT cover any other type of insurance that a company may be offering its employees.

E-mail From: Red
Subject: COBRA does NOT cover everything
Sent: Tuesday, February 17

Are you sure? You mean we've lost ALL the other insurance?

E-mail From: Black
Subject: An Insurance Elephant
Sent: Tuesday, February 17

Yes. Or if it has not already lapsed, it will very soon. And before you overreact, I want you to think of insurance as just another elephant. And attack it in pieces based on your most critical and immediate insurance needs.

1. **COBRA:** From a probability standpoint, and that is what insurance is all about, your most important coverage is medical. That, and dental, falls under COBRA, so deal with that first.

2. **Lapsed Coverage:** Then review all the other insurance that the Company had provided and determine whether it is important enough to replace.

3. **Current Coverage:** And then review all your personal insurance (car, home contents, umbrella, etc.) to make sure you understand exactly what you are buying. And whether there are less expensive options.

E-mail From: Red
Subject: An Insurance Elephant
Sent: Tuesday, February 17

I can't believe this. Just what I want — and need — another elephant to eat! More work. More learning curves. Does it ever end?

E-mail From: Black
Subject: Life is a learning curve
Sent: Tuesday, February 17

In a word — No. I could argue that life is a learning curve, and just when you figure it out, you die, but I know that is not what you want to hear. But here is the good news — your big learning curves will end one day. One reason everything seems so overwhelming is you are being introduced to so many things in a very short period of time. And keep in mind, a typical learning curve does not proceed smoothly — it has peaks and valleys.

E-mail From: Red
Subject: Life is a learning curve
Sent: Tuesday, February 17

With all due respect, I really don't care about the shape of the learning curve. All I know is I need to continue looking through Nick's severance package to try and confirm our COBRA coverage. So bye for now. EOM

After dinner that night I asked Nick about COBRA, and he looked at me as if I was actually talking about snakes. Once I explained what it was, he used the fact he was British as his excuse for not being familiar with the program. I let him off the hook by telling him until today I didn't have any idea what it was either, and that I suspected most people had never heard of it unless they needed it.

We decided, or rather it became obvious, that I was better prepared to handle the insurance issues, and so Nick handed me a stack of documents related to the Company-provided insurance. After trying to decipher everything, I decided it would be easier to call the human resources department first thing in the morning. Black was right — we were already covered by COBRA for medical and dental. I was told we had an initial grace period of three months to pay the first premium, but then it would be due monthly. The long-term health care policy also could be continued as an individual policy. That was the good news. The bad news was that all the other insurance had already been cancelled.

Since I was becoming quite the little expert at making binders and spreadsheets, I started yet another 3-ring binder called, cleverly, Insurance. I laughed at myself for my previous resistance to learning Microsoft Excel as I now used it to create a master list of all our past, current and potential insurance needs. I started with all of the insurance coverage we previously had through the Company and then added in insurance policies that we had taken out independent of them, such as automobile, renter's, etc. Alongside each type of insurance I made columns for the policy numbers, renewal dates, what it actually covered and what our monthly premium was. Or what it had been.

As I was making my new binder, I felt that the lessons I had learned from organizing and analyzing our credit cards (which was only a little over a week ago!) would give me the confidence to tackle this latest elephant. But as I started, I realized I was the elephant. And my name was "Dumbo."

Question Two: What Does Our Current Coverage Cost?

☎ I have just spoken with the human resources department, and you were right about COBRA. Although the remainder of the company-provided insurance has lapsed, I have time to make decisions about our health and dental insurance since we are covered by COBRA for 18 months. It doesn't cover vision, but I'm not too worried about that. I guess I now have to start looking for new policies for life, accidental death and disability insurance.

☎ Whoa. You are not done with the topic of COBRA yet. How bad are the premiums?

☎ I don't know. I didn't ask. I only confirmed we were covered. I looked at one of Nick's old pay stubs and saw the monthly premium. It's not cheap, but it's not as expensive as I expected. I'll worry about the cost later.

☎ Sorry, but you need to worry about it now. The amount on Nick's pay stub was how much you were paying when Nick was still employed. The Company was probably paying a significant amount of the total premium, and you were only responsible for part of it. Group health coverage under COBRA is usually more expensive — significantly more — because now you are responsible for paying the entire premium. You need to find out how much it is going to cost, because unless there are pre-existing medical conditions, I can almost guarantee that you can find other health insurance that will cost less than what it will cost you through COBRA.

☎ And I was so excited to cross COBRA off my list. I should have known this was going too smoothly. OK. I'll call them back and ask about the cost. Maybe you'll be wrong this time!

I was tempted to ignore Black's advice and leave COBRA in place and not think about it so I could focus on the insurance coverage that had been cancelled. But Black's comments made me curious about exactly how much we would be paying for medical coverage. So I called the Company back and spoke to someone who told me the COBRA prices. And then I almost had a heart attack. The cost of the long-term health care coverage, which had been a nominal amount, didn't change, but the health insurance sure did. It was going to cost us over four times (!!!) what we had been previously paying. The amount we had been paying every month was high, but manageable. Multiplying it by four made it astronomical and blew my budget out of the water. I knew that I had to find another health policy. And quickly.

☎ HELP! I called about the cost of COBRA coverage. I can't believe how expensive it is. I hope you're right when you said I can probably get medical coverage for less somewhere else because I certainly can't afford to pay COBRA prices for the next 18 months. I need to find a cheaper policy. NOW!

☎ I was afraid of that. I can make some phone calls and do some research to get you some leads, but I suggest you call the agent you use for your house and car insurance. His company may not offer their own health insurance policies, but I am sure they have a marketing relationship with a company that does. I am positive he will have some suggestions, but remember agents work on commission.

☎ Tim, the agent we used to work with, has recently gone out on his own. We always got along well, so I'll contact him and explain the situation and ask about medical and dental coverage. Down the road, he could probably give us quotes on the other insurance that we've lost.

☎ Once you get him on the phone and explain the situation, he will probably bring up the other insurance anyway. Just tell him your first priority is replacing the COBRA coverage, although you want him to start pulling together the other information.

☎ I think I can only deal with one type of insurance at a time. You know, one bite at a time.

☎ I understand. I am not saying to review everything all at once, but you need to review all your insurance needs to decide what you really need (vs. what was a nice safety cushion before) and how much you can afford to spend.

☎ I understand all that, but right now my only concern is the medical coverage and getting the cost down. Everything else can wait.

☎ Not really. I was going to mention insurance when we were working on your budget, but I knew finding a house and a mortgage were more pressing items and insurance could wait a few weeks. I figured we would discuss all your insurance needs when it came time to change your rental insurance to homeowners' coverage. Looks like that time is now.

☎ Thanks for the warning. This isn't one elephant, it's a stampede. Anything else you're not telling me?

☎ Not that I can think of, but I reserve the right to change my answer if I see more elephants on the horizon. Now back to insurance. As you already know, insurance makes up a big part of a monthly budget. You need to make sure that you are spending this money wisely, not just out of habit or because you had a corporate sponsor paying for it before. You need to be making conscious decisions rather than automatically replacing or renewing insurance.

☎ That makes perfect sense. I just don't want to hear it right now. Or do it.

☎ Me neither. How about you call your agent and let him walk you through the basics? Then if you have any questions, I can fill in the details.

☎ So I can admit to someone else how little I know? Gee, thanks.

☎ How about telling the truth – that you have never taken an interest in insurance before, but you are now. It is not as if you flunked Insurance 101 since it was never offered at school.

I knew better than to comment that it should have been a required course in school. At that point, I wished I didn't have a pragmatic, financial analyst for a sister, but rather someone who would tell me how badly she felt that I was having to learn so much so quickly. I wanted her to tell me how sorry she felt for me and that I was being a saint handling everything. But I slowly returned to reality and realized I should be thanking my lucky stars that I had a no-nonsense, extremely blunt sister who could actively help me with specific advice and instruction (even if she did pawn me off on the insurance agent.)

Question Three: What Are Our Choices?

Since I had no choice except to face the reality of insurance, I mentally prepared myself to go through all our insurance. I soon found out that there were more types of insurance available than I had ever realized. And so I set out to learn about the confusing, exasperating, but necessary world of insurance — starting with what were, for me anyway, the most important policies:

<u>Health Insurance</u>

One thing was obvious: I had to sort out my health insurance immediately since COBRA was unbelievably expensive. I called Tim and asked him to give me a quote to duplicate our current insurance. Within a few hours, he called me back with a quote that was twice what we had been paying, but that was still less than half of the current COBRA cost. It would have been an easy decision, except that he also felt the need to present me with a handful of other options. Each one a little different, each one filled with jargon and descriptions that I felt incapable of understanding. It was as if he was speaking a foreign language. And then the faxes started arriving. And I learned I not only didn't speak the language, I couldn't read it either.

☎ Got a minute? I'm sitting here with a bunch of different health insurance options. I feel like I need a professional interpreter.

☎ I cannot compare the policies without knowing all the details, but I can try to answer any general questions. And you know I am always happy to give you my opinion.

☎ That would be great. Here goes. It seems like my biggest question is whether I want to be in a PPO, which stands for Preferred Provider Organization, or an HMO, which stands for Health Maintenance Organization. From what I can tell, they are similar in that they both have a network of approved doctors, but the PPO gives me the option to use doctors outside the system whereas the HMO doesn't. But the HMO is a fixed monthly fee with us paying small amounts for doctor visits and seems to promote preventative care. The PPO would have us paying a larger percentage of the visits, especially if the doctor is outside the network, but it offers much more flexibility. Does any of this make sense?

☎ Yes. You just explained the difference between an HMO and a PPO.

☎ I liked it much better when we were under the Company plan. They made all these decisions for us, not to mention they paid for most of it.

☎ I understand, but the part about them making all the decisions may not be totally accurate. Many companies offer several different insurance options, so Nick probably had to review them at some point.

☎ Yeah, well, I didn't, so this is all new to me! How do you decide what plan to go with?

☎ Easy to explain, but not an easy decision. First, you might want to call your current doctors and find out if they are part of any HMO. If not, you would have to switch doctors if you choose an HMO plan. What you really need to decide is whether you are more comfortable in a PPO or an HMO plan. As you already know, a PPO gives you more control over your decisions, but you pay more. It is a personal decision, and Nick may have an opinion since he is used to the socialized medical system in England. Bottom line: It is a matter of what you can afford and how strongly you feel about freedom of choice.

☎ If money were no object, I know I'd want the flexibility of a PPO.

☎ OK. Then see what PPO coverage you can get that you can afford. Prices will vary dramatically based on the deductibles, co-pays and maximums.

☎ My agent starting talking about all those things, and I could feel my eyes glazing over. I'm so confused. And I have got a huge headache. Maybe I'm getting Natasha's flu.

☎ Quit overreacting. It is not as confusing as it sounds. The deductible is how much you have to pay before the insurance policy starts to contribute. This is just like your car and renter's insurance, except with medical it is typically an annual deductible vs. a "per incident" one. The higher the deductible, the more you must pay before your insurance kicks in, but the lower the insurance premium. In reverse, if you choose a policy with a low deductible, which means the insurance company starts paying sooner, it will cost more.

☎ I understand the concept. But how do I decide?

☎ Let me finish explaining the other two primary variables, and then I can try and explain how to decide. Or at least narrow it down. Co-pays are the co-payment percentage. It is how much you pay of the total medical bill, once the deductible is met. For example, a 20% co-pay means you pay 20% and the insurance company pays 80%. And maximums are just that — it's the most that the insurance company will pay during the period you are insured.

☎ This is exactly what I'm talking about. It's so complicated. All I want is to pay as little in premiums as possible while still being able to choose our own doctors. At the same time, I don't want a situation where we have to pay a lot for medical expenses or potentially go broke because of a "G-d forbid" situation.

☎ Sorry, but insurance is a question of risks vs. rewards. The decisions are about trade-offs, and so they are not necessarily going to be obvious or even easy. But you just made a few decisions, and I do not think you even realized it.

☎ I did? So tell me. What did I decide?

☎ You said you did not want to pay a lot for insurance, but wanted to make sure you were covered for catastrophes. Which, for what it is worth, is how I think insurance should be used. Take the highest deductible you can tolerate and then have your agent give you the cost for different co-pay levels. Have him use an average annual maximum for the comparison so that the only thing you are analyzing is the cost associated with the different co-pay percentages.

☎ I think that makes sense. Then I can evaluate the benefit vs. cost and decide what we're willing to risk. I have a file with all the girls' medical bills. Should I use that to determine the coverage we need?

☎ You can use it to give you a sense of what the different policies would have paid, but remember you want insurance to cover the risks of the unknown. Too many people focus on getting insurance to cover expenses they know they are going to incur, like doctor bills associated with colds and the flu, and they forget the insurance companies are experts who have already calculated that into their premiums.

☎ OK. I can handle a higher co-pay percentage for the small stuff, but what about the big stuff? A major medical claim would wipe us out.

☎ That is where the maximums come into play. Most policies set an annual maximum out-of-pocket limit on your co-payments and then they cover 100% of expenses over that annual cap. See what kind of options, and the associated cost differences, for the annual caps. And look for a plan that has no lifetime maximum or at least one with several million dollars.

☎ Several million? That seems a bit excessive.

☎ Not really. Serious health problems cost a lot of money and can last a lifetime.

☎ Great. Just what I want. I have to become clairvoyant and be able to see the future to make sure I make the right insurance decisions today.

☎ You are not trying to PREDICT the future; you are trying to PROTECT the future. You need to focus on determining your comfort level in terms of what benefits you want vs. what you can afford or what you are willing to pay for those benefits. And this approach applies to all insurance, not just medical insurance. Think about cost vs. benefit, not only when deciding what type of policy you want, but also when determining if you want an insurance policy at all.

☎ If I have to repeat this thought process with all the insurance, why didn't you send me an e-mail with all these instructions so that I could re-read it over and over and over again?

☎ Because you called me.

She had me on that point, but once I got hold of myself and thought about Black's comments, I was able to ask the right questions (since I already knew I wanted a PPO, and knew my priorities, I could ask specific questions), get the associated costs (I created a Microsoft Excel spreadsheet to compare the costs) and make my medical insurance decisions fairly quickly. That didn't mean it was an easy decision, but at least I could sleep at night knowing my family is protected.

Life Insurance

Next I started to evaluate the life insurance the Company had provided and which had evaporated overnight. To me, life insurance was the most depressing thing to think about because it made me reflect on how devastated I, and more importantly the girls, would be if Nick died. However, I knew it was extremely important that if Nick died, the family would be OK financially. But at least on this front I hadn't been totally in the dark.

IM Still working on health insurance?

IM Nope. Nick took Sawyer out for most of the day so that the house would be quiet and Natasha could stay in bed and rest. Since she was alternating between napping and watching TV, I was able to make significant headway on the medical insurance. Next I'm going to attack life insurance.

IM Want to do this by e-mail so you can save them?

IM Thanks, but I don't think it will be necessary. Life insurance seems more straight-forward, and the good news is that although we lost our company-paid policy, we're OK for now because I made Nick take out an additional life insurance policy when we first moved to the States. So at least on that front I don't feel totally exposed, although I want to increase the amount of the policy.

IM Why did you take out a second policy? Was the Company's policy too small?

IM I never asked Nick how much life insurance the Company provided. I just wanted the peace of mind of knowing we had sufficient coverage, so we took out a separate policy. Now I need to replace the Company's coverage since we lost the life insurance policy as well as an accidental death policy.

IM No comment about your past logic. However, before you mindlessly replace the lost coverage, you need to sit down and realistically think about how much total coverage you need.

IM Thanks for your snide comments. And vague instructions. Do you have a cheat sheet I can use?

IM Nope. Sorry. I never had to analyze life insurance since I never had to support anyone but myself. But you will need to have enough coverage to replace Nick's future income. A quick and dirty calculation would be to take his after-tax income and multiple it by the number of years you would need to replace the income. This number would be on the high side, as it does not take into account the interest income you would earn on the payout, but it would be a good starting point.

IM After-tax? You must be kidding. Because he's a British expatriate and the Company filed all his tax returns, his tax return is almost impossible to understand. Can't I just use the monthly number we need to pay our bills and include extra money for retirement and college?

IM The easiest thing to do would be to ask your agent to help you with the calculation. I am sure they have all kinds of spreadsheets and formulas. It is important for you to make a conscious decision about how much insurance you need vs. merely replacing what you had.

IM Well, thanks for not saying "mindlessly" again, but you're right, I probably would have focused on replacing what we'd lost. In terms of actual need, and based on our monthly expenditures, the separate policy we took out is probably more than sufficient. However, to play it safe, I think I'll ask Tim to help me calculate the amount of insurance he thinks we need. I might ask him for a quote to see what the incremental cost would be to bump it up to the next level.

IM It does not cost anything to get a quote. But remember, even if the amount seems small, over time it adds up. It is not a question of if you can afford it — it is a matter of whether you need it. And speaking of need — I need some sleep, so if you do not have any more questions for me, I am going to bed.

I thought about what Black had said, and the next morning, after talking with my insurance agent, I still didn't have an obvious answer. The increase in what I'd have to pay each month to have coverage equal to the total amount of what we had before Nick was fired was not so large that it was prohibitive, but not so small that it was a no-brainer. It was an amount that made me stop and think. The only good news was that the lessons I learned with the medical insurance made me more comfortable thinking about trade-offs of costs vs. benefits.

IM A quick IM to let you know that I have decided not to increase our life insurance or add an accidental death policy. I'm just going to keep the policy that we already have.

IM Why?

IM If I increased the life insurance, the additional payout would be great, but it's not critical. Plus, for the moment I can't rationalize increasing our monthly premium.

IM Have you considered increasing your current life insurance benefit temporarily so that if something happens in the short term, you know that you are more than covered for everything? I understand you do not want to have to spend the extra money now, but it seems to me that now is when you need the peace of mind most.

IM True, but we'd be OK under the current policy. It's not that I can't swing the incremental cost; I just don't think it's worth the extra money.

IM Good answer! It was a trick question. I wanted to make sure you have been listening. There is no reason, at least none that are legal, to have Nick be worth more dead than alive!

IM Nick makes me mad at times, but never that mad!

IM Then I think the extra money would be better spent on a life insurance policy on you.

IM Why would I need a life insurance policy? Nick is the breadwinner. Or at least he was.

IM How quickly we forget! Was it not earlier this week you were bitching and moaning about everything you do? You are the children's nanny and cook; you are the housekeeper and now the bookkeeper and financial advisor. I thought you agreed you were a CEO, CFO and a COO.

IM I remember. I just don't understand what that has to do with life insurance.

IM Obviously, you have not thought about succession planning. What if something happens to you? Who is going to take care of the girls? Will Nick be in a financial position to stop working to look after them? Will he be able to afford to hire a nanny or caretaker? And where will that additional money come from? Will he have to cut back in other areas?

IM I never thought about any of that.

IM Well, you not only need to think about it — you need to do something about it. You are relatively young, female, normal weight and no pre-existing conditions. (I do not think insurance companies cost-adjust for people with "terminal warm and fuzzy.") And you do not need a huge death benefit, just enough to provide Nick with some assistance. The premium should be very reasonable. Compare the cost to the benefit. A life insurance policy on you is just another way of protecting the future.

IM Makes sense, but right now I need to take my "warm and fuzzy" self to the kitchen to make lunch.

In a million years I'd never have thought of a life insurance policy on myself. I'm completely devoted to my children and would do anything for them, but I also assume that I'll always be around. Confronting the fact that something could just as easily happen to me as to Nick, and how that would affect the girls, wasn't easy. But once I did, Black's suggestion of a life insurance policy on me made perfect sense. When I looked at the cost (which in comparison to Nick's policy was almost a rounding error) vs. the benefit and peace of mind it provided, it was the easiest insurance decision I ever made.

Homeowner's Insurance

With Black's financial expertise and foresight that we should focus on buying a house, our dream was coming to fruition. We found a beautiful Southern Colonial house we could afford in a wonderful neighborhood in Sugar Land, a city on the outskirts of Houston known for its excellent schools and sense of community. However, until we had all the paperwork completed and knew the closing was actually going to occur, I was afraid to say anything and jinx it. But once everything fell into place, it was time to take Natasha and Sawyer to see the house. After running through the entire house, excitedly opening every door, Natasha proceeded to lay claim to her new bedroom. And she proclaimed, "I love my room. I love this house." To which Sawyer screamed her agreement.

But now it was back to business. As Black had predicted in the midst of my insurance nightmare, excuse me, I mean evaluation, I went from having a renter's (contents) insurance policy to needing a homeowner's (dwelling and contents) insurance policy. And because we were closing in less than a week, this elephant went from being on the horizon to being in my face almost instantly. More questions, more headaches, more problem-solving.

☎ I can't believe this week! With everything going on in preparation of closing on the new house, Nick's working on a business proposal and can't help with Sawyer. So I'm having to juggle insurance phone calls between everything else.

☎ Can the calls wait until tomorrow?

☎ No, both our real estate agent and mortgage banker called to tell me that I'll need proof of insurance in advance of the closing.

☎ Well, it should not take long for your agent to put it in place.

☎ That's what I thought, too, but when I called him, he told me how he was very sorry, but that he can't write us a policy. Something about how Texas is going through some homeowner's insurance quirks and few companies are writing new policies. But he gave me a few referrals, and to make a long story short, I finally found an agent who represents companies that can write a policy.

☎ I am confused. It sounds like you resolved the problem pretty quickly.

☎ Yes and no.

☎ What does that mean? Bottom line — do you need me for something specific or is this just a rant and rave session?

☎ Sorry. I guess it's a bit of both! The agent is asking me whether I want replacement value, which will have a high premium, or a flat rate, which will have a lower premium? Obviously, I prefer to spend the least amount of money on the premium, but still have sufficient coverage. What do you think?

☎ Thank you. Finally a specific question, rather than talking in circles. You were starting to sound like Nick. Let me give you an extreme example. The house burns to the ground. Do you want insurance that will pay enough to rebuild the house and replace the contents, or do you want a settlement check that is equal to the purchase price of the house and a fixed amount for the contents? It is cost vs. benefit — just like all the other insurance that we have talked about this week. Think back to our conversation about medical insurance.

☎ OK. I would prefer the replacement policy, but it's significantly more expensive. But just for the record, this sounds totally different from our medical insurance analysis.

☎ So just like with the medical insurance, you knew what type of coverage you wanted; now you need to find a way to lower the premium. How about increasing your deductible?

☎ Like I did with the medical insurance? OK, I was a little slow to see the similarity. It seemed so different.

☎ In terms of specifics it is. The point I was trying to make is that once you understand how insurance works, which it sounds like you now do, you need to focus on what is important to you and whether it is cost-effective. I believe in replacement value with a high deductible because I know that I won't submit small claims to the insurance company. Not to sound redundant, but always take the highest deductibles you are comfortable with and remember you are buying protection against catastrophic losses, not the little stuff.

☎ You don't sound redundant — just logical and consistent.

Black may have been in an impatient mood that day, and I understood why she could lose patience with me, but even when she's snippy, she still makes sense. But at least I was done with insurance for awhile. As I started to sort laundry, I was thrilled to have such simple decisions like whites vs. darks, warm vs. cold water, and then the more difficult bleach or no bleach! After the past few days of making serious decisions, I loved the fact the worse thing that could happen is something red would sneak into the white wash and Nick would end up with pink underwear!

Insurance Questions Are Never Ending!

E-mail From: Black
Subject: Homeowner's & Other Insurance
Sent: Thursday, February 19

Do you have any more homeowner's insurance questions? I feel like I did not spend enough time helping you get through it — I was in a rush to get to a meeting. I will be back online after dinner.

Meanwhile, I pulled together the following list of types of insurance — not to cause panic, but merely so that you will see you can get insurance for lots of things. (Some of which seem ridiculous to me.) Regardless of the type insurance, the thought process remains basically the same. And remember, insurance companies did not get big all by themselves. They could never have done it without people who are willing to pay for insurance. And that is what the insurance companies are banking on … and making money on.

Health
• Medical • Dental • Vision • Daily Hospitalization • Long-Term Care

Income & Life
• Disability • Life (Term vs. Whole Life) • Credit Life and Disability

Assets
• Household (dwelling and contents) • Mortgages (Disability and Death)
• Home Warranty Plans • Renters (contents) • Automobiles • Personal Property
• Jewelry • Liability • Umbrella

Other
• Computers, Electronics, etc. • Pet Care • Travel • Special Event

E-mail From: Red
Subject: Homeowner's & Other Insurance
Sent: Thursday, February 19

What a list! I promise not to ask questions about all of them. I know that I keep asking stupid questions and bothering you about all this insurance stuff when I'm sure you have more important things to do.

E-mail From: Black
Subject: Insurance is Important
Sent: Thursday, February 19

No problem. Insurance is important. And confusing. And time-consuming.

E-mail From: Red
Subject: Insurance is Important
Sent: Thursday, February 19

Tell me about it! The good news is that I have made all my medical and life insurance decisions. And after our conversation this afternoon I called Jerry, our homeowners insurance agent, and requested a few different quotes and should be able to make that decision tomorrow.

E-mail From: Black
Subject: Insurance is Important
Sent: Thursday, February 19

Good. You are making great progress, not to mention you seem much calmer tonight than you did this afternoon.

E-mail From: Red
Subject: Insurance is Important
Sent: Thursday, February 19

I am. Oh, I never told you, but yesterday I spoke to our agent about our car insurance. I had him explain all the various options regarding deductibles and personal liability coverage and a few other issues. He gave me several different quotes, and I decided I was comfortable with a higher deductible than we had before so that we can lower our monthly premium.

I remembered your comment about insurance being protection against catastrophes, and it has become my insurance mantra. I realized that we'd probably never put in a claim for car repair below a certain amount. So why carry a low deductible and pay a high premium?

E-mail From: Black
Subject: You get an A+ in Insurance
Sent: Thursday, February 19

Gee — I guess you have been listening. And learning.

E-mail From: Red
Subject: You get an A+ in Insurance
Sent: Thursday, February 19

I'm trying. For example, our real estate agent warned me this afternoon that once we close on the house, I'll start getting offers in the mail about mortgage insurance. So I put a note in my file to talk to you about that some time in the next few days.

E-mail From: Black
Subject: You get an A+ in Insurance
Sent: Thursday, February 19

No problem. But it will be a short conversation. On the surface, they seem logical, but typically mortgage insurance policies are only necessary if you do not carry sufficient life insurance. However, mortgage disability coverage is a totally different issue.

E-mail From: Red
Subject: You get an A+ in Insurance
Sent: Thursday, February 19

That makes sense, since I know Nick's life insurance policy is large enough to cover the mortgage; so unless the mortgage insurance rates are incredibly cheap, I can probably just stick to our current life insurance. But you're right about the disability issue. In the last few days I found out that since Nick is only recently self-employed, disability insurance is almost non-existent or very expensive. But if we can get mortgage disability insurance, that would be great.

E-mail From: Black
Subject: You get an A+ in Insurance
Sent: Thursday, February 19

Just make sure to read the fine print. And make sure you can cancel the policy at whatever time you think you are past the point of needing it.

E-mail From: Red
Subject: You get an A+ in Insurance
Sent: Thursday, February 19

Good point! I keep thinking about insurance as a forever thing, but I guess it doesn't have to be that way — sometimes I can use insurance as a temporary measure.

I know I'll be talking to our insurance agents in the next few days, and I'll make a note to ask about mortgage disability insurance. I don't want to assume that the offers I'll be getting in the mail are necessarily going to be the best.

Instead of making a note, I called our agent and in my usual fashion began with, "This may be a dumb question." He interrupted me. He said he wished all his clients were as dumb as me, that he was very impressed with my logical approach to insurance and my ability not only to make a decision — but to make an informed decision. For me, especially given the circumstances, it was the ultimate compliment.

IM I'm finished! I'm so excited. I made my final insurance decisions this afternoon, and all the policies are now in place. I even set up separate subcategories on Microsoft Money for insurance so that I could see not only the total monthly amount that I'll be paying, but the breakdown between the different policies. I feel so relieved knowing that this is behind me now.

IM Congratulations. You did a great job. Now all you have to do is remember your "insurance mantra" when it is time to review the policies.

IM Excuse me? Are you raining on my parade?

IM What are you talking about? I said you did a great job. You understand what you are paying for and your insurance decisions were all intelligent, conscious decisions.

IM I was referring to your comment "review the policies."

IM Sorry, but insurance is like all your budget line items — you need to review them on a regular basis. Needs and circumstances change, and you want to make sure your insurance coverage reflects those changes.

IM You don't mean I have to review them every month when I pay the premium, do you?

IM No, but insurance companies send out policy renewal notices 30–45 days in advance, and I use them as reminders to review the policy details and not just automatically renew.

IM You mean you get quotes from different companies every year? Do you switch insurance companies often? I'd think it would be a pain if you have to switch a policy to another company, even if you have a good agent.

IM This is another one of those "do as I say, not as I do" moments. First of all, remember our medical and dental policies are provided by Larry's company. Secondly, our agent works for a specific company and so he is not able to write policies from various insurance companies.

IM Then how do you know you are getting the best deal?

IM Do not know — do not care. We have good coverage with a reputable company. The cost of the policy is not really an issue with Larry, so I have not bothered to look at other options even though, as you now know, there are many different companies out there offering insurance at different prices. I like our agent and he gives us good service, so I have no desire to change agents. Some people actually buy insurance direct and avoid using agents altogether, but that thought would never cross my mind.

IM Or mine. I barely made it through everything with the help of several agents. I can't imagine doing it on my own.

IM And I hope you never try, but if you do — do NOT call me for help.

IM No worries there, but finish your thought about the review.

IM OK. You should not assume that you are always getting the best policy for your money by renewing the policy. For example, your history with the company may warrant discounts, any pre-existing medical conditions may have improved, a different insurance company may have more (or less) competitive rates than it did in the past. If you have a good agent he (or she) will automatically do those things for you, but you may want to ask them to do it for you annually so they know it is something you expect. I do not think it is necessary to review everything every year, although it would be a nice goal, but you do need to do it every few years.

I was thankful that I had wonderful insurance agents to walk me through all of this. I was learning from Black that instead of ignoring the things I didn't understand, I could find people who were experts.

12

Desserts Spelled Backwards
Is Stressed. And Vice Versa.

IM You OK?

IM Yes. Why?

IM You usually call me on Saturdays on your way to Weight Watchers, so I was wondering if something was wrong.

IM Nothing wrong. But nothing right either. I was so exhausted this morning that I overslept and decided to ditch both Weight Watchers and my usual Saturday morning grocery run.

IM Maybe you are coming down with Natasha's flu.

IM No, I'm not sick. Unless you count that I'm sick of feeling tired all the time. Between Natasha being home with the flu last week, Nick being busy the past few days and so unable to help with Sawyer, and my feeling like I spent the entire week dealing with insurance, I feel totally wiped out. I'd love to crawl back into bed, but that will never happen.

IM Look on the bright side — you survived the week.

IM Gee, thanks. But what about next week? We close on the new house on Wednesday morning and that night the puppy (which seemed like a great idea when you and I ordered her last summer) arrives from Australia. Just in time to be underfoot while I'm trying to pack and move. My life is insane!

IM Not really, just busy. Is there anything left to do before closing?

IM Not that I know of, but that's subject to change.

IM Have you scheduled the move yet?

IM No. I told our landlady late March, but I haven't called the movers yet. I'm dreading this move. I have lost count of how many times we've moved, but each time it's a huge amount of work. And that was before I had two young children AND a puppy added into the mix.

IM Yes, but Nick was going to work every day during those moves, plus most of those moves were before you used my color-coded labeling system. This one should be easier.

IM I'm not sure if Nick being around will be a help or a hindrance, but I forgot about your system. It did make a huge difference during our move to the States. I hope you saved the instructions. And if it isn't too much trouble, can you make those wonderful labels for the boxes again? They were great, and definitely made things easier. Anyway, the bottom line is that there's no such thing as an easy move.

IM Maybe not, but you have always moved from one country to another. Now you are only moving from one ZIP code to another. Since it is only crosstown, you can do it in stages if you want. Plus, you have the luxury of having over a month to do it.

IM As if I have nothing else to do all month! What are you suggesting? Move everything myself in Nick's SUV?

IM Not everything, but believe it or not, Nick and you can do a lot using your cars. I once moved all my kitchen stuff and clothing by the carload. In a two-seater Mercedes roadster!

IM I can't imagine you having enough kitchen stuff to fill a shopping cart, let alone a car, even one with only two seats. But moving your clothing, shoes and handbags is another story. I'd have thought that would require a fleet of moving vans.

IM Whatever. The point I was trying to make, which obviously escaped you, is that by moving things in stages I was able to have my kitchen set up and all my clothing in place in advance of actually moving in. It made the place instantly livable, which in turn eliminated much of the usual stress associated with moving.

IM That makes sense. Too bad you don't have a color-coded system for making my life less stressful.

IM No color codes, but I can come up with plenty of suggestions.

IM Is one of them "go back to bed and pull the covers over your head?"

IM Or you could do what I do ... run five miles.

IM Yeah, right! Any better suggestions?

IM Research shows that pets can reduce stress. Maybe you should get a puppy.

Another flippant comment. Another day without sympathy. Some things never change. Or maybe things change and I failed to notice them — like my life. In reality, by this point I had gotten over the worst of the crisis, but I had gotten so accustomed to being in panic mode that I didn't know how to operate any other way. All I wanted to do was escape — if only for a short while.

Who Said "Time Out" Was A Punishment?

When our financial crisis started, being able to blow off steam and vent to Black usually made me feel better, but not this time. Now, once again, I felt like I wanted to get into my car and run away.

E-mail From: Red
Subject: I Have Had It!
Sent: Saturday, February 21

I understand that:

1. Having your husband fired is STRESSFUL
2. Taking over financial responsibilities is STRESSFUL
3. Realizing you owe lots of money is STRESSFUL
4. Buying a home is STRESSFUL
5. Getting a puppy is STRESSFUL
6. Moving is STRESSFUL

I could add more to the list, but these are the highlights. So my question is — if any one of the above is stressful, what are ALL of the above?

E-mail From: Black
Subject: I Have Had It!
Sent: Saturday, February 21

I understand. I can remember a 10-day period where I was fired; Larry and I were moving in together in a new house; and Daddy, 2,000 miles away in New York, was diagnosed with cancer and needed emergency open-heart surgery before they could treat the cancer.

E-mail From: Red
Subject: I Have Had It!
Sent: Saturday, February 21

But you didn't have two kids. And you didn't have money problems!

E-mail From: Black
Subject: Stress ... is not a competitive sport!
Sent: Saturday, February 21

This is not a contest. I was trying to tell you I understand. And that I have been there.

E-mail From: Red
Subject: Stress ... is not a competitive sport!
Sent: Saturday, February 21

Unfortunately, knowing I'm not the first person to be stressed out does NOT make me feel any better. And wasting time on the internet accomplishing nothing isn't going to help either. I'll call you later. EOM

I knew I was under a lot of pressure, and I was frustrated that I couldn't find a release valve. Black was trying to make me feel better by explaining that she understood, but I surprised even myself when I realized I really didn't want sympathy or understanding this time. I wanted answers. Or at least suggestions. But how was she to know that?

IM Sorry about my e-mail earlier today. I'm miserable and tired and feel like I'm at my wit's end.

IM I could tell. I started to tell you to take a "time out" but it would only have prolonged the conversation, not helped it. It is funny ... when you are a kid, you think of time out as a punishment. And then when you grow up, time out becomes an elusive dream.

IM True. Very true. I wish someone would make me sit in the corner all alone or go to my room; even without dinner, it would still be OK. I'm fed up with everything and everybody, and I don't see any relief in sight.

IM Then make it happen.

IM Well, Miss Know-It-All, what do you suggest? How do you escape when the world seems to be closing in on you?

IM Me personally? Like I said earlier, when I need a short break, I run five miles, but to totally escape I play with cars! Why do you think I race?

IM Sorry, I just remembered I got so involved with insurance this week that I forgot to ask you about your day at the track. How was it?

IM Great. Racing is how I escape. Track days are wonderful, and race weekends are even better. Talk about a total escape. They are relaxing weekends spent with fast cars and good friends. And lots of interesting conversation.

IM Excuse me? Racing a Ferrari is relaxing? I find that hard to believe. Maybe if you were a spectator, but surely not as the driver.

IM Think of racing as a high-speed chess game. Lots of strategy. Lots of quick thinking. You have to be 100% focused, because the wrong move could result in damaging the car and possibly hurting yourself and others.

IM Sounds more like high-speed stress. How can you find that relaxing?

IM Because I am focused on learning the track, improving my lap times, and racing to the best of my abilities. I cannot think about anything else. My day-to-day life, and its problems and responsibilities, do not fit inside my helmet. And when I get off the track, I am with friends who share my passion for racing, so conversation and camaraderie come easily. For me, it is a perfect way to relax.

IM I'm not sure I understand your relaxation methods, but I can see where racing a Ferrari would be an escape from reality. Just owning one is an escape from reality! For us mere mortals, books and movies will have to do.

IM Well, those are still much better escape vehicles than alcohol. And on that note I need to log off so I can get dressed for Saturday night at Tony's, which requires me to drink enough wine to get through dinner with Larry. We can talk more tomorrow.

Although I couldn't help but question how racing could be relaxing, I definitely didn't question the desire to escape. I used to find time to catch a movie or get away to a quiet place with a magazine or a book for a few hours; but once Nick got fired, taking time for myself seemed like a selfish luxury. However, Black's comment about using alcohol (even if it's fine wine) to escape reality concerned me. I didn't mention it to her, but I did feel a little better knowing she recognized the situation. I was starting to wonder if she was having problems of her own, and I felt guilty burdening her with mine.

Do Not Confuse Time Alone With Escape Time

IM Good morning. Quick question: when was the last time you got away from everyone?

IM Yesterday afternoon. After lunch I left the girls with Nick and went grocery shopping and then ran a few other errands. Why?

IM I meant time away, not time alone.

IM What's the difference?

IM "Time alone" means without anyone with you. For instance, running errands by yourself or working in your office without the girls around would be time alone. "Time away" means time with no other objective than doing something for yourself. When was the last time you went to a movie by yourself?

IM A movie? You must be joking. I barely have time to sleep let alone the luxury of having an extra two hours to go to a movie.

IM You used to find the time on Sunday afternoons. What happened?

IM To you, it might be old news, but a month ago Nick got fired. I was supposed to go to the movies with a friend that Sunday, but I obviously had to cancel.

IM I would have gone anyway, just to escape, but I understand you cancelling it that weekend. How come you did not reschedule for the next Sunday? Or the one after that?

IM By then I felt our finances were so desperate that I didn't want to waste the money. I figured the money I'd spend on the movie, the popcorn and the Diet Coke would be better spent on something more important.

IM Did you ever think about going to the movie and skipping the popcorn and Diet Coke?

IM No! The popcorn is the real reason I go to the movie, but I have to buy a ticket to get to the concession stand. The movie is the excuse for me to sit alone with my popcorn.

IM OK. But even with a big bucket of popcorn, the movie is still much cheaper than seeing a shrink.

IM Are you trying to tell me something? Do you think I need a shrink?

IM Not until I heard your popcorn confession. I understand cancelling the movie because of the money, but why did you cancel the afternoon altogether? A break of any kind would have been good for you. Even if it was only to visit over coffee.

IM Because YOU told me to stop wasting money on frivolous things, like Jamba Juice and Starbucks!

IM My comments about Starbucks and Jamba Juice were in the context of a trade-off. Using Starbucks as a destination to visit with friends or escape with a magazine is very different than it being purely a coffee habit. You cannot always put a value, either in monetary and/or time terms, on doing things for yourself.

IM I wasn't. I was only trying to explain (or maybe defend is a better word) why I cancelled my Sunday movie.

IM And I am trying to make you look at things differently. Do you still feel like a movie will break the budget?

IM No. Now that I have a better handle on our finances, I know we can afford the movie and the big bucket of popcorn. But now I'm not sure I can afford the time.

IM You cannot afford not to go to the movies, or at least take some time for yourself. What is your excuse for not going this afternoon?

IM I promised Natasha we would go shopping for a special toy to welcome Woof, which is what she has named the puppy.

IM Interesting name. Legitimate excuse. But take out your calendar and make an appointment with yourself to go to a movie next Sunday. I do not care if it is a comedy or a tearjerker. I do not care if you have to ignore everything else on your "To-Do" list. I do not care if you have to skip a shower or a meal. Just go.

IM Fine. Enough already. I get your point. EOM

This IM with Black caught me off guard, and at first I was annoyed. I felt I needed to defend myself and point out that I don't do things with friends just for the activity — I do things with my friends to spend time with them. But then I realized that was exactly what I had NOT done when I cancelled my afternoon out. And it made me realize I had to start looking at things differently. And maybe a little more honestly.

I spent Sunday relaxing with the girls, knowing that almost everything was done in preparation of closing on the house and the arrival of Woof. I even made time to do my Sunday night review of the upcoming week. When I looked at my calendar, I saw

I could theoretically schedule time for myself every Sunday afternoon and so set up a 2-hour "movie break" as a recurring appointment. The amazing thing was that just knowing I had time blocked off for me provided a sense of relief. Not to mention something to look forward to. And by Monday night, I was already counting down the hours until Sunday.

IM I'm furious, and I have to vent to someone who will understand.

IM Glad to help. Vent away.

IM Tonight at dinner I mentioned to Nick that I was exhausted and that I wanted to go to bed early.

IM Bet he liked that idea. Wink-wink.

IM I'll ignore that. So Nick says – and you're going to love this — that he doesn't understand why I'm so tired. He goes on to say that I had almost the entire day to myself because he watched Sawyer in the morning and even took both girls off for ice cream after he picked up Natasha from school. He finishes his little "aren't I wonderful" speech by saying he's surprised that I didn't enjoy my day off more!

IM I wondered why I had not heard from you all day. So what did you do on your day off? Eat bonbons and watch soap operas and Oprah?

IM You know what my lists look like, so don't even go there. And Nick doesn't understand that just because I'm "alone" doesn't mean that I'm doing nothing!

IM Hey, only yesterday you asked the difference between "time alone" and "time away," so why do you expect him to know? Are you saying you think he is smarter than you?

IM Cute. But in case you haven't noticed, I am NOT in a cute mood!

IM Yeah, I picked up on that when you asked permission to vent.

IM And to think I felt guilty about my Sunday movies. Not anymore! The fact I try to squeeze so much into my day, including getting up before the birds so that I have some quiet time before the girls wake up, means I have earned my movie time even more.

IM No argument from me. I am sure that when Nick worked in an office, he did not consider it a "vacation" day when he did not have any meetings or appointments. It meant he could work on those things that required his undivided attention, but he was still working. You might want to remind him of that next time.

IM Nah. That would be like wrestling with a pig.

IM ???

IM "Never wrestle with a pig. You both get dirty, but the pig likes it."

IM Maybe you do need professional help! Or at least some sleep. EOM

I needed a way to relieve my stress. I could hear myself saying the most outrageous things and recognized my behavior was out of character. Nothing serious, just snippy comments or slamming of drawers and doors. It was as if I was having out-of-body experiences and I was standing next to myself. Except it wasn't the real me. I knew I had to do something about it. And soon. I only hoped Sunday was soon enough!

Self-Preservation Is Not Selfish

E-mail From: Black
Subject: Stress Management
Sent: Tuesday, February 24

After our IM last night I did some research. Here is an 8-step stress management technique I found that might help you.

1. Picture yourself near a stream.
2. Birds are softly chirping in the cool mountain air.
3. No one but you knows your secret place.
4. You are in total seclusion from the hectic place called "the world."
5. The soothing sound of a gentle waterfall fills the air with a cascade of serenity.
6. The water is crystal-clear.
7. You can easily make out the face of the person you're holding underwater.
8. See? You're smiling already.

Have a great day!

Black's e-mail certainly made me smile. But my stress was due to many things, not just one person. Was Black trying to tell me something about her life with her e-mail? I thought about it for a few minutes, but then decided I was probably overreacting. After all, Black has never been one to drop subtle hints. Bomb shells, maybe. But subtle hints? Never!

IM I loved your e-mail. Obviously, I can't "drown" my problems, but I sure need some other ways to reduce stress. Any ideas?

IM Here are your options:

A: Identify and eliminate things that are causing you stress.
B: Adjust your attitude and/or outlook.
C: Find a way to temporarily escape.
D: All of the above.

IM I vote for C. Listing what's causing me stress won't eliminate any of them. And I'm not sure what you mean by adjusting my attitude or outlook.

IM Change your perspective and how you look at things.

IM Still not sure what you mean. Give me an example.

IM OK. If I get annoyed or frustrated with Larry, I realize the best way to a man's heart is through his chest with a sharp knife!

IM Funny, but not a real answer.

IM Realer than you realize. One of the health columns in The Wall Street Journal referenced research that shows a connection between laughter and health, and how laughter reduces a stress hormone.

IM Thank you for that scientific study, but besides male-bashing jokes, do you have any advice which is a bit more practical?

IM That was practical. You need to try and lighten up. First of all, worrying about what has already happened is a total waste of time. Worrying about what might happen is also a waste of time. I know that things happen for a reason and things will work out, one way or another, and so I look ahead and do not dwell on the past. I may not be able to control the situation, but I know I can control how I deal with it — and that eliminates much of the stress in my life. And if I can laugh about any aspect of it — that makes things even better.

IM I guess we look at things differently. I don't think I can put myself in your shoes (beside the fact I can't afford them) and look at things that pragmatically. But I know there are times you are under stress because you get pissy with me.

IM True. And when I sense a "pissy" mood, as you call it, I go for a long run and think things out. Because running is a rhythmic activity (as is vacuuming, or so I am told), it allows my body to get into its own rhythm and then my mind is free to work out problems, find solutions or merely daydream. I usually come back with a plan or at least a clearer perspective on things, which makes me feel much better.

IM I don't picture myself in your running shoes, either! And vacuuming was not exactly the suggestion I was hoping for. Any other suggestions?

IM I will save the "Escape through Exercise" lecture for another time. Right now, you need to acknowledge that stress is going to be part of your life. Although you cannot avoid it, you can learn to deal with it. Find an activity — it could be as simple as a walk in the neighborhood or reading a magazine at Starbucks — that functions as a temporary escape. Let Nick and the girls know that you need some time away. And then last, but not least, schedule it. Put it on your calendar like an appointment. And make it a priority.

IM You make it sound so easy.

IM It is. Do not complicate it.

The realization that I needed to make more time for myself and take better care of myself was the easy part. Figuring out how to implement it, on the other hand, was more difficult. It meant re-prioritizing, first in my mind and then on my lists and calendar.

E-mail From: Black
Subject: Sleeping on the Job?
Sent: Tuesday, February 24

I called a few minutes ago, and Nick said you were taking a nap. I am glad you finally decided to do something for yourself. Meanwhile, I put together a list (since I know you LOVE lists) of ideas for ways to temporarily "escape" from your day and/or life. They are in no particular order, although I think anything related to exercise would be your best bet — both mentally and physically.

- Sneak a nap. (I put this as #1 so you could feel a sense of accomplishment.)
- Get a puppy. How can you not feel better playing with a puppy? (I put this as #2 since you will accomplish it tomorrow night.)
- Have a "time-out" place in your house, backyard or within walking distance of your house. Let everyone know you are "off limits" when you go there.
- Take a book or magazine and go hide somewhere or curl up in the park. Don't tell anyone where you are going, and only emergency phone calls are allowed.
- Exercise … start walking. It is free and easy to do. No special equipment required. Ideally, go by yourself.
- Exercise … work out with a tape or DVD.
- Exercise … join a gym and start taking classes. (I thought you once did yoga.)
- Learn a new sport or start doing a favorite sport again.
- Listen to music you enjoy or that brings back fond memories. (I turn on disco music since it makes me want to dance.)
- Relax with a movie YOU want to watch (on television, on your computer, in a theater).
- Spend time with friends — arrange a lunch, a walk, a talk, a "girls" night out.
- Find a charity or hobby and make time for it.
- Go to a museum, gallery or crafts show. (Personally, I love to go to exotic car dealerships after the new models are released.)
- Expand your horizons: learn about wine, gardening, anything you find interesting.
- Book a massage, a manicure or a pedicure.
- Start a "sunny day" list of tasks. There are always low-priority things that can be done outside: taking care of correspondence, reviewing paperwork, cleaning out the garage, washing the car. Start a list, and when it is a beautiful day, do one of those "outdoorsy" items and accomplish two things — enjoy the weather and cross a low-priority item off your list.

- Have a "rainy day" list too. Same concept, different weather. Things like clearing stuff off your kitchen counters, alphabetizing your spices (kidding!), reorganizing or tidying up the girls' rooms. Clutter makes everyone feel stressed out. (Remember how therapeutic it felt when you went through the piles in your office. Apply that feeling to other rooms.)
- Start a journal. Levenger has a great 5-year journal, and if you take the time to focus on the highlight of the day, it puts everything else in perspective and reduces the effect of any low points.

E-mail From: Red
Subject: Sleeping on the Job?
Sent: Tuesday, February 24

Glad to see "Nap" was on the list, as mine felt great! I decided I needed some "down time" so I laid down, although it was a real struggle to overcome the pangs of guilt. I'm sure it'll get easier in time, but for the moment I'll really have to force myself to do things for myself. However, I must admit I do feel better — both physically and mentally — so I guess that's an incentive for making sure I remember to give myself some personal time. Even if I do feel like I'm "cheating" on my family.

E-mail From: Black
Subject: What Did They Get Cheated Out Of?
Sent: Tuesday, February 24

I cannot believe you took some time for yourself merely to maintain your sanity and feel more rested. That is a cruel thing to do to your family. Very cruel. And inconsiderate.

Fine. Maybe I was being too hard on myself, but initially it did feel as if I was neglecting my responsibilities. The flip side of the coin was that I knew this was the "quiet before the storm." That once we close on the house in the morning I'd be up to my ears in boxes and packing, and the only time I'd have for myself would be whatever time I stole. And so I told myself that scheduling time for me was no different than scheduling any other important activity.

Escape Through Exercise

The rest of that week was incredibly hectic. The combination of preparing for the move (and I must admit Black's color-coded moving system was going to make this the easiest move I had ever made) and the arrival of Woof made the days extremely chaotic. I was thrilled when the girls wanted to take a break and go to the park that weekend and leave Woof at home. Funny, somehow I think they needed the quiet time too. As I watched the girls play, I noticed a few runners go by and it made me think of Black.

I have always admired Black because she can put on running shoes and take a mental break from her day, not to mention the physical benefits derived from her workout routine. And I have always envied people that go to the gym on a regular basis as they obviously have more spare time than I do. Then I realized that it might be that they just prioritized it higher.

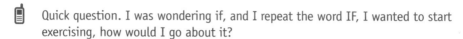 Quick question. I was wondering if, and I repeat the word IF, I wanted to start exercising, how would I go about it?

☎ Hello. Hello. Who is this? You must have the wrong number.

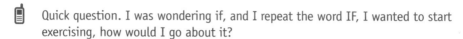 I didn't say I was going to do it, I said I was wondering.

☎ And what brought this on?

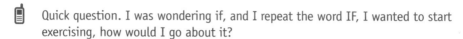 Primarily the obvious — health and fitness and weight control. But watching you use it as a way to temporarily get away from life and reduce stress is also a motive. Although I have no desire to run five miles.

☎ What happened to your Sunday movie? Are you trying to tell me you are not going tomorrow?

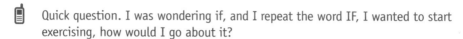 I'm not answering that question until you answer my question. If I wanted to start an exercise program, where would I start?

☎ The first step is to make it a short-term priority.

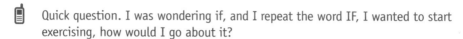 Short-term? No, I want it to become something I do on an ongoing basis, not just a quick fix.

☎ I understand, but if you make it a long-term goal, you may procrastinate starting. If you make it a short-term project, once you start experiencing the benefits, you will become addicted. I bet it will go from being a scheduled task to a way of life within six months. It is similar to when you started Weight Watchers. Initially it was to lose weight, but then it became a logical way of eating.

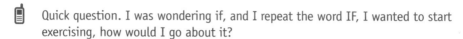 We'll see. For the moment, keep in mind I don't intend to become fanatical like you; I just want a normal exercise program.

☎ First, you need to find something that you enjoy. It can be as simple as throwing on sneakers and going for a walk. Or you can rent a yoga tape or go to a Pilates class at the local gym. Or come over here and work out in our gym.

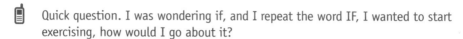 This sounds like it may take more time than I have available at the moment. I think I'll wait until I'm settled in the new house.

☎ No! What did I just say about procrastinating? Exercise does not require hours of time. And it does not have to be in a gym. You can start with 10-minute sessions at home and gradually increase them. The key is to start. And I would suggest doing it first thing in the morning.

📱 But that would mean getting up even earlier than I already do and you know I'm not a morning person.

☎ Not necessarily. Get up at the usual time and do the exercise first. Before you get side-tracked by other activities like wasting 15 minutes IMing me. Plus you will not be awake enough to change your mind.

📱 That all sounds very logical, but I have a feeling that something is going to fall by the wayside, and I'm guessing it's the exercise.

☎ That's why for the first few weeks, or maybe even months, you need to schedule your exercise time as appointments. Ones that are etched in stone. Once you start, it will not take long for you to feel the results — physically you will have more energy, and mentally you will feel more confident and in control. And trust me, over time it will become addictive.

📱 Somehow I don't picture me ever becoming a gym bunny, hopping my way to happiness. But I'd certainly be happy to be in better shape — mentally and physically.

☎ I can remember what you looked like in that Winnie-the-Pooh Halloween costume, and I am picturing you in a bunny outfit hopping down the treadmill. It is a great visual. Hilarious, in fact!

At first I was annoyed that Black was so amused. Then I had to admit the thought of me on a treadmill was amusing, not to mention the thought of me on a treadmill in a bunny costume. I decided to start working out, and although I'd have loved to join a gym, I wasn't willing to make that kind of financial commitment. But I did go shopping. I looked at hand weights and various workout tapes and DVDs. I started to call Black to ask her advice, but decided I'd rather make a mistake on my own than get myself roped into a more extensive workout program than I really wanted.

And so on Sunday night I started my new workout program — a yoga tape. I decided to do it at night, because years ago when I did yoga I found it very relaxing and it made falling asleep easier. But on the third night I didn't have the energy or desire to work out and I didn't keep my exercise "appointment." I remembered Black's advice, and the next morning I worked out. She was right, a morning schedule would probably be easier to stick with, although working out first thing in the morning was a struggle. I hoped that would improve over time.

Sometimes "Me First" Should Come First

Although that week was hectic, I was starting to understand how having time during the day to be alone and clear your mind, even just a walk around the block, could make a big difference to your well-being. The problem was that shortly after I started to feel better, I started to feel worse. Worse to the point I barely had enough energy to get out of bed.

IM I know it is only Thursday, but any ideas what movie you plan to see Sunday?

IM If that's your way of making sure I go to a movie, then it failed. I'm not going this Sunday.

IM You better have a damn good excuse.

IM Does "doctor's orders" count?

IM Only if you tell me what is going on.

IM Earlier in the week I started feeling really tired. At first I figured it was from all the packing and the fact my body wasn't use to exercising. Yesterday I took it easy, but I still didn't feel any better. In fact, when I got home from picking up Natasha, Nick said I looked awful and suggested I lie down and take a nap. I must have looked really bad for him to notice!

IM Quit the editorial. Get to the doctor part.

IM This morning I barely had the energy to get out of bed, and that was when Nick insisted I go to the doctor. It turns out I have walking pneumonia. I went to the doctor and Clive told me to stay in bed for a couple of days and do nothing.

IM Then why are you on IM? You should be in bed!

IM You must be joking. Clive means well but doesn't understand that doing nothing is a luxury right now — not an option.

IM Well, "Wonder Woman," I think it is you that does not understand. It is not an option. It is a necessity. Let Nick handle things for a few days. Trust me, everyone will survive.

IM But there are so many things I need to do. Life doesn't stop just because I'm sick.

IM True. But the bottom line is that unless you take care of yourself, you will not be able to take care of your family.

IM I understand the logic, but it's difficult for me to just stop and crawl into bed, as much as that's what I want to do. I feel like I'm letting the family down. I'm not trying to sound like "Wonder Woman," I'm just being honest.

IM Let me give you an analogy. If you were on an airplane with the girls and you lost altitude and the oxygen masks came down, would you put the mask on yourself first or the girls?

IM I'm not sure I feel up to one of your stupid quizzes.

IM Humor me. Answer the question.

IM OK. They say that adults should put their mask on first and then help their children, though I must admit I have never understood that since my instinct as a mom is to help my child first. Did I pass or fail?

IM Airline one, Red zero. The airline knows it is in the best interest of the child for the adult to be safe and secure. If the adult is not stable and calm, then helping a scared, helpless child is going to be extremely difficult.

IM Great. The next time I'm on an airplane and the oxygen masks fall down, I'll remember this conversation. But what exactly is the point you're trying to make? Maybe it's the fever, but I don't understand.

IM If you do not take care of yourself and you get sicker, then you will be of no use to anyone. For now, that means following doctor's orders and taking a few days to rest. But even after you get over this, you need to start taking some time for yourself to make sure that you stay healthy – both physically and mentally – so that you can be there for everyone that needs you. Get off the computer and climb into bed. Now! EOM

You Can Run, But Can You Hide?

I spent the next few days in bed, as instructed by my doctor, but more importantly as demanded by Black. I might have had enough strength to do a few things around the house, but I knew I wasn't strong enough to argue with her. But the time in bed wasn't a total waste. In fact, far from it.

E-mail From: Red
Subject: Saturday Night – I am alive
Sent: Saturday, March 6

Quick update: I'm starting to feel better and things are slowly returning to normal. (Whatever normal is!) I actually stayed in bed and away from the computer (and my lists) for two whole days. Well, almost stayed away from my lists. I did work on paper copies of the ones related to the move, but I did it in bed between naps. Tonight I am starting to feel semi-human again, and although I'm not quite ready to start working out again, I do feel like I can probably handle some light packing and other small jobs tomorrow.

Hope you had a wonderful dinner at Tony's. Something really delicious, like that Dover Sole you love. (It always reminds me of when Natasha was born and you were the first family member to come visit us in Amsterdam and stayed at the Amstel Hotel. I never found a better place for Dover Sole.) FYI, I had bland chicken and white rice. Yum Yum.

E-mail From: Black
Subject: **Saturday Night – I am alive**
Sent: Saturday, March 6

Welcome back to the land of the living. Glad you are feeling better. Do not overdo tomorrow. And I doubt you will do it, but how about keeping your Sunday afternoon movie date with yourself? Tell Nick it is doctor's orders — the movie is quieter than an afternoon at home with the girls.

P.S. — Tony's was Tony's — excellent food, the Saturday night regulars, dinner conversation consisted of my monologue and I drank too much wine — in other words, things are normal here too.

I knew I was going to have to ease back into getting ready for the move and so the next morning I starting packing some boxes and figured that would be the extent of today's exercise program. And the extent of my energy. By lunch I was more than ready to take a two-hour break. And although Black doubted I'd take the time to go to a movie, I decided that was exactly what I'd do.

☎ I called the house to check on you, and Nick said you just left to go to a movie. Good girl.

📱 Yeah. I couldn't pass up an opportunity to prove you wrong.

☎ Well, you do sound better. Glad I could help.

📱 This might sound crazy, but just getting into my car and driving away from the house — knowing that I'm not trying to squeeze a million errands into the next two hours — feels fantastic. Although I do feel a little guilty.

☎ Get over it! If you are feeling better just driving to the theater, imagine how good you will feel after popcorn and a movie. Anything else before I hang up?

📱 What's the rush? Hate to hear me gloat about you being wrong?

☎ No. Hate to take up any of your escape time. Quit talking me to and enjoy your solitude. And your triumph. Now hang up.

And that's exactly what I did. I'd already told Nick not to call unless it was an emergency — a real emergency — not an "I can't find Sawyer's Nana doll. Do you know where it is?" type emergency. As I walked into the theater, I felt like I was escaping from a war zone into neutral territory. A place where for the next two hours I could pretend that the rest of the world didn't exist, or at least could survive without me. I got my usual order (a Diet Coke and the largest popcorn) and sat through the previews, looking forward to the movie and the popcorn. I have always waited until the feature film starts before I start eating. Black, on the other hand, buys the smallest popcorn and considers it an accomplishment to have it finished before the previews end.

IM How was the movie?

IM Great. Well, the movie was mediocre, but that's OK. The objective of going to the movie was to be entertained and provide an escape, and it succeeded on both fronts.

IM So I take that to mean you feel better.

IM Yes. Much. Is there something wrong with me? I really enjoyed being somewhere no one could bother me.

IM There is nothing wrong with you. Nothing that an electronic shutdown won't cure.

IM An electronic shutdown? What's that? And where do you come up with this stuff?

IM Think about it. We have become a society that walks around with phones in our ears, a Blackberry in our hands and an addiction to text messages and e-mails. Has anyone ever stopped to ask what is so important that we have to be available all the time?

IM I need the school, or Nick, to be able to get in touch with me if something happens to one of the girls.

IM Fair enough. But you do not use your cell phone only for emergency calls. We talk on it all the time ... when you are in the car, when you are grocery shopping or even when you are with the girls at the playground. And usually the conversations are not very important, or at least are ones that could wait.

IM Says the woman who is tethered to her Blackberry. So what's your point?

IM First, in defense of my Blackberry, I use it because I typically do not answer my cell phone. In fact, if I am in the middle of doing something at home, I do not answer the land line either. So if someone really needs to get in touch with me, I tell them to send me an e-mail. I have several e-mail addresses, but only the high-priority/limited distribution addresses go to the Blackberry.

But the point I was making is the fact we feel the need to be connected all the time adds to our stress levels. There is no getting away, no leisurely Sunday drives, no peaceful strolls through the park ... unless you have an electronic shutdown.

IM That makes perfect sense. And I agree. That's probably why I felt so good about going to the movies. It wasn't only a physical escape from everyone and everything; it was also a legitimate reason to electronically disappear.

IM Which is what I am about to do. EOM

I thought about when I bought my cell phone, and I had to laugh. The salesman started to explain all the options, and I had to stop him and tell him I only needed to know how to use the phone and save contact information. He looked at me like I was a dinosaur, and I guess when it comes to electronic gadgets, I am. Plus, a telephone shouldn't need instructions!

But I did like Black's suggestion of an electronic shutdown. I could start limiting the amount of time I spent (wasted) on the computer by trying to only check e-mails in the mornings when I woke up and at night once the girls were asleep. I realized I really didn't have to spend as much time on the computer as I thought I did.

Recess Isn't Only For Kids

I could tell my stress levels were generally dropping. Of course I could attribute a lot of it to the fact that I was initially stressed out by all the unknowns in my life, which eventually were working themselves out. And even when the outcome was not exactly what I'd have wanted, I tried (not always successfully) to stop worrying about the things I couldn't change.

I was able to see the importance of having several different escape routes and realized these breaks didn't require more time out of my day — they merely required better use of my time. It meant focusing on being more productive to make sure I'd have sufficient time left over to escape. And as my life started to fall back into a routine and my reliance on Black to make it through the day, or at least the next crisis, decreased, I had even more time available. And so I decided to add one more recurring appointment to my calendar.

IM Glad you're online. What are you doing Wednesday night?

IM Is this a trick question?

IM No. I know Larry takes Brittney and Chelsea to dinner on Wednesday nights, and I was thinking we could schedule dinner and a movie. Unless you're possessive of your Wednesday nights alone.

IM It is not that I want to be alone; I just want a break from having to do a monologue ... which is what dinner with Larry has become. I am running out of material.

IM Want to talk?

IM No. That is the problem. I want to listen for a change, rather than being the only one talking. But to get back to your question ... are you talking about every Wednesday night? Like a recurring appointment?

IM Yup! Every Wednesday, all things being equal.

IM Is this to replace your Sunday matinees, or are you going to "cheat" on your family twice a week? If the latter, you are such a slut!

IM I guess it was too much to expect a simple yes or no.

IM Your expectations of me are sometimes way too high. When have I ever given you one-word answers? Wednesdays work for me, but what brought this on?

IM Getting sick. Getting new priorities. Realizing that time for me is important to reduce my stress and maintain my sanity. Scheduling time for me is now one of my priorities, rather than being at the bottom of my list of things to do. I know I'm doing something beneficial for both me and the family, even if it might look to others like I'm wasting time or being selfish.

IM Think of it as your adult recess. A grown-up version of snack time or recess at school. Where kids take a break from their studies. They get some nutrition and exercise and have fun while they are recharging their physical and mental batteries.

Adult recess? She was right. Once I started scheduling time for myself, I found the breaks allowed me to come back refreshed and more focused on the tasks at hand. I learned there's no escaping stress, so you better have a game plan to deal with it. The key is to make sure that I don't sacrifice my own time, even when my lists provide ample excuses for doing so, unless the specific task is truly more important than my self-preservation!

13
Managing Your Home With Dollars And Sense

IM   What are you doing up so late?

IM   I'm doing house work.

IM   At this hour? Even Martha Stewart is probably asleep by now.

IM   I wish I was too, but a house never sleeps. And I'm running out of hours in the day.

IM   And you are forgoing sleep for housework? That is a bit extreme, especially since you will be moving in a few weeks. Leave the floors dirty!

IM   NOT housework. House Work. Two words. Paperwork and administrative tasks. Not to mention everything associated with moving.

IM   I gave you my moving system. That should make things easier.

IM   Absolutely. It's a great system and will make a HUGE difference, but it won't help me with all my other house-related tasks. At the risk of sounding incredibly naïve, I never realized how much work it takes to run a house.

IM   That is because Nick used to take care of most of it. And before that you lived with Mom and Daddy. Now that you have entered the real world, you have to deal with reality. Sorry.

IM   I know you love reminding me how I avoided so many adult responsibilities for decades, but I have already admitted – countless times – that I was an ostrich. But I'll say one thing — life as an ostrich was much easier.

IM   I bet my ostrich handbags would disagree with you. Anyway, I think you are making a bigger deal about home management than is necessary. You have already demonstrated you have the skills and systems to take care of administrative and decision-making issues. And do not forget that the "warm and fuzzy," which is what makes a house a home, has always been your specialty.

IM   That's all fine and good, but I'm still running out of time. Any bright ideas on how I can conjure up more hours in the day?

IM No, but look at the bright side ... if you survive the next month, the worst of it will be behind you.

IM That's the bright side?!

IM Yes. Since the major tasks — packing and moving — have deadlines, they will somehow get done regardless of how many hours you have in the day. Everything else will get done in due time. And let me guess – you have already started a "New House" checklist.

IM How did you know? In fact, that's one of the things I'm working on tonight.

IM I am clairvoyant. And guess what will be the best part of the next month ...

IM Yes? This should be good.

IM I will be out of town for almost two weeks! The next time Nick plans to get fired and you decide to move into a new house, please give me a little more advance notice.

IM Chicken!

IM Hey, I would rather be a chicken than an ostrich. EOM

The timing in terms of taking my head out of the sand was less than ideal. Nick and I had lived in five different countries and six different residences (I finally counted), and all but one had been either rented houses or corporate-owned apartments. Obviously, when you're an occupant versus an owner, your level of responsibility is significantly less. In addition, we were usually on a generous company-paid housing allowance and the Company paid for all the moves. Plus, since we knew each residence was only a temporary situation, we didn't really look at our houses as part of our future.

The end result was that the impact of any house-related decisions was fairly minimal. Any time during the past 15 or so years would have been a perfect time for me to learn about home-management issues. But no! I timed it perfectly. I waited until the decisions would be more important and mistakes more far-reaching.

Management Aspects Of The House

I woke up the next morning feeling better. As Black had reminded me, I did have the skills necessary to juggle all my house work tasks. Of course, life never happens as we plan it and a house is an ongoing challenge — or nightmare depending on the day — with even the most ordinary and seemingly benign events having logistical and financial repercussions.

☎ Just checking in. Plus, I wanted to let you know I sent you an e-mail about your "house work" ... 2 words.

☎ I doubt I'll get online for awhile. It's been a yucky morning.

☎ Yucky? Is that a technical term? What happened?

☎ The downstairs hallway toilet backed up, and I have spent the last hour cleaning up the mess. Why couldn't it have waited another few weeks? Then we wouldn't be living here anymore, and I wouldn't have to deal with it. Now I have to call the plumbing company. And then I get to hang out and wait for them. What a great way to waste time. And money.

☎ Weren't they just out? I hope you have them on an annual maintenance contract.

☎ Yes, but that was for a different bathroom. And no, the owners don't have them on a contract. Our rental contract stipulates that we pay for things like plumbers, unless it's a major problem.

☎ That is usually the case with rental properties, but I thought you might have put them on a maintenance contract. You might want to consider doing that in the new house.

☎ Won't need to. The sellers have included a one-year "Home Warranty" insurance policy.

☎ I am not exactly sure what that covers, but you might want to review the small print. It still might make sense to consider an annual service contract. At least find out the cost and compare it to the minimum call-out rate. Figure out the break-even point.

☎ Plumbers are so expensive. I'm not sure I want the cost of an annual contract.

☎ I understand. I am merely suggesting you consider it and make an informed decision. And it is not something you have to do today. It can wait until after the move.

☎ I don't even know if we're going to have problems with plumbing in the new house. I may not need them again in the next 12 months.

☎ Or you might need them several times. You are thinking in terms of fixing problems, and I think of service contracts as preventive maintenance. I keep a running list by trade (plumbing, electrical, heating and air conditioning, etc.) on what needs to be repaired, cleaned or checked. Most things are not urgent and so do not require immediate attention, but when the list becomes long enough, I schedule a convenient time to have them come out. I try to catch things when they are small vs. letting them turn into a major problem or an emergency.

☎ But I thought service contracts were for repair work only.

☎ Some are, but many companies offer a contract that gives you repair work and general maintenance and service.

☎ I didn't know that. OK, I'll put it on my list. Is it just plumbers, or are there other maintenance contracts I need to consider?

☎ Not exactly sure. I know we have one with the air conditioning company. And I wish we could put our painter, Johnny, on retainer.

☎ Why? Changing room colors monthly? How many shades of off-white are there?

☎ I wish that was the case. This house is at an age when the wood windows and doors are going to need replacement, and I am trying to avoid that until we move into the high-rise. For the last few years I have had Johnny's crew come out and power-wash the house and check the caulking around the windows and doors every six months to try and prolong their life. When they find wood that is beginning to rot, we can do repair work instead of waiting until the entire window or door needs to be replaced.

☎ Sounds like your painters have job security.

☎ Yes. Sometimes I think more than I do.

☎ Should I read something into that comment?

☎ No. You should hang up and call the plumber.

Which is exactly what I did. And although I knew it was wasted money, there really wasn't anything I could do about it. However, I knew the time spent waiting around could be put to good use — between packing and getting better organized for the new house, I had a lot to keep me busy.

E-mail From: Black
Subject: **"House Work" ... 2 Words!**
Sent: Tuesday, March 9

Part of my "job description" is taking care of Larry's house. Basically all he does is pay the bills (well, technically he does not even do that ... I pay all the bills and tell him how much to deposit in the checking account) and I take care of everything else. I went through my house files to see if I had any checklists or notes you might find useful, but could not find any. However, since I know how much you love checklists, I put together the following:

1. **Tasks Completed**
   ☑ Determine budget
   ☑ Selection of house
   ☑ Mortgage
   ☑ Insurance
   ☑ Purchase house

2. **Immediate Issues**
   ☐ Pre-move preparation
   ☐ Deciding what to sell vs. move
   ☐ Physical move

3. Ongoing Issues
☐ Budget & expenses
☐ Insurance
☐ Maintenance

4. Long-Term Issues
☐ Capital improvements

E-mail From: Red
Subject: "House Work" ... 2 Words!
Sent: Tuesday, March 9

You're right — I love checklists, but I REALLY love the section with the items that are already checked off! As far as the ongoing issues, all the day-to-day bookkeeping is already on Microsoft Money so I can track the expenses and update my budget as necessary. Insurance is already filed in its own loose-leaf binder, and I have another binder for all the closing documents. There's a drawer full of miscellaneous papers and user manuals at the new house, and I'll put them in Ziploc bags until I get a chance to go through them. And although the maintenance issues will wait until after the move, I'll start lists by trade.

FYI, I'm planning on having at least one garage sale and have started accumulating those items in the garage. And between your moving system and my Microsoft Excel spreadsheet, I think I have the move fairly well organized. So the only question I have is about the pre-move preparation. What exactly do you mean? I have already turned on the utilities and have an appointment for the phone service. I plan to have a cleaning service come in a day or two before the move. Is there anything else I need to think about?

E-mail From: Black
Subject: "House Work" ... more thoughts
Sent: Tuesday, March 9

A few things come to mind

- **Maintenance:** Add "Review Inspection Report" to your list of things to do. I am sure there are assorted items the inspectors found that were not important enough to require immediate attention, but you should add them to your maintenance list by trade. In fact, if I were smart, I would order an inspection of Larry's house to see if there are any things I should be aware of, but I am not really that interested in making more work for myself since we will be moving.

- **Pre-Move (Capital) Improvements:** I know I put capital improvements under "Long-Term Issues" but if there are any items (within your budget) that are easier to accomplish before you move in, you might want to consider doing them now. I know you mentioned wanting to re-paint some of the rooms (which technically is maintenance, not capital improvements) and since you have the luxury of having full access to the new house while you are still living in the rental house, that might be the perfect thing to do now.

- **Your Lists:** Make sure to print out all your lists, including at least a week's worth of your daily lists, before you pack up your printer, in case you have any problems hooking it up in the new house. In fact, when you back-up Franklin Planner, e-mail me the back-up file so I have it … just in case.

Well, that response was pretty straight-forward, with the exception of one item — Black's reference to her house as "Larry's house." It was the second time she did that today, and I was a little concerned. But not concerned enough, or maybe not brave enough, to broach the subject with her.

Customizing Your House Into A Home

The more I thought about it, the more I liked the idea of painting some of the rooms before we actually moved. I realized moving might scuff or scratch the new paint, but it would be easier to touch up a few spots than it would be to paint entire rooms full of furniture. Not to mention that thinking about decorating issues was far more interesting than organizing and budgeting "house work."

Black always seemed to have a "career." When she retired from the corporate world, she entered the construction phase of her life. First, it was an addition on their (Larry's?) house, followed by a significant remodeling of the upstairs. Then they bought land in Arizona and Vermont, and she was in charge of those plans. Vermont got cancelled before it was built, but Arizona had recently broken ground and was a two-year construction project. Black was also working on elaborate plans for a high-rise in Houston.

E-mail From: Red
Subject: "House Work" … more thoughts
Sent: Wednesday, March 10

I love the idea of painting now, but I'm not sure it's within our budget. What would you guess it would cost?

And as far as doing any other capital improvements, the only other things on our list are major: redoing and updating the entire kitchen and building a second floor over the garage. I don't see either of these projects happening for years. If ever.

E-mail From: Black
Subject: "House Work" … more thoughts
Sent: Wednesday, March 10

Re: Painting. I have no idea what it will cost, especially since I have no idea if you want to do all the rooms or just some of them, but the best way to find out would be to call Johnny and ask. Remember when you first moved to Houston and you hated the color of some of the downstairs rooms and were desperate to repaint them? I called Johnny to get the name of a less expensive painter for you, and was surprised to learn that he had different price points depending on your objectives. Since it was a rent house, you went with the cheapest option. It is a matter of thinking and planning. Obviously, you would not want to invest in the same quality of paint job in the girls' bedroom or playroom as you might for the dining room or your bedroom. Keep in mind you can paint expensively or you can paint economically. (Or you can do it yourself … and I will pay to watch!)

Re: Capital improvements. Garage addition, I agree. But what were you thinking in terms of the kitchen? I might have some ideas.

E-mail From: Red
Subject: House "Work" … more thoughts
Sent: Wednesday, March 10

The kitchen? What would you know about kitchens? Can you even remember the last time you cooked?

E-mail From: Black
Subject: From the non-cooking kitchen expert
Sent: Wednesday, March 10

Just because I do not cook does not mean I do not know anything about kitchens. In fact, I am becoming quite the kitchen expert. The Arizona house is going to have two kitchens — one for general use and one for caterers. And the high-rise is going to have a state-of-the-art kitchen. I have even been consulting with the chef from Tony's to better understand what is needed in terms of appliances and work flow. And even in the current kitchen, which was your basic spec house vanilla, I changed a few things to make it look more like a custom home.

So let me repeat my question: What exactly do you want to change about your kitchen?

E-mail From: Red
Subject: From the non-cooking kitchen expert
Sent: Wednesday, March 10

Everything! Initially, we thought we wanted to reconfigure the room by knocking down walls. Then we realized that we like the current flow of the kitchen, although we hate the color of the walls. Even without it being a total overhaul, there are a lot of big-ticket items: new cabinets, better appliances, granite countertops, converting the coat closet in the kitchen to additional pantry space. It's a long list, and the numbers will add up very quickly.

E-mail From: Black
Subject: Kitchen Project … one course at a time
Sent: Wednesday, March 10

I agree your list has some expensive items, but the kitchen is the room you are going to use the most. You need to take that into consideration when you prioritize your home-improvement budget. Have you thought about doing some interim work? There are several things you can do now that might not break the bank, but would make a big difference.

Like what? I don't want to do anything where I spend money for a short-term fix that will have to be redone later, which is why I decided to wait on the kitchen until we had saved enough money to do the whole project.

My pro-bono kitchen designer thoughts:

WALL COLOR

- Easiest thing to do, especially since you hate the color of the kitchen (and I cannot say I blame you) is to repaint it now.

CABINETS

- Replacing cabinets can be very expensive, but painting them or changing out only the doors can give you years of enjoyment.

- Or something as simple as changing or upgrading the door knobs/pulls to something you would want to keep long-term. I did this when we first moved to this house. It was an easy (and relatively inexpensive) change that made a huge difference.

PANTRY SPACE

- Redoing the coat closet to give you additional pantry space will require carpenters, painters and maybe an electrician. It may not be worth the time or the expense.

- Think about how you want to use the additional storage (maybe surplus storage vs. daily access?) and let me know as I may have some suggestions. Every time I move, I seem to live in The Container Store trying to figure out how to organize everything in the drawers and closets. And sometimes when you have a lot of space, it is even more of a challenge because you almost have too many options. Anyway, I am amazed at how many solutions they have to help maximize the efficiency of limited space, like a coat closet. I can almost guarantee you can buy what you need to make your current closet work at a fraction of what it would cost to remodel it.

APPLIANCES

- Appliances are a significant part of the cost of remodeling a kitchen. If you can afford it, you might want to consider getting them one at a time and sooner vs. all at once and later.

COUNTERTOPS

- Countertops are the least of your worries and can be replaced when you have the money. Depending on what you want, some are more kid-friendly than others, so you might want to wait until the girls are grown or at least a little older.

Thanks, Martha! Say hello to my sister Black when you see her. But seriously, what great ideas. Especially coming from someone I know prefers shoe racks to spice racks.

I especially love the idea of redoing my coat closet. I don't know if I showed you, but in the back of the closet is a door which leads to a storage space under the staircase. I figured it was going to be a total waste of space and I'd just throw luggage in there, but I think you've just given me a wonderful idea as to how to use that as my surplus pantry.

Any chance you can meet me at The Container Store so I can start looking at storage ideas? I'm REALLY excited!

I was thinking of the kitchen project as "all or nothing," but once I read Black's suggestions I realized we could do some of it immediately. And the best part was that some of the smaller, less expensive changes would actually make the biggest difference. I was also excited about changing wasted space into usable space.

📱 Where are you and what are you doing?

📱 Sitting in carpool line. Where are you?

📱 Just leaving downtown. I thought we could meet at The Container Store, but I forgot it was school pickup time. We can do it another day.

📱 What were you doing downtown?

📱 I had a meeting with the high-rise architects. This place is going to look amazing when we are finished. Although it is going to be fairly contemporary, all the woodwork will give it a feeling of warmth. I will be so glad to get away from the traditional décor of our current house.

📱 We're so different. For me, the more traditional, the better. I love the warmth of an older home. And cozy rooms.

📱 But that is because you are warm and fuzzy. For me, it is just a house. I tried to make Larry's house feel like a home, at least for the girls, which is why I did that major renovation to their part of the house. But the rest of the place is just a house. At least with the high-rise and the house in Arizona, I will feel like each is partly mine since I am putting my heart and soul into the designs.

📱 I may regret asking this, but since you're the one that started this conversation, here goes — what's going on with you and Larry? You have referred to your home as "Larry's house" on more than one occasion. And your last comment really concerns me.

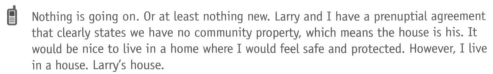 Nothing is going on. Or at least nothing new. Larry and I have a prenuptial agreement that clearly states we have no community property, which means the house is his. It would be nice to live in a home where I would feel safe and protected. However, I live in a house. Larry's house.

 I had no idea that was how you felt. Does Larry know how you feel?

Sort of. He knows my history. When I moved to Houston, I bought my townhouse and it was my first real adult "home." I kept it as a rental property when I got married the first time, and moved back into it (after a major renovation) when that marriage ended. After I moved in with Larry, I turned it back into a rental property and did not sell it until we had been married about five years.

Well, you must have felt like you no longer needed it if you sold it. That says something positive about Larry and you.

Not really. The truth is it says more about the real estate market. It was a good time to sell, and my long-term tenant was looking to buy a unit. When I sold it, Larry commented he never understood why I had kept it that long. However, instead of having a business discussion, I told him it had always been my security blanket. I guess it was my way of trying to start a conversation. I was never sure he understood or cared to understand. But it really is not important.

Are you sure about that? I have always thought of a house as a home, a place you share with your loved ones. And that it should be made as warm and safe as possible, so that no matter what's happening in the outside world, once you go inside and close the door, you can be yourself, knowing that you're loved and wanted.

Like I said, you are the warm and fuzzy one.

I wondered what was going on with Black. I had never heard her express these kinds of sentiments before. I do know that before my life had changed so dramatically, I probably wouldn't have heard her words with the same intensity. But today this conversation really hit me and made me realize how important having a home was to me. And maybe even to Black, although she wasn't willing to admit it.

Bigger And Better May Not Be Better

When we first moved to the States, Black had tried to convince me that we needed to buy a house. At the time I didn't understand why, and rather than ask her to explain, I merely told her we preferred to rent. I now know that she had been looking at it from a financial viewpoint, whereas I was thinking of it as another temporary residence since Nick and I had talked of one day moving to Vermont. In any event, there was no question that I'd come a long way since then (of course, considering where I started, there was no way to go but up!), but my days of learning were definitely not over.

☎ Hello. Catch you at a bad time?

📱 Not really. Just standing here keeping an eye on Nick. We, and I use that term loosely, are looking at a new TV for the living room.

☎ What happened to the old one?

📱 Nothing, but when we move, it's going upstairs into the family room, and so we'll need a TV for the downstairs living room. And since that room is between our bedroom and the kitchen, that'll be the one we'll use the most. My concern is Nick is wandering dangerously close to those huge flat-screen TVs.

☎ They are definitively male magnets. Boys and their toys!

📱 That's a rather sexist comment coming from a woman who races cars! Anyway, I can't believe how much they cost. And personally, I don't think they're worth it.

☎ The boys or the toys?

📱 Either. Both. But especially the TVs.

☎ I know you are through the worst of the financial crisis, and maybe Nick wants to celebrate a little, but before he pulls out his credit card, you might want to step back and question whether you need it or just want it.

📱 Since I rarely watch TV, I definitely don't need it. Or want it. But you're right, and I agree. I'll call you back later. Right now, I think I might need to rein him in before he buys out the entire store.

I caught up with Nick and found him watching a huge state-of-the-art TV, and before I could try and talk him out of it, he said the picture was unbelievable. I agreed it was unbelievable, but I was looking at the price tag. It was more than we had earmarked for a new TV and, even with the special financing available, it didn't seem worth it. But before I could say anything, he showed me a few more reasonably priced TVs that he thought were much better buys. I replied, "You're right. This is unbelievable." He thought I was talking about the TVs when in all honesty I was thinking how unbelievable it was that he wasn't going for the biggest and best. I guess he had been listening to me when I talked about family finances, which was both surprising and impressive! We jointly selected a more reasonably priced model that would give us years of use. And without years of credit card payments because we bought it outright.

E-mail From: Black
Subject: None of My Business ... But Still Curious
Sent: Saturday, March 13

When you get this, please give me an update ... I do not care how much you spent, but I am curious ... what television did you end up buying?

E-mail From: Red
Subject: None of My Business ... But Still Curious
Sent: Saturday, March 13

A large, but not huge, flat screen that was reasonably priced AND on sale. (As an aside, Nick even commented that his new flat screen is much better than Larry's old fat TV. As you said, boys and their toys!) Now I'm thinking of taking the money we saved on the TV and putting it towards a new armchair for our bedroom.

E-mail From: Black
Subject: REALLY None of My Business
Sent: Saturday, March 13

Excuse me? You saved money on the television and you're going to spend the savings? Here is a novel concept ... how about saving your savings? I think you should be focused on the bigger picture (no pun intended) and not the financial implications of any single purchase, whether a television or an armchair.

E-mail From: Red
Subject: REALLY None of My Business
Sent: Saturday, March 13

Ah — but we had already budgeted an amount to spend on stuff for the new house, and the TV was in the budget. Gotcha!

E-mail From: Black
Subject: Next Lesson: Assets vs. Expenditures
Sent: Saturday, March 13

Well then, it is time for your next lesson. Now that you have experience and confidence (or is that cockiness?) with budgeting, you need to start looking at your expenditures in terms of increasing your assets. You are already aware of the need to decrease your liabilities by paying down debt, so it goes without saying you should not incur any more. Now you need to focus on spending money on assets vs. spending money on "stuff."

E-mail From: Red
Subject: Next Lesson: Assets vs. Expenditures
Sent: Saturday, March 13

Isn't that what we did when we decided to buy a house instead of throwing money away on rent? Anyway, we budgeted money for stuff for the new house.

E-mail From: Black
Subject: Next Lesson: Assets vs. Expenditures
Sent: Saturday, March 13

But it is "stuff" nonetheless. And not necessarily "stuff" that adds value. I will acknowledge that some things, like the new television, have enjoyment value (vs. financial value), but all your future expenditures need to be intelligent. Is it a new armchair for the bedroom or are you replacing an old one for the hell of it? Just because you included it in the budget or can afford it does not necessarily make it a smart use of your money.

What was she talking about? For the same amount of money we could buy either an expensive TV or a reasonably priced TV and an armchair. The answer was obvious. But once I got over being annoyed with Black for questioning my decision, I started calmly thinking about it, and I began to understand the point Black was trying to make.

Budgeting: Always For The Future And Sometimes For Fun

Nick had transferred his Company retirement account from England into the States earlier in the month and we had earmarked an amount for the house (the down payment, as well as "start-up" costs), and I needed to update my budget to reflect those numbers. I wanted to make sure we controlled ourselves and stayed within that budget. And although our actual move date was next week, I was determined to have as much of my financial and management systems updated and ready-to-go before I physically moved the computer and printer.

E-mail From: Red
Subject: Budgeting 101 – Is there an advanced class?
Sent: Wednesday, March 17

Until recently, most of the money we've spent has been routine recurring-type expenses, but now I want to set up additional accounts to plan and manage special or onetime expenditures. I need to do this ASAP because we're spending a lot of money on the actual move and buying things for the new house, not to mention home improvements such as the painting. I feel like I'm spending more money than I'd like. At the very least, I want to be able to budget for the next few months to make sure we're not spending more money than we can afford.

E-mail From: Black
Subject: Budgeting 101 – Is there an advanced class?
Sent: Wednesday, March 17

Wow. Give me a second to get over the shock ...

E-mail From: Red
Subject: Budgeting 101 – Is there an advanced class?
Sent: Wednesday, March 17

Hey, you're the one who created this monster.

E-mail From: Black
Subject: Microsoft Money Monster
Sent: Wednesday, March 17

I know, and I am so proud.

E-mail From: Red
Subject: Microsoft Money Monster
Sent: Wednesday, March 17

Do not — repeat do NOT — get mushy on me. I need answers, not accolades. And I don't have a lot of spare time at the moment for sarcasm.

Right now I have a monthly budget amount that we can spend on house-related expenditures, plus an amount we earmarked from Nick's retirement account for "new house" costs. But this doesn't seem specific enough. I'm afraid that we'll spend it (especially with all the little stuff we keep buying) and I won't have anything to show for it.

E-mail From: Black
Subject: Microsoft Money Monster
Sent: Wednesday, March 17

You already know how to budget, so this should be easy. Budgeting for onetime expenditures is basically no different. It sounds like you have two streams of available money — the monthly amount you already have for house-related expenditures (is this separate from recurring bills like utilities and insurance?) and the lump sum. As far as how to allocate the lump sum amount in your budget, you can either set it up as a monthly amount for a specific number of months, or you can use the total amount. It is more of a psychological decision.

As far as actual budget decisions — remember when you were trying to pay down your credit card debt and you would compare the importance of a new purchase against using that money to pay down debt? Now just modify the thought process.

E-mail From: Red
Subject: Microsoft Money Monster
Sent: Wednesday, March 17

I don't have a problem with the budget process, but I do with the execution. We never seem to have money left at the end of the month even though I have budgeted "discretionary" spending categories. Maybe I'm crazy, but psychologically I feel like I shouldn't include the lump sum money anywhere in the budget or the checking account. Maybe I should keep it in a cookie jar, and when the jar is empty, we stop spending.

E-mail From: Black
Subject: Budgeting 201 – Special Expenditures
Sent: Wednesday, March 17

Well, it sounds like that is really not much different than what you are doing. For you, the key may be to NOT have the money in the same account as all your recurring expenses. Pull the discretionary money out of the account at the beginning of each month and put it in a separate savings or investment account that is specifically designated for onetime house expenditures. Put the lump sum amount in that new account too. That will force you to decide whether any given expenditures are important enough to dip into the "special" account.

Since you already know how to use Microsoft Money categories, you can earmark the money in as much detail as you feel necessary — for now, it may only be the move and any other start-up type expenses. Generate a monthly report. (If you want, I can show you how to use bar graphs to make it instantly obvious where you stand.) And then display or file it so you will see it throughout the month. In time you will start to think about adding to the special fund vs. mindlessly spending money.

This strategy will also come in handy when you want to budget for other non-routine household expenditures, whether buying a new computer or building an addition above the garage.

E-mail From: Red
Subject: Budgeting 201 – Special Expenditures
Sent: Wednesday, March 17

That's a great idea   taking the money out at the beginning of the month. How about if we opened different bank accounts earmarked for different objectives vs. putting everything in one? Then we could watch the various totals grow, and when we hit our goal in any given area, we could spend that money accordingly.

E-mail From: Black
Subject: Budgeting 301 – Do What Works Best for You
Sent: Wednesday, March 17

Whatever works best for you. My personal preference is to have one long-term investment account and one savings account that is my "emergency" or short-term account. But if psychologically multiple accounts work best for you and Nick, then go for it.

The key is for you and Nick to sit down and think about what you want to do with your money and then set realistic goals and objectives. And work towards them. Remember, even if one month's deposit is not as much as you would like, you will still see the account growing, which will help keep you motivated.

How did Black know that was what had prompted this conversation? I knew we were still paying off last summer's California vacation. I had come to the painful realization that although I had carefully planned the trip in terms of logistics and activities, Nick had never planned for how to pay for it. I didn't want to be the one responsible for making that mistake again — with vacations or house-related expenditures.

You Can't Ignore Contingencies And Emergencies

IM Glad I caught you online. Are you still working on the "new house" budget?

IM No. I finished that, and I'm now cleaning up my list of things I need to do before the move and the first few days after the move. Why?

IM I was going to tell you to remember to budget for contingencies and emergencies. Make a note somewhere and we can talk about it some other time.

IM Great. Unlike you, we do not have unlimited funds! And let me guess — I need to make that a higher priority than any other goals we might have, such as a summer vacation.

IM That is your call, but if you do not put money away for contingencies and/or emergencies and something happens, like the air conditioner dies or you need roof work, you will have limited options. You would then either have to eat into the accounts already set up for other plans or borrow money. (And pay interest!) But if you put money aside to cover unexpected events and they do not happen, then that money just stays there as a safety net.

IM OK. That makes sense. I'm just getting depressed about having to add yet another "withdrawal" into our monthly budget. There seems to be no end of expenses.

IM Welcome to being a homeowner!

IM Gee. Thanks. Got any good news?

IM It is not a permanent monthly expense. Once you reach your "contingency and emergency goal," you can earmark the monthly amount for another purpose. Just remember, if you have to use this contingency money, you need to make sure to replenish it.

IM So tell me, what's it like to not have to worry about all these house-related expenses and contingency budgets? To be able to enjoy where you live and not worry about the financial stuff?

IM Wish I could. You must have me confused with my husband. Remember, it is his house I live in. But before you read too much into that comment — do not worry. I have no plans to move out of his house and into yours.

IM Darn! The girls would love it and you could build an apartment over the garage. Which reminds me — I also need to plan for non-financial emergencies.

IM Such as?

IM You have an amazing financial brain, but you don't always think of the non-financial things. It's not always about money. Sometimes it's about what has to be done. I'm talking about things like a fire escape plan, emergency contact lists or being prepared for hurricane season.

IM I am not going to ask how your train of thought jumped from an apartment over the garage to contingency planning, but, just so you know, I actually have most of those plans in place already.

IM I should have guessed. When you get a chance, send me a copy. And before you say anything about budgeting for these "non-financial emergency plans," I already know they'll have a cost, such as supplies and fire extinguishers, but I'm guessing the cost isn't significant enough to worry about.

IM The costs are actually insignificant if you were to do a risk/reward analysis.

IM No, thanks. I'll leave the number crunching to you and take your word for it.

My thought process jumped from the addition over the garage to non-financial emergencies because Black had once mentioned if we ever decided to build over the garage, we should make sure to include an emergency generator. She explained that since we live in a city prone to power outages due to hurricanes (Welcome to Texas!), we should consider making it a stand-alone self-sufficient "safe house." So garage additions to generators to hurricanes to protecting oneself to making general plans for an emergency — a thought process that made perfect sense. At least to me.

Seven Simple Questions

At last! Amazingly enough, especially in light of the last few months, we were finally in our own home. I could hardly believe it. I was exhausted from the move, but incredibly excited. It was a time of hard work, but also, surprisingly enough, of reflection. The first weeks after we moved into the house provided significant opportunities to spend money, and because it was now our home vs. a rent house, it would have been easy to rationalize many of the expenditures. But this wasn't only a new home, it was a new beginning and a new me — with a new understanding of financial matters. And I decided a checklist of questions would help me stay focused.

E-mail From: Red
Subject: My Turn to Send a Checklist
Sent: Saturday, April 3

I know you don't worry about money and probably haven't done a budget in years, but I have developed a "Think Before I Spend" checklist and I'm so proud of myself that I had to share it with you.

1. Can we afford it? And do we need it?
2. Is it an asset?
3. Pleasure or pain?
4. Short-term or long-term?
5. Does it provide a valuable service?
6. Why am I buying this?
7. Will it hold its value?

P.S — You can laugh or make smart-ass comments if you want, but I don't care!

E-mail From: Black
Subject: My Turn to Send a Checklist
Sent: Saturday, April 3

I am impressed with your list.

P.S. — The only comment I have is that your comment about me and money is wrong. I want you to know I recently looked at my spending and did a ballpark estimate of how much money I need on an annual basis to survive.

E-mail From: Red
Subject: My Turn to Send a Checklist
Sent: Saturday, April 3

WHAT??? WHY???

E-mail From: Black
Subject: My Turn to Send a Checklist
Sent: Saturday, April 3

Long story … rather not put it in an e-mail. All I will say right now is that after looking at your list of questions, I am not sure many of my expenditures would pass your test! Or at least the questions that I understand, because a few of them are … to use one of your phrases … as "clear as mud."

E-mail From: Red
Subject: My Turn to Send a Checklist
Sent: Saturday, April 3

They make sense to me! Would you like for me to send you seven separate essays explaining each question? Want examples too?

E-mail From: Black
Subject: This is a Test!
Sent: Saturday, April 3

That would be great! It will give me something to read when we get home from dinner at Tony's and Larry starts snoring on the couch.

Was she kidding? Or was she trying to make me think through this list again? That's one of the problems with Black. Between her sarcasm and pragmatic approach to things, I can never quite figure her out. Or is that part of her plan too? Well, regardless of her intent, I knew these questions made sense. And I could explain them. And probably get an A+ on the essays. However, if I was graded on my past execution of the theories, I wouldn't do as well. But I did go back and rethink my list, one question at a time, and wrote myself some notes.

> ## 1. Can We Afford It? And Do We Need It?
>
> - *Obvious, but often ignored questions*
> - *Don't have to point out the obvious to Black!*

Black seems to have an uncanny knack of always calling when we're about to spend money. For example, the day Nick was out looking at TVs and later that same afternoon when I was going to spend the leftover money on an unnecessary armchair. And just last week she caught us in the act again when we'd innocently gone out for a few small items:

📱 Catch you at a bad time?

📱 Not really. We're looking at outdoor patio furniture. We stopped by Lowe's for a few small hardware items and a garden hose, but then we noticed they're having a great patio furniture sale.

📱 What is wrong with all the old stuff?

📱 It wasn't ours; it came with the rent house. So we need to buy patio furniture. We're now trying to decide whether to get an entire collection or only buy specific pieces. As long as I have you on the line, what do you think?

📱 I think it is not my money, so I do not vote. Plus, I have no idea how much the furniture is compared to how much you budgeted. Or if there is a significant discount for buying the entire set. Or if you are thinking of buying the furniture outright or paying it off in installments. I will leave you alone to think. Bye.

Black made some great points and it reminded me of the painful lessons I'd already learned about credit cards. If we put the patio furniture on a credit card with the intention of paying it off over time, the purchase would end up costing us significantly more once we included the interest expense. We decided not to buy the entire collection, only key pieces that we wanted and needed, and would be able to pay in full when the bill arrived. We'd enjoy not only the furniture, but also the wisdom of our purchase.

2. Is It An Asset?

- Or just an expense?
- Obvious questions –

If you understand assets and liabilities

One evening when I was initially working on the budget for the new house, I decided to ask Black a decorating question. I should have guessed it would turn into a finance class. About window treatments, no less!

💬 Quick question: What do you think about us replacing some of the custom drapes that came with the house with plantation shutters?

💬 Personally, I think rolls of brown wrapping paper would be more attractive than some of those drapes.

IM They're not that bad, just not our taste. Sorry I even asked. I should have known better.

IM OK. First question. What is making you choose shutters over new drapes?

IM Nick and I both love shutters, and they suit the house and our furnishings really well.

IM Second question. Did you look at the cost of shutters?

IM Yes. Once I starting thinking about replacing the drapes, I did a cost estimate and realized the incremental amount to do shutters (vs. new drapes) was actually money well spent, because the shutters would be a permanent addition to the house and would have a resale value, whereas drapes don't.

IM Now I am impressed! You came up with that all by yourself?

IM Not exactly. You mentioned it once, and I made a mental note.

IM OK, then I am impressed you remembered. Last question. Do you think this expenditure must be done now or could it wait?

IM It can wait, although I'd prefer to do it sooner than later. I was really trying to decide whether or not to include it in my home improvement budget.

IM It sounds like financially you knew what to do ... which means you were looking for free decorating advice. You used me!

IM Like I already said — sorry I even asked.

But I did get the answer I wanted. I have always liked the look of plantation shutters, and when it came time to select window treatments for our new house, I was thrilled that I'd be able to rationalize purchasing them — if not immediately, then in the near future. The key was to decide whether a purchase was an asset — either on its own (such as a painting or a piece of antique furniture) or as part of a home improvement (such as shutters or building an addition).

3. Pleasure Or Pain?

- Is buying the asset a smart use of money?
- Does it provide enough pleasure and/or value to be worth the cost?
- Is financing required? Is it worth the interest payments (pain)?

 Hello. Just checking in.

We're just leaving the bank. Nick wanted to see about financing options if we decide to build a guest suite above the garage.

Last conversation we had about home improvement, you were not sure you wanted to spend money painting the kitchen. Now you want to add square footage?

You know how Nick is about pipe dreams. It was something the previous owners had mentioned as a selling point, and we were in the bank taking care of other stuff and he brought it up. The terms weren't bad at first glance, but as you taught me, the interest expense definitely adds up. Wonder if Mommy would contribute to the cost, since she'd be the one getting the benefit of the guest suite.

And Mom giving you money would be pipe dream #2. It seems a bit crazy to spend money for a suite that only the occasional guest will use. And you already have a guest room, granted it is relatively small.

True, but a guest suite above the garage would be a great space. Especially since it would be in a separate building and overlooks the pool.

Sounds wonderful. Houseguests might never want to leave, which is probably a good reason NOT to do it. However, if you told me you were going to start saving to build a game room that the whole family could enjoy, that would make sense to me.

That's a great idea! I vote for pipe dream #3.

For now, the addition over the garage was truly a pipe dream. However, I included a line item in my budget for the garage addition, although I was not yet prepared to actually start earmarking any of our available funds for so large an investment.

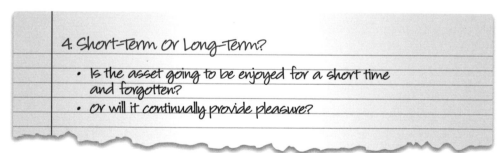

4. Short-Term or Long-Term?

- Is the asset going to be enjoyed for a short time and forgotten?
- Or will it continually provide pleasure?

I was still thinking of assets. The fact the garage was a significant long-term investment didn't mean all long-term investments had to be huge expenditures. But in order to make sense, they had to stand the test of time.

☎ I want to ask you a question. But let me preface it by saying that I'm not looking for an opinion on the specific selection, but rather on the thought process.

☎ A partial opinion? That is asking a lot of me.

☎ Do your best. The patio furniture was just delivered, and I can see we're going to need more shaded area in the backyard. Nick suggested we buy a Live Oak tree. And before you claim not to know what that is, it's the type tree that you have in the front of your house. They're expensive, but if we buy a smaller, and therefore less expensive one, over time it'll grow into a wonderful addition to our backyard.

☎ Good thing I am not allowed to voice an opinion on the selection of a tree because when Larry and I first moved in and worked on the landscaping, I wanted to remove the Live Oak. The landscape architect convinced me to keep it, and it has grown into a wonderful shade tree. However, I still think it looks like something out of Gone With The Wind.

☎ But that's your favorite movie!

☎ But not because of the trees. OK, I snuck in my opinion ... now back to your thought process.

☎ Well, we think they're wonderful. But do you think it's money well spent?

☎ Do you remember when you struggled with the decision as to whether or not to buy a pool heater at the rent house?

☎ Why can't you ever just give me a straight answer?

☎ Because that is not as much fun. Back to the pool heater. What did you decide? And why?

☎ We bought it. We rarely used the pool because it was always so cold. Once we heated it, we used it all year round. And loved it. It was a great decision.

☎ So on a "cost-per-use basis," it made sense?

☎ Absolutely. And a lot more sense than all those pool floats and toys that we buy and which either get thrown away after one summer, or used once or twice and then forgotten.

☎ And that was an investment at a rent house. Now we are talking about a purchase for your own home. I do not know how long you plan to live there, but a Live Oak's life is measured in centuries. So in terms of "cost per year" it is a bargain!

We bought the tree and every day I see it from my bedroom window and enjoy it. In fact, I'd argue that it's going to grow into one of the best — and maybe smartest — purchases that we made for the house.

5. Does It Provide A Valuable Service?

- How do you value an intangible?
- Does the service
  - make life easier?
  - reduce stress?
- Does the service provide a better level of service or expertise?

I typically think of purchases as tangible things, but sometimes they're intangible services. Sometimes they're even both — dinners out provide both food and service. However, the service decisions can become tricky. Things like paying someone to do something you are capable of doing becomes an issue of putting a value on your time. When Nick was fired, I immediately stopped using a cleaning service, although Nick never thought about buying a lawnmower and doing the yard.

☎ Have a minute for me to vent? I just got off the phone with Mommy. She was giving me grief because I mentioned I was trying to schedule the electricians to do some new wiring, and I wanted them to be done before the painters got there.

☎ I know Mom can rub you the wrong way at times. Are you sure you are not overreacting?

☎ Not this time. She made a point of saying that Daddy always used to do all kinds of electrical and plumbing projects around the house. And then she reminded me that they even painted and hung their own wallpaper. She made a snide comment that it must be nice to have enough money to hire electricians and painters.

☎ Daddy was good at fixing things. He was a mechanical engineer with the hands of a surgeon, and he did not mind doing handyman jobs. Nick does not fit that same description.

☎ No kidding! Nick would try to fix something if I asked him, but the reality is he'd probably make the problem worse. Then I would end up spending MORE money to get it fixed correctly. Nick is a marketing consultant, not an electrician or a plumber. That said, he's very creative and is wonderful at hanging pictures and offering decorating ideas.

☎ Well, I am married to an engineer, but I still use professional electricians and plumbers. And it is not because Larry cannot fix things. He can, but prefers to pay someone else to do it. Even when it would be quicker to do it himself.

☎ You must be kidding. That's ridiculous.

☎ There was a time when I mentioned some of the door pulls on the kitchen cabinets needed to be tightened, and he suggested I call the painters to come by and do it. I was too embarrassed to call them about something so mundane, so I just did it myself. All it took was a screwdriver and about 15 minutes!

☎ So he won't do anything around the house?

☎ I can barely get him to change a lightbulb. I think the only reason he does is he knows if he does not do it promptly, then I will ask him to bring me the six-foot ladder so I can change it myself. Or worse, I will parade past him with the ladder.

☎ Why do I have a feeling you really would do that?

☎ Because I did. And he was not amused. Funny, he does not mind paying someone else to do something, but he cannot stand the thought me doing it if he will not. Talk about competitive!

☎ It sounds like we can both rationalize the expense of paying someone else to do work around the house because it avoids unnecessary grief. But for me there's the value of knowing the job is being done promptly and correctly. I guess the bottom line is that the cost of peace of mind, as well as harmony in the house, can be just as valuable as saving money.

☎ You have to ask yourself whether you can afford the service and whether it provides sufficient value. And trust me when I say … money cannot buy happiness, but it can sure be used to avoid conflict.

> ### 6. Why Am I Buying This?
>
> Because …
> - I want it?
> - My neighbors want it?
> - The advertisers want me to want it?

It's so easy to get wrapped up with having what everyone else does. The comparisons are so convenient to make — starting with the appearances of your house and yard, not to mention the car on your driveway, and continuing throughout the house. Kids come home talking about the neighbors' "cool game room" or husbands drool over electronic gadgets and large flat screen TVs. And I admit I can't help but envy large pantries and closets with customized built-ins. But the point is when it comes to a house, there's always bigger and better.

IM Nick and Natasha came home from our new neighbors and were excited about some new video game or something called Zeebox or Whybox. Any idea what they are talking about?

IM You need to get out more. They are talking about the Xbox. It is a video game console system.

IM I still have no idea what you're talking about.

IM It is a "black box" that is used for playing video games.

IM Like the games Natasha plays on my computer?

IM Yes. Only the console hooks up to your television and provides much higher quality graphics and audio. Several different companies make systems; Xbox is Microsoft's entry into the market and is the first to use a hard drive to save games. Their primary competition is Nintendo and Sony, and it is a hot market.

IM Great. Something else electronic. Are they all the same?

IM Not really. They differ in the computational power of the console (but similar to computers, the latest is often the greatest) and which exclusive games they may offer. For "gamers" that is often the deciding factor.

IM That is way more information than I wanted. So are you a gamer? I think I'm going to need to learn the lingo since I have a feeling Natasha and Nick are going to try and convince me we need one.

IM Last time I played a video game was Pac-Man, and it was an arcade-type machine in a bar, so that probably was in the early '80s.

IM So how do you know all this? And why?

IM From Jeff and Carolyn. And from reading The Wall Street Journal. There was a recent article on Microsoft's marketing strategy on Xbox pricing. They really are not very expensive, but Nick certainly does not need one.

IM Cheater! And you're right about the "need" comment. Up until today I don't even think he knew what they were.

IM A good rule of thumb is that if you have to ask what something does, then it is probably something you do not need and can live without.

IM Does that include husbands?

IM Interesting question.

I hate to think how many things we bought over the years because they were either highly advertised or because our friends, family or neighbors were getting them — mistakes we made because we were busy keeping up with the infamous Joneses.

7. Will It Hold Its Value?

- or will it become a garage sale item?
- This is NOT a ridiculous question!

E-mail From: Red
Subject: My Turn to Send a Checklist
Sent: Saturday, April 3

I went back and reviewed my list of questions and most of them seem very obvious to me. The only one I think you might find "clear as mud" is the last one, since it refers to garage sales. I doubt you have ever been to a garage sale, let alone had one.

I had two garage sales before we moved to get rid of stuff we no longer wanted. After all, it made no sense to spend money moving things you no longer want. Anyway, when I saw how little you can sell things for (especially in comparison to the original purchase price), I was shocked. After you had "scolded" me about wanting to buy a new chair for the bedroom, I was still thinking about buying it and even went so far as to start thinking about selling the old chair in either a garage sale or the local paper. But once I realized I'd get virtually nothing for it, I had to admit to myself that the new chair would be worth significantly less than the purchase price, and so I decided the enjoyment factor wasn't worth the difference

I don't know if any of this makes sense to you, but it sure makes sense to me!

I wasn't expecting my logic to make sense to Black. The last thing I expected was that it would be the logic she used, albeit at a very different price point, for her own purchases.

IM Glad you are still online. I was kidding about the essays. As long as your checklist makes sense to you, that is all that matters.

IM Well, the garage sale one was the only one I planned to explain anyway. Did it make sense?

IM Perfect sense. In fact, it is the same logic I use whenever I ask Larry for jewelry from Bulgari.

IM I can hardly wait to hear this logic!

IM It really pays to have friends in the jewelry business. I always knew the resale value of most jewelry is never close to its original purchase price, no matter how great a deal I got. But years ago, Phil and Pam let me know the exception is a handful of upscale jewelry houses, such as Bulgari, whose pieces – in addition to being beautiful — hold their value. So whenever Larry offers to take me jewelry shopping, I always suggest we go to Bulgari.

IM Isn't this the same logic you use for your Hermes handbags?

IM Yes. And on that note, I will say ... Good night.

I was glad I had gone back and re-read my list of questions because I knew they'd guide me in the future. But this last conversation with Black made me realize that many of my questions were relevant regardless of your financial situation.

A House Full Of Money Or A Home Full Of Love?

Our new house truly was a home. From the minute I first saw it, let alone moved into it, I was in love with this house. It had a wonderful warm feeling to it and, most importantly, it had a huge kitchen that instantly became the heart of the house. We were lucky to have found it and even luckier to have been able to buy it.

I was very excited about our future. Maybe the new house was a new beginning on many fronts — and the fact I finally had learned about budgets and financial control would make all the difference as I now knew I could manage our home efficiently and cost-effectively. The combination of Nick getting fired and the good fortune to have a significant retirement package that allowed us to buy our own home made me appreciate, more than I can ever say, how a house is so much more than a structure filled with furniture and things.

14

I Don't Want AstroTurf —
I Want Something Real

IM Hello.

IM So you decided to return?

IM What are you talking about?

IM I spoke to Nick earlier today, and he said you ran away from home. I took that to mean you needed some alone time. So I left you alone.

IM I caught a movie with my friend Chris. And this should amuse you — she said your life was like a movie. She wondered what it'd be like to live in a beautiful house, drive expensive cars, have a wonderful husband and never worry about money.

IM Excuse me while I throw up.

IM I told her that sometimes the grass looks greener somewhere else because it's AstroTurf. After she stopped laughing, she asked me to explain.

IM Hey, that is my line! So what exactly did you explain?

IM I told her that sometimes other people's lives aren't as perfect as they seem.

IM There is an understatement.

IM And I changed the topic from you to Nick and me, explaining that after Nick decided to go out on his own (FYI, that's Nick's "party line"), we were forced to reevaluate our life and our priorities. And I realized the life we appeared to be living wasn't who we really were and, more importantly, it wasn't the life I wanted to live.

IM I am impressed.

IM Me too. And surprised that I admitted it to Chris. But I think I may have finally stopped envying other people's lives, especially now that I realize their lives might not be as perfect as they seem.

IM If you only knew ... And I agree with everything you said. Is there a point to this IM other than letting me know my life looks like a movie? And keep in mind, if we add you to the script, it becomes more of a soap opera.

IM Thanks a lot. And yes, there was a point. Now that the worst is behind me, I have been thinking about the future. I want a future with real grass, not AstroTurf. I have decided I want a lush, beautiful, real lawn. And I want a garden too!

IM Now I really am going to throw up. But since it is very difficult to garden in the dark, can this project wait until tomorrow?

IM Sure. Night-night.

Visualize Your Garden Before You Start To Plant It

It was hard to believe it had only been two months since Nick got fired. So much had changed. I felt I was ready to take on the challenge of truly planning for the future rather than just reacting to events or merely dreaming about what might be. And I was prepared to face the reality that I was, yet again, at the beginning of another learning curve. The good news was that this time it was a positive road — that of planning for the future — rather than trying to correct the mistakes of the past.

IM I have been thinking about your IM last night. Do you really want to start planning for the future?

IM Yes. I thought that I'd start putting aside a little extra money each month into a "future" account.

IM Logical start. Any idea what you are saving for?

IM The future.

IM No kidding. How can you save for the past? I meant, what specifically are you saving for?

IM The usual things – college for the girls, retirement, etc.

IM I think the time has come to discuss long-term financial planning.

IM I'm not sure I'm ready for an advanced level of finance. Can't I just start saving more money?

IM All we are going to do is adjust your approach to financial matters from being reactive to being proactive. Now instead of reacting to events, you can start dreaming about the future and taking steps to make it reality.

IM So if I dream about George Clooney, financial planning will make him appear?

IM I could probably come up with a financial scenario that might make George accessible … but I was thinking more along the lines of that second home Nick and you have always dreamed about.

IM But that's just a dream and, given our current finances, it may be more of a hallucination.

IM Let me use your garden analogy. You are standing on an empty lot that is covered with dirt. How do you plan to get your luscious yard of real grass? And your beautiful garden? Twitch your nose and have it appear? Or, are you going to go back to your magic wand?

IM I guess "hire a gardener" isn't the correct answer?

IM A gardener can maintain the yard and garden, but first you need a landscape architect to help you design it. And the first thing they will ask is, "What do you have in mind?" The second question will be, "What is your budget?" To get the end result you want, you are going to have to plan it. The good news is that there are people who can help you plan it, plant it and make it grow. Call me later when you have time to talk.

I knew just wanting a healthy financial and personal future was not going to make it happen. I had to plant it seed by seed, be patient and then give it a chance to grow. Still it would have been nice if I could randomly scatter assorted packets of seeds and then keep my fingers crossed that it would rain and everything would sprout exactly as I wanted it to.

☎ OK, let's talk about financial planning. What should I plan for?

☎ I can tell you how to plan for it. I can even offer suggestions on types of things that you might consider including in your plan, but I cannot plan your future for you. Everyone is different. Nick and you have to decide what is important to both of you.

☎ I'm confused. Aren't we just planning how to put away money for the future?

☎ The reality is you have a problem budgeting for short-term house-related expenses. Correct me if I am wrong, but you recently complained that you would spend your entire monthly budget and were not even sure what you were spending it on. So what makes you think you can put away money for the future? Do you honestly believe if you have no goals or objectives, that you will have the will power and fortitude to save a significant amount of money? Can you honestly tell me you will NOT rationalize short-term or medium-term expenditures, thinking that you have plenty of time in the future to save for the future?

☎ That was rather blunt, wasn't it?

☎ Yes. If you are serious about planning for the future, you have to be committed — or at least receptive — to the process. If you are not, this conversation can wait. Your call.

☎ Go ahead.

☎ Long-term financial planning requires that you identify not only what you want but when, so that you have time to work toward the goals. For example, if you want to plan for the girls' college education, you stand a better chance of accomplishing that goal if you start when they are young rather than when they start their junior year in high school. Same thought process with second homes and retirement.

☎ Those are daunting thoughts that will add up to a huge number. I'm not sure we can handle all of that. In fact, I am beginning to regret wanting to plant this garden.

☎ No one is forcing you. And I am not saying everything you might ever want is going to make it into the final plan. I am saying that you have to decide what is on your list before you can start to put together a plan for achieving it. However, I can guarantee with almost 100% certainty that if you do not plan for it, it will not happen.

☎ So where do we start?

☎ Start at the end and work backwards. If you do not know where you want to go, how can you decide the best way to get there? Getting in the car and driving will get you somewhere, but not necessarily where you want to be.

☎ Can you be a tad less theoretical and a bit more specific?

☎ Fast forward 20 years. Where do you see yourselves and the girls? Where do you want to be living? What do you want to be doing? What do you want for the girls? And are these goals in sync with Nick's? You cannot do this alone.

☎ You mean I have to stay with Nick for another 20 years?

☎ If that is a snide comment, fine. However, if you are planning to be a single mom, that will drastically affect the plan.

☎ I was kidding! Picturing us in 20 years is a great idea. And it seems like common sense. I hope the whole financial planning process is as straight-forward.

☎ Long-term financial planning is very logical. It is a matter of realistically identifying what you want long-term. The complications come once you calculate the associated financial requirements and then have to decide what you can realistically afford and what type of investment strategy will help you achieve those goals.

☎ Stop! We just hit the confusing part.

☎ You stop. It is just like when you were learning about budgets and insurance and all the other financial issues you have recently mastered. It is confusing because it is new to you. The confidence will come, trust me. First, you need to think about the big picture. Then you can focus on the financial specifics — the tools and experts that can help you reach your long-term goals.

☎ The experts? Like you?

☎ No. I am an amateur. When the time is right, I will introduce you to some pros. Right now you need to think about where you want to be in 20 years, and I will think about how to explain the basics of financial planning to you.

I needed to sit down with Nick so we could discuss what we wanted our "garden" to look like, what was important to each of us and to the family. I knew I didn't want AstroTurf, which is why I stuck with the garden analogy although I am not a gardener. To me, garden is a noun, not a verb. But that doesn't mean that I don't know what I like and dislike. (Similar to Black and her kitchen planning expertise.) And in terms of our future, I was definitely in a better position today than I was a few months ago to know what was important and what was not.

Planning And Planting Seed By Seed

E-mail From: Black
Subject: Looking Down the Road
Sent: Monday, April 5

I have broken the process down into six steps for ease of discussion. The first five are fairly straight-forward. Once you work through them, I can help you with the last one.

Steps
1. Visualize your goals (garden)
2. Identify your current situation
3. Estimate the cost of your goals
4. Calculate the shortfall
5. Determine if the goals are financially achievable
6. Establish a savings and investment plan

Step 1: Decide what you want long-term. A good place to start is to list your top three or four objectives. Make sure they are:

- **Realistic/Achievable:** Set yourself up for success, not failure.
- **Appropriate:** In other words, consistent with your lifestyle and values.
- **Time-Specific:** For example, college for the girls, retirement when Nick reaches 65.
- **Quantifiable/Measurable:** You need to be able to estimate the total dollar amount needed. This will also allow you to establish interim milestones.

Step 2: A summary of where you stand today. You have a pretty good handle on your situation, but it would be helpful to have a current cash-flow worksheet and a complete balance sheet listing all your assets and liabilities, both short-term and long-term. You are going to need this when you get to the last step, so you may as well update it now.

Step 3 & 4: Are basically just arithmetic. Once you identify and quantify your financial goals and compare them to how much you have in assets, you can calculate how much you will need to save to reach your goals.

Step 5: Will be a ballpark number not an exact calculation, but it will be a good indication of whether the goals are realistic and achievable in the given time frame. Keep in mind the more you save and the longer it is invested (Step 6), the more your money will grow so you will not need to save the full amount. However, there are some issues related to risk tolerance and investment strategy that will ultimately affect this calculation. For the first pass we can use an average interest rate. I know Microsoft Money has a worksheet to do this calculation, but when you get to this point, I will help you with it. Obviously, if the goals are not realistic and achievable, then you will need to make adjustments. Either in your long-term goals, your current spending levels, or both.

Step 6: Can wait for now. I do not want to overwhelm you.

E-mail From: Red
Subject: **Looking Down the Road**
Sent: Monday, April 5

Steps

1. OK. Visualizing the future will give Nick and me something new and positive to talk about.
2. I can do math.
3. I can do math, but may need help with the cost estimates.
4. I can do math.
5. Makes sense. But why can't we keep everything in savings accounts and use current interest rates? I'm not sure I'm ready to get into investment strategies and putting our money at risk.
6. Too late, I'm already overwhelmed. Also see note 5. If we just keep the money in interest-bearing accounts, we don't have to work on an investment plan.

E-mail From: Black
Subject: **You Sound Like Mom**
Sent: Monday, April 5

As you know, after Daddy died I started managing Mom's money. Up until then Mom only liked savings accounts because, like you, she had no tolerance for risk. The fact Daddy had dabbled in the stock market and lost money, combined with the fact Mom's generation remembered the Stock Market Crash of 1929 and the Great Depression that followed, made this a very logical mind-set. It took me a while to even get her to listen to me about stocks and bonds, but I soon realized even an asset allocation that focused on maximizing income (vs. asset growth) would not give her the security she wanted. She was more receptive to tax-saving strategies, and so I was able to get her comfortable with the idea of laddering municipal bonds.

E-mail From: Red
Subject: **You Sound Like Mom**
Sent: Monday, April 5

You lost me right after savings accounts, but I don't want any further explanation right now. I bet Mommy asked you a million and one questions!

Subject: You Sound Like Mom
Sent: Monday, April 5

Of course she did. Mom is Mom. But to her credit she asked some very pertinent and intelligent questions. And based on her questions and concerns, I was able to come up with acceptable answers and solutions.

E-mail From: Red
Subject: You Sound Like Mom
Sent: Monday, April 5

Mommy's constant questions drive us crazy, but I can't see anyone ever getting the better of her.

E-mail From: Black
Subject: Mom was Vulnerable
Sent: Monday, April 5

Maybe. But what if I was not around? After Daddy died, Mom was upset and distracted and feeling overwhelmed and alone. Daddy had various life insurance policies which now had to be handled, and many of the companies were offering investment "opportunities" in lieu of lump sum settlements. Mom handed me all the associated mail, and in the stack I noticed some of it had even been sent by companies in response to the public death notice. It made me see how easily women could be taken financial advantage of; especially women of Mom's generation whose husbands typically handled all the finances. After all, it is a very vulnerable time and not having some financial experience makes a woman a very easy target.

E-mail From: Red
Subject: Mom was Vulnerable
Sent: Monday, April 5

True. And it's not like she could have turned to me for advice. My only advice would have been to ask you. I guess Mommy and I took it for granted that you would help her with all the financial details. There was never a question whether you would do what was right for her — not what you wanted to do or what might benefit us later. But you hear and read about shysters who prey on older women, robbing them of their life savings. It's despicable.

E-mail From: Black
Subject: Mom was Vulnerable – Many Women Are!
Sent: Monday, April 5

WARNING: It is not limited to older women. Women a lot younger than Mom who come into money, either through inheritance or divorce or some other financial windfall, have lost plenty of money through either disreputable or bad financial advice. Not to mention … just stupid spending.

I have always wondered why more women do not realize the importance of understanding finances and financial planning. Just think about all the women who will need financial planning in their lives: women who never marry, women who marry and end up divorced, and women who marry and outlive their husbands. The only ones who can chance letting someone else deal with the topic for them are married women who stay married to financially astute husbands who remain healthy and outlive them. The odds are not in our favor!

And I want to stay on topic, but you need to realize women are not the only ones. In this area, men have equal rights too. Regardless of your sex, without financial knowledge you are exposed to financial risks.

E-mail From: Red
Subject: Mom was Vulnerable – Many Women Are!
Sent: Monday, April 5

I get the point. I'll learn as much as I can and hope I never have to do this alone, but at least I'll know I'm prepared. At the very least, I'll try to learn enough to always make sure I ask questions and don't just blindly accept someone's advice. And one of these days I'll get you to explain to me what you explained to Mommy. But not tonight.

Me? I'm conservative by nature and definitely not a risk-taker. I was hesitant to do anything beyond putting our money into a traditional bank account. I thought the other options were not much better than taking your money to Las Vegas and betting your future on the roll of the dice. However, it was comforting to know that I wasn't the only one in the family Black had needed to educate about the virtues of financial planning.

Investment Options – Your Gardening Tools

I found the thought of investments and long-term planning overwhelming. But that was how I felt about insurance when I first started dealing with it. So maybe I just needed to keep an open mind. And hope some of this financial stuff would magically sink in.

☎ Quick question. Within a few weeks of Nick being fired, you were going to transfer his retirement accounts from England. I remember Nick and you met with a bank about handling the transfer, and they suggested rolling over the money into retirement plans they had available. About the same time, I introduced you to my tax accountants, UHY Advisors, because Nick was going to need tax advice. At that meeting they also told you about their investment services. I never asked, but what did you end up doing?

☎ We went with UHY Advisors. We liked the idea of one-stop shopping, so decided to let them work on our taxes and handle the transfer. Most of the money transferred over last month. Why? Are you going to suggest we talk to them about financial planning?

☎ So they are handling the retirement accounts?

☎ Yes, but we haven't talked to them about financial planning.

☎ Excuse me, but what do you think the retirement accounts are? Plus, they are part of your long-term financial portfolio. You need to review how that money is invested as a starting point for both your investment portfolio and your investment education.

☎ Thanks, you have an uncanny knack for making me feel stupid. Anyway, since the money basically just got here, I'm not sure they have done much with it. In fact, I'm not sure whether we discussed what we were going to actually do with the money once it arrived, other than to make sure it arrived. I'll look at the monthly statement and see if I can decipher it. Expect questions. Lots of questions. I know you're not going to let me off the hook, but I feel I earned the right to at least say — I hate this!

☎ I never said I expected you to love doing this, but which do you hate more — learning something new or feeling stupid? Have a nice day!

I knew I wasn't going to be able to avoid the topic, so I thought I'd be clever and buy a book to teach me the basics. That way I could impress Black with my newfound knowledge. I logged on to Barnes & Noble and did a search on "Personal Finance," and it came up with over 14,000 titles! That alone was so daunting, I decided to wait and let Black spoon-feed me what I needed to know.

E-mail From: Black
Subject: Investments 101 – Stocks & Bonds
Sent: Tuesday, April 6

I know you did not ask for this yet, but here is a sneak preview of the three primary investment vehicles you will need to understand and consider. Obviously, bank and money market accounts are the most conservative, and you will keep some of your money in them. Of the remaining options, some are more conservative (bonds) while others are more growth-oriented (stocks). I have intentionally not included hedge funds, commodities and collectibles (like art and wine) because I do not think these should be included in your asset allocation.

Bonds

- When you buy a bond, you are basically lending money to the entity that is issuing the bond. When the bond is issued, it includes a specified maturity date which is the date the principal will be repaid. They are typically issued at a specific interest rate (a fixed rate), and interest is typically paid semiannually or annually.

- The issuing entity can be either a company or a municipality (city, county, state or other public agency). The latter bonds are referred to as "munis" and are typically exempt from federal income tax.

- The value of the bond fluctuates with changes in interest rates in an inverse relationship. In other words, if interest rates increase, then the value of your bond decreases. And vice versa. However, keep in mind that only affects the price you would get if you sold the bond prior to maturity; otherwise, the bond will make the stated interest payments and will be redeemed at full value at maturity.

- There are many variations on the basic concept, but the major differences are related to the type of institution issuing the bond, their credit worthiness and the length of maturity.

Stocks

- Basically, you own shares in a company. In a perfect world, as the economy grows and companies grow with it and earn greater profits, stock prices would follow suit. But we both know the world is not perfect!

- The key to success is to have diversity in your stock holdings. The more uncorrelated (reacting differently to the same market events), the better. As an aside, the reason Daddy lost money in the stock market is he owned stock in one or two companies and did not spread his risk across companies, industries and sectors. He was rolling the dice, betting on a specific company.

- There are several ways to invest in stocks. You, or your stockbroker or investment advisor, can select the individual stocks for your portfolio or you can let a mutual fund manager do it for you.

Mutual Funds

- A mutual fund pools the dollars of many people to, in theory, invest more efficiently than individuals could.

- Investors typically purchase the funds because they do not have the time or expertise to manage their own portfolios and so "buy a piece" of a larger, professionally managed portfolio.

- Mutual funds span the spectrum of risk/return ranging from money market funds to bond funds (higher yields than money market funds, but they fluctuate with interest rates) to stock funds (offer greatest long-term potential for appreciation, but also the greatest short-term volatility).

- There are thousands and thousands of mutual funds with different objectives, areas of specialization and fee structures.

Let me know if you have any questions or want to discuss this further.

E-mail From: Red
Subject: Investments 101 – Stocks & Bonds
Sent: Tuesday, April 6

Thanks. Glad you sent this information in an e-mail. I'll only have to read it a few hundred times before it starts to make sense. Meanwhile, here's my question: If I'm very conservative and not willing to take any risk, why would I consider anything riskier than bank and money market accounts and maybe — repeat maybe — bonds?

Subject: Investments 101 – Diversification and Asset Allocation
Sent: Tuesday, April 6

I do not want, nor do I plan, to be your investment advisor, but I will try and explain the underlying logic.

Risk Tolerance

You, like Mom, are what would be considered a very conservative investor. However, the safest investments are also the ones that typically have the lowest rate of return. In some extreme examples, you may not even keep up with inflation, and you will not earn any value over time.

The possibility of greater returns comes at the expense of greater risk of losses (risk/ return trade-off). Philosophically, you may be willing to accept financial objectives that are not focused on eliminating as much risk as possible, but instead optimize your returns as much as possible given your specific situation. Obviously, we all would like to continually earn high returns year after year. However, if you lose sleep when your investments take a short-term drop, chances are the potential for higher returns over the long-term from those assets may not be worth the stress.

Nick and you need to ask yourselves if you are willing to risk some money for the possibility of greater returns. We already know your risk tolerance is lower than mine, and I would guess Nick is somewhere in the middle … but there is no way of knowing without asking. It is something the two of you need to discuss.

Diversification

The key to a successful investment strategy is diversification, or dividing your assets among several different investment vehicles. The same logic that is used with investing in stocks applies to the entire investment portfolio. Think of the old adage, "Do not put all your eggs in one basket." When it comes to investments, if you are properly diversified, there is less risk that all your investments will falter at any given time. In reality, some investments rise when others fall, which smoothes out the volatility of the total portfolio. For example, generally the bond and equity markets move in opposite directions, so if your portfolio is diversified across both areas, negative movements in one will be offset by positive results in the other.

Asset Allocation

Asset allocation is an investment portfolio strategy that takes diversification one step further and determines the percentage allocation of different investments. One rule of thumb used to determine the percentage a person should allocate to stock is to subtract their age from 100. In other words, if you are 40, you should put 60% of your money into stock and the remaining into bonds, real estate and cash. If you are 80, only 20% should go into stocks. In general terms, that might make sense, but obviously it does not take into account other important information such as whether or not you are a parent, a retiree or a spouse. You and I are a perfect example of why this is too generalized. Since you are five years younger than me, you would have 5% more allocated to stocks than I would.

However, I do not have any children and my risk tolerance is much higher than yours so, in reality, I probably would be willing to allocate significantly more of my portfolio to stocks than you would.

All of this leads us back to the initial steps of "planting your garden." Once you identify your current situation, your future capital needs and how much time you have to grow your investments combined with your risk tolerance, the decisions regarding asset allocation will become clearer.

E-mail From: Red
Subject: **Investments 101 – Diversification and Asset Allocation**
Sent: Tuesday, April 6

Clear as mud! Now I know why I didn't major in Business.

Everything Black took the time to explain to me was important and made sense in a conceptual way, but the fact still remained it was incredibly confusing. And more than I could handle. I began to think it might be best to return to my ostrich days. But if I put my head back in the sand, what kind of garden could I grow? A cactus garden?

But then I realized that working on a strategy didn't necessarily obligate me to move forward on the implementation of the plan. And that I had nothing to lose, except maybe the time invested in the process. And that if nothing else, my time wouldn't be wasted since it would be an investment in my financial education.

Finding A Financial Planner To Help Plant Your Garden

I thought, yet again, about how fortunate I was to have Black in my life. I wondered who other people turned to when it came to money. You can't blindly trust people merely because they seem to have financial expertise.

IM I can honestly say that until recently it hadn't really made much difference to me what you studied in school or what you did for a living. But I'm so happy that you decided to become a financial analyst! Not only have you helped me enormously during our crisis, but now you can help us plan financially for the future.

IM I am happy you are happy, but here is where I may disappoint you. Although I have done a significant amount of financial analysis over the years, I am NOT a financial advisor. I have an MBA in international finance, but that does not qualify me as an investment advisor.

IM I thought you said when we got to the point of establishing an investment plan, you'd help us.

IM I did and I will. I did — by letting you know I am not the right person. I will — by helping you find the right person. Financial services is one of the largest, maybe the largest, industries in the world. But you have to be careful. It seems almost anyone who offers financial recommendations can appear as if they are financial advisors — accountants, bankers, insurance agents, stockbrokers — the list goes on and on.

IM I know. I remember when we were talking to the bank about moving the retirement account, and they were telling us about all their investment opportunities. You pointed out that they were trying to "sell" us their products, not necessarily recommending the best investment vehicles.

IM I am impressed. You were paying attention. It does not mean the bankers' advice was bad or it was not a good investment, I just wanted you to understand the bankers' motives.

IM I understand. But what are our options if you can't help us with our financial planning? Unlike Larry and you, we don't have millions to invest. How can mere mortals like us handle financial planning if we can't afford to hire expert financial planners?

IM I am not sure you can afford NOT to hire a financial planner. Not unless you plan on becoming an expert yourself. And have the time and desire to manage your own money. And the discipline to execute and monitor the plan.

IM Well, that is clearly not an option. Have any others?

IM You can hire a planner by the hour. Which is a great option for people who want to get started and learn the basics, much of which I have already explained, and they will get into more detail about your specific needs. Or you can go with one of the large investment brokerage houses, like Merrill Lynch. They all provide financial planning services. But whether you go with a planner or a brokerage house, the key is to understand what you are paying for, what they are qualified to do and also their motives.

IM Where do I start? How do I know who to call?

IM You do your homework. That is what I had to do when we decided to change investment advisors. I put together a list of potential companies based on my own experience as well as recommendations from OUR accountants. Hint-hint!

IM So UHY Advisors can do this for me?

IM Yes. They mentioned their financial services when I first introduced you to them. Call them and explain you want to meet with someone from their financial planning group to set up an initial consultation and have them explain their process.

IM I feel like Dorothy from The Wizard of Oz — the answer was there all the time. But why couldn't you start out by telling me to call UHY Advisors?

IM Because, Dorothy, I needed you to follow the "road" so you would better understand the answer. Anyway, I used them when we interviewed investment and asset management firms. They put together the initial questionnaire, coordinated the meetings and summarized the results. Obviously, it was something they were well-qualified to do; but since they would be working with the investment firm regarding tax planning, I thought it was important to include them in the process from the beginning.

IM That all makes sense. And thanks for giving me the answer. What would I have done without you?

IM You would have asked people you know for recommendations. And then you would have had to interview them, etc. There are guidelines and checklists I could have provided, but I did not see the value in you figuring all this out for yourself. Just remember — you owe me for the countless hours I saved you. EOM

I didn't have a problem setting up the initial meeting, but I did wonder whether I'd feel comfortable bombarding them with all my questions. It was one thing to look stupid in front of your sister, but it was entirely different when it was with a business firm that knew Black well. I was afraid their expectations of me would be tainted, thinking that as Black's sister I'd be far more knowledgeable than I am. It was ironic — starting in kindergarten and continuing for years, teachers would ask if I was Black's sister, mostly wanting to know if I was going to cause as much trouble as she did and require special attention. More often than not, I denied being related to her. However, this time I'd have to admit to the truth, and this time, I was the one who would require extra attention.

📱 Got a minute? I have a curiosity question.

☎ Go for it.

📱 I was thinking about our conversation about UHY Advisors and the fact you used them to help pick an investment advisor. Didn't you once use Merrill Lynch? Did you drop them, or do you use multiple financial companies? I realize you have way more money than Nick and I do, but is there some logic to having multiple accounts?

☎ Yes and no. I do not want to confuse you at this juncture, but as I mentioned, there are many different types of financial companies. Brokerage houses are different than investment advisors. It is a function of their primary duty and responsibility. Years ago, before I had any significant savings, I opened a Merrill Lynch account so that I could start somewhere. My account manager tried to get me to sit down and do a long-term plan and strategy, but in my youthful arrogance I felt since I had a finance degree, I did not need any help.

📱 With all due respect, I'm not sure you have totally outgrown your arrogance, but this is amusing, so please go on.

☎ Most of my saving was done via company retirement accounts. However, I did carefully review the options available to make sure I maximized their value and minimized my tax situation, but other than that I did nothing regarding my own personal finances. The small amount of money I had at Merrill Lynch was kept in money market accounts earning minimal interest. Occasionally I would dabble in one or two stocks, but I had no real plan.

📱 So you were no better than Mommy or me? I feel better already. Much better.

☎ It gets even better. Or worse, depending on how you look at it. When I was fired from my last full-time job, I exercised significant stock options which made me a millionaire. Or at least I was on paper, since I sold some, but not all, of the stock. I put the cash in the money market accounts at Merrill Lynch. It was not until after I worked with Larry's investments for several years, all of which were managed by registered professional investment advisors, that I decided to let an investment advisor handle a portion of my money. I let my money, which by then was a significant amount, just sit there for years earning minimum returns instead of growing.

📱 What was your logic?

☎ Rationalization is a better word. When I did not have much money, planning for my financial future did not seem as important as building my career or establishing a lifestyle. It was not until after I exercised the stock options that I had any significant money, and by then I was living with Larry. I started doing consulting work, and shortly thereafter Larry and I got married. At that point I figured I would never have to worry about money again and so focused on Larry's financial investments instead of my own.

📱 That all makes sense. But it does sound like, "Do as I say, not as I do." Now who's acting like Mommy?

☎ Valid point. But as I mentioned, over time I did transfer some of my own money to the investment advisors I was using for Larry's money. However, I assumed I would stay married to Larry forever. And that was probably not a smart approach, at least from a financial perspective, to planning for the future. That is why I have recently been looking at my financial situation from an entirely different perspective.

📱 What are you saying? Are you trying to tell me something?

☎ All I am saying is that I have money in several different places because I never took the time to sit down and come up with a long-term plan. I basically did nothing. Which in reality was a decision ... and it was NOT a smart one.

📱 And so what has made you decide to do something now? What has changed?

☎ The only thing that has changed is that I realize I need to look at my financial situation independent of Larry and plan more wisely for the future. I plan to send out

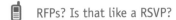

RFPs to the financial companies that currently either hold or invest my money, as well as an investment advisor I have known for years who has started his own firm.

📱 RFPs? Is that like a RSVP?

☎ RFP stands for Request for Proposal. Bottom line is, I have to do the same thing you are doing regarding financial planning. The only difference is I have a stronger financial background.

📱 And more money!

☎ And a more expensive lifestyle to support. But the fundamentals are the same: What do you have? What do you need? Can you get there from here?

It was hard to imagine Black and I doing the same thing at the same time. Nick and I have bank accounts. Black has investment accounts. I guess I now had to stop thinking of financial planners and investment strategies as something that's exclusively for the Rockefellers and Kennedys of this world.

Where There's A Will, There's A Way

📱 I'm so mad at Nick, I could kill him!

📱 Any particular reason, or are you planning on using the life insurance money as a jump start on your long-range financial planning?

📱 Never thought of that. What a great idea. Do you have step-by-step instructions?

📱 Never mind. Start over. Why do you want to kill Nick?

📱 OK. Maybe that was a slight exaggeration. Stupid little things he does. And doesn't do. Nothing important — only annoying. Especially when I'm busy and he's just watching TV.

📱 And that, your honor, is her sole defense for repeatedly stabbing her husband with a kitchen knife. Somehow, I do not think it would hold up in court. Unless, of course, you have a female judge and a jury of wives.

📱 That's funny.

📱 Well, if you decide to go through with it, make sure the knife is sharp and Nick's Will is up-to-date. I am assuming, of course, that both Nick and you have Wills. If not, you need to. In fact, that is probably the first thing you need to do in terms of planning for the future.

📱 Somehow planning for your death seems the complete opposite of planning for your future, but yes, we both have Wills. Not sure how current they are, but we have them.

📱 Good. It is amazing how many people never bother to do a Will.

📱 Really?

📱 Really, but I know you did not call to talk about Wills. Do you have something you need to talk about, or did you just call to vent?

📱 Just to vent. Sorry. Talk to you later.

I hadn't thought about our Wills in years. Nick and I made sure to get our Wills done when I was pregnant with Natasha. We wanted to make sure there wasn't any question about things like who would take care of her in case something happened to both of us, who would make the financial decisions, etc. But that was years ago, and since then things had changed. Even though I was thinking about long-term planning, I never would have thought to include reviewing and updating our Wills as part of the plan if Black hadn't mentioned it.

💬 Sorry I could not talk earlier. So, did you decide to let Nick live?

💬 Yes, but I looked at our Wills and saw we haven't updated them since before Natasha was born.

💬 You do need to update your Wills. Especially since you were living overseas when Natasha was born. You need to make sure those Wills are valid here.

💬 I know, but Wills are such a morbid thing to think about.

💬 Dying without a valid Will is a more depressing thought. What if something were to happen to both Nick and you? I would hope your old Wills would hold up in court, but what if they did not? Or what if there were delays? Would you want the State to appoint a trustee? Since the girls are minors, would you want the State to appoint temporary guardians?

💬 I get your point. I'll give updating our Wills a very high priority on my "to do" list.

💬 I review my Will every year around my birthday. I look at it as celebrating another year of living, instead of what will happen if I die.

💬 You're weird. And why would you need to review your Will every year?

💬 Things change. People change. Who you love and trust can change. Remember, Larry and I have no community property, and I have no children. When I die I want to make sure my estate is handled according to my wishes. And although my Will rarely changes, sometimes I do change the other associated documents.

💬 Whoa. Two things. First and foremost, I'm not sure exactly what you mean by Larry and you have no community property. Are you taken care of if something happens to Larry? And second, what other documents are you talking about?

IM Depends on what happens to Larry. If he were to die — yes, but to what extent I do not know as I do not have a copy of his Will. If he was to be seriously ill — I would hope so, but again I do not know to what extent as I do not know who he has appointed as Power of Attorney and any instructions he may have given them. If we were to get a divorce — nope. The prenuptial agreement states I get nothing but my cars, jewelry and clothing. Not even a place to live. So as you can see, there are various documents — not just the Will — that control the future. Too many to explain on IM. I will send you a list later.

IM Why would you agree to something like that? Sounds like you're at his mercy.

IM Not important now. The bottom line is, that is our deal. We can talk about it some other time. Not today. Meanwhile I will put together that list for you. EOM

IM You cannot end this with an "EOM"

IM Yes, I can. EOM

At this point I wasn't sure whether or not I was overreacting, but I was sure that Black was well aware of her situation, and if anyone could handle it, she could. Talk about someone who was able to pragmatically approach the future — and even generate a list of documents necessary to do so! I couldn't help but wonder how many documents this would take. I thought the Will took care of almost everything. It explained what we wanted done with our assets, who we wanted as the girls' guardian, and who we wanted as Executor of the Will to make sure everything was done as specified. It turned out that our Wills handled everything once we were dead, but not if we were somewhere between "alive and functioning" and dead. Then we would be in limbo land and potentially at the mercy of others.

E-mail From: Black
Subject: **Life & Death Documents**
Sent: Thursday, April 8

More free advice — I guess I am now your pro bono attorney. Not all of these may be necessary, but it is the list of documents I review every year for my birthday. I know you find that "weird," but I have been doing it for so many years that it has become a tradition. Obviously, it is not important when you actually review them, but it is important to make sure you review them (and update, if necessary), on a routine basis.

And remember, you get what you pay for, so here goes:

1. **Last Will and Testament**
   Although I review this annually, it only changes when there is a major life event. For example, when I got married, when Natasha was born, when Daddy died.

2. **Personal Belongings Letter**

   Over the years, as I accumulated jewelry and cars and other personal belongings, I decided to handle specific bequests by a separate letter that is referenced in my Will. The letter changes every year or so, but I can do that myself, and then I send it to the attorneys for safekeeping along with my Will. (And I know you are coveting my black Hermes JPG Birkin bag!)

3. **Power of Attorney — Medical**

   This document designates who can make health-care decisions on my behalf should I be unable to make such decisions.

4. **Power of Attorney — H.I.P.A.A**

   This supplements the Medical Power of Attorney. The Health Insurance Portability and Accountability Act of 1996 ("HIPAA") established privacy rules that restrict the information that health care-providers are allowed to release about your medical condition and treatment. The penalties are severe, and so health-care providers are very cautious. This document clearly states that any information released to the designated parties will not be a violation of the privacy rules of HIPAA.

5. **Directive to Physicians**

   The Medical Power of Attorney authorizes who can make the decisions, but it does not give them any idea of my wishes. This document clarifies whether or not I want life-sustaining treatment if I am terminally ill or diagnosed with an irreversible condition.

6. **Power of Attorney   General**

   This document becomes effective only upon my disability and requires that two licensed physicians unanimously determine that I am unable to act. The document then designates who can handle all my financial, business and legal affairs.

7. **Burial and Funeral Instructions**

8. **Letter with Miscellaneous Information**

   This includes things which logically do not fall anywhere else, but would be important in the case of my death. For example, the location of safety deposit boxes and their keys, the combination to my safe, passwords to access my internet accounts, etc.

That e-mail made me realize that planning for the future meant planning for both the good and the bad. It still gives me an eerie feeling knowing that, given the amount of life insurance we have, the girls' financial future is probably more secure if we're dead than alive. And the thought of Nick or me being seriously ill or incapacitated is extremely depressing. But there's also a feeling of resolve and satisfaction knowing that we have plans in place. Black made me realize that if we weren't prepared for the worst possible scenarios, then the reality of the situation could be catastrophic. However, by planning for the worst we could then focus on working towards our goals for the future, something

I was ready to get back to since it was a much more cheerful topic than planning for our death. In fact, I was looking at long-term financial planning with a much more enthusiastic attitude than I had previously.

Learn The Basics And Understand Why

Although I was still apprehensive about long-term financial planning, there was one thing I clearly understood. And that was that I needed (and wanted) to continue my education and have some understanding of basic investment concepts. Black seemed addicted to *The Wall Street Journal*, always referencing it for one thing or another. After buying several issues at Starbucks, I decided to get a subscription.

I soon realized there were many things a novice like me could learn from the paper. Although I tend to skip the "Money and Investing" section, I find a lot of relevant financial information in the "Personal Journal" section. And I must confess my favorite section is the Friday "Weekend Journal," because it always includes one or two great entertainment and travel articles. The look of shock on Nick's face when the first issue arrived was worth the subscription price alone. And when my Mom saw several issues in the kitchen, she commented about Nick's copies of *The Wall Street Journal*, never even thinking that it was my subscription!

☎ Two quick things. The first is to tell you that I have set up a meeting with UHY Advisors for April 19th to discuss financial planning.

☎ So I can hand you off to them then? Great! And the second thing?

☎ Recently in *The Wall Street Journal* there have been a bunch of articles about brokerage accounts and issues about commissions. I don't really understand all the various fees for different services, but it seems like there are all these hidden costs, etc. It's beginning to scare me.

☎ Hold on. You were doing what? Excuse me, to whom am I speaking?

☎ Very funny. Yes, I was reading *The Wall Street Journal*. Get over the shock and back to the issue of fees and hidden costs. Do I need to be concerned?

☎ Concerned? No. Aware? Yes. Don't get too worked up over a few articles. Keep in mind many readers of *The Wall Street Journal* do their own investing, and the articles and warnings are more relevant to them than someone who is using a qualified advisor.

☎ OK. But now I feel like I have opened a financial Pandora's Box. The more I'm learning, the more confused I'm getting, because there's so much information and detail out there. Do I really need to go down this road? There must be a better way.

☎ To an extent you are right — there is a lot of information and detail. But you do not need to fully understand all of this, unless of course you find it interesting. Your job is to learn and understand the basics related to your specific situation, and then ask questions when you want or need more information.

☎ But how will I know when I need more information? And how do I know what are the right vs. the wrong choices?

☎ I know you want specific answers, but the reality is that long-term financial planning is not black and white. It is an ongoing process, and as things change, so will your plan. But as you continue to learn more, you will understand more. You may come across something you think is interesting, but you may not be sure if it is relevant to your situation. Research it. *The Wall Street Journal* has a great online article search. Or ask me about it. If I cannot help you, then ask your financial advisor. You could start a list similar to the ones you keep for your electrician or plumber.

☎ Great — another list! I'm sorry to be such a pest, but I'm uncomfortable with all of this.

☎ You may be uncomfortable, but that is only because you are thinking of all the things you think you do not know. I do not think you realize how much you have learned in the past two months and the fact you probably now know more than many people.

☎ Yeah. Right. You may not remember this, but I have said it before — you're not very good at warm and fuzzy. But thanks for trying to make me feel better.

☎ I am not being warm and fuzzy. I am stating the obvious. So remind me how many more days there are before I can hand you over to the financial experts?

I knew I was a good student — not that I was necessarily the smartest or the quickest to understand a concept, but rather one who would work at it. And I started to look at our initial long-term planning consultation with UHY Advisors as a "meet the teacher" appointment. However, I wasn't expecting a homework assignment, at least not so soon.

IM Glad you are online. I need help with a homework assignment.

IM Natasha is only in Pre-K. You cannot be in over your head already! Or is it computer related?

IM Cute. Neither. It's from UHY Advisors. When I called to set up the appointment, I asked if I needed to bring any financial documents or be prepared to discuss anything in particular, and was told no.

IM And you need help doing nothing?

IM Would you let me finish? I just received information from them about setting up a savings plan for college for the girls. We haven't even had our first meeting! It seems to me like they are fast-forwarding the process.

IM Are they trying to get you to make a decision, or are they just sending you information about the new 529 Plans? And when you initially spoke to them, did you mention planning for the girls' college education?

IM How did you know it was about 529 Plans?

IM Because they are "the" topic of discussion when it comes to planning for college expenses. Plus, you already use UHY Advisors for tax planning, and that is the underlying value of the 529 Plans. But before you panic, keep in mind they are probably just sending you "food for thought" before next week's meeting. Have Nick and you even talked about college for the girls? I know when I went to graduate school in England, I was the anomaly over there. It seemed like so few women even went to college.

IM You are always the anomaly! But it sounds like I don't have to figure this out by next week, so that's a relief. Thanks.

Black and I grew up in a house that valued education, and so it was expected that we'd go to college. Nick grew up in England at a time when only a small percentage of men, let alone women, continued their education past high school. But it was an unspoken understanding that he too expected our girls to get a college education. And although we hadn't yet put together a list of our long-term financial goals, I knew we needed to think about being prepared for the high cost of college.

E-mail From: Black
Subject: Tax Planning & Saving For College
Sent: Tuesday, April 13

I know I get to "hand you off" next week, but before you ask my opinion on 529s, I thought I would volunteer it.

The plans are named after section 529 of the Internal Revenue Code, and were designed as a tax-advantaged investment to encourage savings for education. They really came into prominence with the Economic Growth and Tax Reconciliation Act of 2001. I did some initial research to see if they made sense for Larry, but I must warn you I have not looked into them recently and things may have changed. Now that I have prefaced this with a disclaimer, and knowing you get what you pay for, here goes:

1. First and foremost, you must take care of your future first and maximize the amount you contribute to tax-sheltered retirement accounts. Remember the airplane analogy — in case of an emergency, put on your oxygen mask and then tend to your kids. You are the stronger, more able person, and you can help your child much better if your financial future is secure.

2. The college financial aid system penalizes you for saving money outside of retirement accounts. And some schools may treat these assets as the child's when determining financial aid.

3. Without going into the specifics of any of the 529 plans, the main shortcomings are:

   a. Money must be used for educational expenses. If for some reason you do not need the money for educational purposes, there is a penalty for withdrawal.

   b. Future changes to tax laws could negatively impact their value.

4. The upside is that the money inside the plan compounds tax-deferred (just like in a retirement account), but when the money is withdrawn, it is taxed at the student's tax rate — which is presumably lower than the parents'.

5. There may be other considerations in terms of asset protection (bankruptcy, divorce, etc.), but since I was only looking at it in purely financial terms, I did not research that aspect of them.

Hope this helps.

E-mail From: Red
Subject: Tax Planning & Saving For College
Sent: Tuesday, April 13

Yes and no. Overall, I think it just makes the issue even more complicated. I can't help but wonder — and worry — about what we'll do if we can't save enough to pay for Natasha and Sawyer's college education. It's so expensive, and it's getting worse. And now that Nick's out on his own, I have no way of knowing how successful he'll be.

E-mail From: Black
Subject: Other Ways To Fund College
Sent: Tuesday, April 13

Sorry. I was not trying to make the situation worse. I was just explaining one investment vehicle that can be used to fund education. Keep in mind I received almost no financial help from Mom and Daddy when I went to college. I took out student loans, and worked summers and part-time during the rest of the year. And when I did my graduate degree, I was working full-time until a scholarship let me take the last semester abroad.

E-mail From: Red
Subject: Other Ways To Fund College
Sent: Tuesday, April 13

But that was because you pissed off Mommy. If you had apologized to her, they'd have paid for more of it. They did for me.

E-mail From: Black
Subject: Other Ways To Fund College
Sent: Tuesday, April 13

Big deal. We both still managed to get an education. Although I might argue about the value of your Theater Arts degree.

To the day I die, I don't think I'll ever truly understand Black's carefree attitude about serious matters. But I guess that is because I look at things from a totally different perspective. She has this uncanny ability to remove the emotions from decisions that are usually very emotional. I hoped I could be a little more like her when it came to thinking about long-term planning. Or at least I would try.

In preparation for the following week's meeting with UHY Advisors, Nick had pretty much decided he was going to let me steer the ship since I had been handling all the current finances. Having said that, I knew he had definite opinions on how the money should be invested, so I tried to sit down and discuss our current financial situation and general financial goals with him, but didn't make much headway. I hoped the meeting would at least provide a framework that I could use for future discussions, but since I wasn't expected to "be prepared" for this meeting, I wasn't overly concerned that we didn't have a list of our future goals.

Black had gone out of town for the weekend to a Ferrari event that benefited Make-A-Wish, and I didn't want to bother her. I figured this was a well-deserved escape for her. And so I was on my own, so to speak. I tried to focus on what Black had been telling me about my "better than most people" understanding of financial matters, as well as her many informative e-mails. Monday morning I felt semi-ready for the meeting and packed those e-mails along with a file full of personal financial information. Sort of my financial security blanket. Plus, I knew I could always preface my questions with disclaimers like, "this may be a stupid question, but ...," "I'm not sure this makes sense, but ..." and my favorite, "I know my sister knows this, but I don't so could you please explain ...".

E-mail From: Black
Subject: Meeting with the Financial Advisors
Sent: Monday, April 19

I know you have already left for your meeting, and by the time you get this e-mail I will have been "dumped" for more qualified advisors. However, I have one more comment. I know you love the quote that "the grass may be greener because it is AstroTurf." Well, in keeping with your corny garden analogy, I need to tell you a secret ... The grass is greenest where it is watered.

Hope the meeting went well. Really well.

15
I Need A Warning System

🔋 Good morning. I figure you are in the car on the way to your meeting with UHY Advisors. Any last minute questions?

🔋 None that I can think of. In fact, I think I might actually see light at the end of the tunnel. Then again, maybe it's an oncoming train.

🔋 I love your eternal optimism. How about accepting things as they are? Acknowledging things happen for a reason. And if it turns out to be an oncoming train, just get out of the way.

🔋 Well, aren't we philosophical this morning?! What happened to you this weekend?

🔋 How much time do you have?

🔋 Nick and I are about to pull into the parking garage, so unless it will take less than two minutes it will have to wait.

🔋 It was one of the best weekends of my life. In fact, it may have saved my life.

🔋 WHAT?! You better explain yourself. And quickly.

🔋 It is a long story. All you need to know for now is that it involved Ferraris, a Lambo and Make-A-Wish.

🔋 A Lambo?

🔋 Yes, a Lamborghini. Call me after the meeting.

🔋 Count on it!

I could understand how a weekend that combined cars and Make-A-Wish could be wonderful. But save her life? That sounded a bit dramatic, even for Black. And of course I loved the fact she intentionally timed it so that she wouldn't have to explain herself. I was sure this would be interesting, but right now I needed to focus on more mundane things; like long-term financial planning.

Do Not Fear The Negative ... Remember The Positive

☎ OK. We're home. Tell me about your weekend!

☎ Like I said earlier, it is a long story. And it can wait. How did your meeting go?

☎ I'm not answering your question until you answer mine.

☎ Fine. As you now know, long-term planning requires you to decide what is really important to you, and what you are willing to sacrifice in the short-term in exchange for the long-term. I thought about that this weekend. In fact, I thought about a lot of things. The fact I was around people with money (or at least who drove expensive cars) and the event benefited Make-A-Wish gave me plenty of food for thought. I guess you could say I had my own personal long-term planning meeting. No other attendees required. And so, I ask you again, how did your meeting go?

☎ So you're not going to tell me what you figured out? Or how this saved your life?

☎ No. Suffice it to say I learned, no make that remembered, a lot about myself this weekend. Life decisions are a lot like financial decisions in that there are always trade-offs. I have been thinking about mine. I know what I traded and why. Now I am trying to decide if they were reasonable trades. I guess you could say I am revising my risk/reward analysis. And before you ask ... no, I am not done calculating yet. So, for the last time before I hang up ... how did your meeting go?

☎ Good and bad. Good in that it looks like we're headed in the right direction. Bad in that I don't think I could handle going through another crisis like this. Besides becoming clairvoyant or buying a crystal ball, how do I make sure that I don't go down this awful road again?

☎ I am confused. You jumped from heading in the right direction to being on an awful road. What are you talking about?

☎ Sorry. I'm referring to the road I have been traveling ever since Nick was fired. The one littered with financial mistakes. A road we ended up on because Nick never stopped to ask for directions, and I assumed he knew where he was going. The one with lost values. And no signs indicating what is really important.

☎ You forgot the "Men Working" sign.

☎ Cute, but I'm trying to be serious.

☎ OK. Then seriously, I am not sure the road was as awful as you make it sound. It was bumpy, and it may not have been the most direct route, but it did take you to a better place. And as long as we are using a road analogy, remember life is not a destination, it is a journey.

☎ I didn't ask the meaning of life. I asked how not to make the same mistakes again. And can we stop with the road analogy?

☎ Yes, but you are the one that started it, and I refuse to use your stupid gardening analogy, although I will admit I thought about AstroTurf this weekend. How about we use Weight Watchers?

☎ Why do we need an analogy? And what would you know about Weight Watchers?

☎ There was a time when Larry and the girls joined Weight Watchers. Unbeknownst to them, I read all the materials and followed along.

☎ You must be kidding. You on Weight Watchers? Here's a news flash — you don't start Weight Watchers at a size 2! You'd be lynched if you walked into a meeting.

☎ I understand that, but I knew my eating habits could stand some improvement and their program is more about smart eating than merely dieting, although their marketing hook is weight-loss.

☎ That's very true. But what does that have to do with my awful road? I can hardly wait to see how you connect these dots.

☎ How much weight have you lost?

☎ 35 pounds.

☎ And much more to go?

☎ None. I hit my target about six months ago, and I'm now on maintenance.

☎ And have you put any weight back on?

☎ Not for long. I admit I sometimes get offtrack, but that's why I still do the weekly weigh-ins. If I gain a few pounds, I just start counting points again until I lose the weight.

☎ So you do not wait until you have gained 10 or 15 pounds?

☎ That's a stupid question. I know how difficult it is to lose weight. Why would I wait?

☎ You wouldn't wait. That would be stupid. Even if you were not actively on the Weight Watchers program, you cannot get away from the fact that you now know about the system and how it works. Look at Mom. She has not done Weight Watchers in decades, but she still remembers the success she had with the program.

☎ OK, so I know how to control my weight. When are you going to connect the dots?

☎ I just did. The logic is the same with your fear of going down your "awful road" again. You learned from your mistakes, and I doubt you would repeat them. The fact you are concerned about heading in that direction proves my point.

☎ You couldn't just say that to start with?

☎ No, because you were the one who started this conversation with your road analogy. Anyway, sometimes I think we learn more from our mistakes or failures than we do from our successes. Or maybe the lessons are just more memorable. But instead of fearing the negative, you need to remember the positive.

☎ You're in a very weird mood. I'm starting to get worried.

☎ You worry too much.

I'm sorry, but there was no getting around it: Black was in a strange mood. But regardless of her approach to things — whether philosophical or pragmatic — they still made sense.

📱 I'm sitting in carpool line and have been thinking about how little you really said about your weekend. I know Make-A-Wish has been an important part of your life for a long time, but do you expect me to believe that this is what made you start thinking about the trade-offs you have made in your life?

📱 No, but you need to understand the only reason I went to the Ferrari event was because it was a fund-raiser for Make-A-Wish, and they specifically asked if I would bring my Make-A-Wish race car.

📱 I understand the motive was Make-A-Wish, but something else must have happened.

📱 I flew up on Friday in time for the silent auction. Saturday morning, I got up early and ran and when I got back to the hotel they were unloading cars from the transport. I had never seen my two cars next to each other, and for some reason when I did ... it really hit me ... how lucky I was not only to have one Ferrari, but two.

📱 And you say I miss the obvious?!

📱 Do you want me to continue, or are you going to keep interrupting?

📱 Continue.

📱 The participants met for breakfast and the start of the rally, which for me was more of a scenic drive than anything else. There was something very special about those hours spent on wonderful, winding roads. We stopped for lunch, and of course it being a room full of motor heads, the car stories started flying and continued again that night at dinner. Since I had the only race car displayed at the event, it got a lot of attention, both in the parking lot and especially at Sunday's concourse, and allowed me to share the Make-A-Wish story with so many people. And on Sunday the guest of honor at the brunch and awards ceremony was a wonderful Wish child. I then flew home and met Larry and the girls for dinner. End of weekend. Any questions?

📱 I still think there's more than you're telling me. For example, explain to me why Larry didn't go. And you still haven't said a thing about the Lambo.

He had the girls, and although I invited them all, he did not want to go. He made it sound like the girls would not have enjoyed it, but I think it was more that he did not want to go. Remember, this is a man who almost never accompanies me on race weekends. Anyway, things happen for a reason.

And the reason is?

The weekend gave me a chance to think about things and what is really important to me and why. If Larry and the girls had been there, I probably would have been focused on making sure they were having a good time. Instead, it turned out to be a selfish weekend.

Since you refuse to talk about the Lambo, I guess I might as well focus on Make-A-Wish. For the record, I would hardly call raising money for Make-A-Wish selfish. I don't know how you can emotionally handle working so closely with seriously ill children.

Easy. I focus on raising money. I do not deal directly with the Wish kids and their families, although I have tremendous respect for the volunteers that do. I have gotten directly involved with the kids once or twice, but the emotional attachment was more than I could handle.

I know I could never do it. Ever since I had the girls, I have a hard time even watching news reports about children who are missing or who have been hurt or killed. I can't imagine being personally involved with seriously ill kids, especially when some of them are the same ages as Natasha and Sawyer.

I understand. It makes you realize how lucky you are to have two healthy children.

I am. Believe me. I'm curious about something, though. As children, we were never exposed to charity, so what got you involved with Make-A-Wish? Even Natasha has asked me about Make-A-Wish, because she has seen the kids' artwork at your house and recognizes the logo from seeing it on your race car.

It was years ago. I was invited to play in a Make-A-Wish golf tournament, and at the dinner some of the kids came out and told their Wish stories. They mentioned their illnesses and the doctors and the hospitals in passing — as if it was just a minor detail in their stories. But when they talked about their wishes, it was with such excitement and pure happiness that it was overwhelming. A few weeks earlier, I had received a huge bonus at work and so I was feeling flush with cash, and when I saw the power of a wish — the hope, the joy, the strength it could provide — it made me look at money in a totally different way. When you meet children who are seriously ill and you realize no amount of money can "fix the problem," but yet something as simple as wishing for a puppy or to meet a celebrity can make such a huge difference in their lives, then you are reminded of what is really important in life. And what is not.

Wow. I don't think I have ever heard you this passionate about anything.

 Probably not. Make-A-Wish has been an important part of my life for a long time. I know I am very fortunate in many respects, but sometimes I get wrapped up in day-to-day life and forget that. I may have problems with one of the cars, or I am annoyed with Larry, or it is just a bad day, Make-A-Wish reminds me that my problems or frustrations are minuscule in the scheme of things.

 This is a side of you that I rarely see. I'm impressed. And proud.

 Thanks, but Make-A-Wish does far more for me than I do for them. Partly as a substitute for not having children of my own, but more importantly as my reality check on life. It is my constant reminder of what is important. And although I may not be able to cure the kids, the fact I can make their lives a little better by helping grant wishes is the least — the very least — I can do in return.

 I think I'm now beginning to understand how and why this weekend was so important to you.

It was amazing. It was one of those rare times when Black didn't make any flippant comments. And that alone got my attention. Before this conversation, I thought her involvement with Make-A-Wish was very generous, both of her time as well as her money, but I attributed much of it to the fact she had surpluses of both in her life. But once I realized this went back to her corporate life, years when she might have had spare money but was working ridiculous hours, I gained a new respect for her commitment. And then when she explained how it has become her "reality check" on life, I began to understand that we all probably need something to help us remember what's genuinely important.

My "Most Important" List

☎ Got a few minutes? I'm cooking dinner and have a few questions.

☎ So why are you calling me?

☎ I have been thinking about this morning's meeting with the financial advisors. And your weekend. And everything you said about Make-A-Wish.

☎ And?

☎ And I need your advice. Organizing and managing financial priorities seems fairly straight-forward, but I'm struggling with the personal ones. How do I make sure I don't lose track of what's important?

☎ You do what you are doing right now. You think about it.

☎ Fine, but how do I remember to do that? Wasn't it only this morning that you told me this weekend may have saved your life because it reminded you of what was important? I thought that rather dramatic, but it does prove even you can forget to think about the truly important things in life.

☎ OK, so I am ... busted. Guilty as charged.

☎ I'm not sure this is an innocent vs. guilty issue, unless there's something you aren't telling me. All I'm asking is how to make sure I don't lose track of what's important. I have learned so much in the last few months, and I don't want to get so wrapped up in day-to-day living that I forget to focus on what's truly important. Plus, I want to make sure I am teaching the right values and priorities to the girls. I know Make-A-Wish is your reminder. Any suggestions for me?

☎ Different things work for different people. For some people, like me, it is charity work. For others, it is organized religion. For you, it might be quiet time alone, or when you are watching the girls at the playground. Given how addicted you are to lists and schedules, maybe you should just put it on your Franklin Planner.

☎ For some reason that sounds very shallow and superficial. Things to do today: buy groceries, take Woof to the vet, remember what is important, teach the girls values, clean out the refrigerator.

☎ You asked for a way to remember. I gave you several choices. Pick one or come up with one on your own. And as far as how to teach the girls, they will learn by example. But if you are really concerned, start a list of "Values and Priorities" and review it with all your other lists every Sunday night. Oh, I forgot, that would make you sound shallow and superficial. Never mind.

☎ Isn't it time Larry and you went to dinner?

But it was a good idea, especially since it would serve two purposes — it would be my personal reminder as well as a list I could use with the girls. Even as I was cooking, I started writing down concepts I believed were important (Black was right, there's no way to stop me from writing lists) and before long I had a hodgepodge of random thoughts.

IM This is late for you to be logging on.

IM It's the first chance I had to get on the computer all day.

IM Let me guess, you are working on your "Values and Priorities" list.

IM How did you know? Am I that predictable?

IM In a word — yes. So, how is your list coming? Care to share?

IM Not yet. It's a work-in-progress.

IM Well, do not get too wrapped up in trying to create an all-inclusive, perfect list. Remember, Charlton Heston only brought down 10 commandments from Mount Sinai, and they seemed to cover everything important.

IM Is there a reason you didn't say "Moses?" You do know that was the Biblical character he was portraying, don't you?

IM Yes, but I was trying to make a point about creating a list that covers general topics vs. getting too specific. Not start a religious conversation.

IM OK. Point made. Not sure I can keep the list down to 10 key items, but I'll try.

IM Try coming up with a single sentence describing your purpose in life.

IM Why would I do that? And what would make you even suggest it?

IM It was something I was thinking about today. During my years in corporate life, I wrote many Mission Statements, but until this weekend it never dawned on me to write a personal one. And before you ask, a Mission Statement is a short paragraph, or sometimes just a concise sentence, that summarizes the purpose of the business and what is most important to the company. It is not a specific list of goals or objectives. It is more a sense of its reason for being. If used correctly, a Mission Statement communicates focus and helps keep a sense of direction.

IM Sounds too business-like for me, but I'm curious — what would your Mission Statement be?

IM Not exactly sure. EOM

At first, the personal side seemed like it would be impossible to organize, but once I took a step back and looked at the assorted ideas and concepts I had accumulated, I could see how they could be grouped into general topics. But not a single sentence, or even a short paragraph.

Values: Sometimes Neglected, Hopefully Not Forgotten

Although I was now working on a list as a way to make sure our family's underlying values wouldn't be neglected, I also knew that merely having a list wouldn't guarantee success. I was concerned that even if I got to the point of having a review system, like I did with my financial objectives and my Sunday night review of my Franklin Planner lists, it might not get the attention it deserved. I have great systems. I have great intentions. The problem is that life keeps getting in the way, and it's so easy to let things slide from day-to-day.

IM Good morning. You are up VERY early. Still working on your "Values and Priorities" list?

IM Not at the moment. I'm way behind in entering American Express receipts, and I want to find out why our last bill was so much more than the previous months. I kept putting off the task because I was doing other things, but it's become a large pile of receipts and so now I have a "project" on my hands. Any more thoughts on your Mission Statement?

IM Still thinking. My life was so different before Larry and I got married. My fundamental values and the things I find important have not changed, but I feel like my hopes and dreams have gotten lost. And stupid little things — like my birthday resolutions — have even disappeared.

IM Birthday resolutions?

IM Everyone has New Year's resolutions, and I bet most people do not stick with them for more than a month or so, if that long. So every year for my birthday, in addition to reviewing my Will, I used to give myself a present of something I wanted to do. I realized the last time I did that was the year Larry and I got married. My resolution was to start working out in a gym, and I have been doing that three times a week ever since.

IM At least that isn't as morbid a birthday gift as a new Will, but I really was asking about your hopes and dreams.

IM They are all part of the same thing. Hopes and dreams are the things we want to do with our life. Resolutions are merely small goals and objectives that take us in the right direction. Some are fairly simple. For example, I want to start taking piano lessons again. And learn to speak Italian.

IM And the not-so-simple ones?

IM Too complex to IM. But before you start worrying, I will tell you they are nothing new. Just things I have not thought about in a very long time. And most, if not all, of them are things I have tried discussing with Larry over the years. In fact, one year when he asked what I wanted for our anniversary, I told him "gift certificates" redeemable for one-hour conversations. Instead, he bought me a diamond necklace.

IM How sad. Although you have to admit that a diamond necklace isn't a bad gift.

IM It is a great necklace, but not what I wanted. I think birthdays and anniversaries are a perfect time to reflect on what would make you happier and then do something about it. Or at least talk about it. And if nothing else, use these occasions as reminders to think about what is important. For example, Larry's birthday is a few weeks away, and I plan to buy myself new golf clubs.

IM Don't you mean buy HIM new clubs?

IM No. He just bought new clubs.

IM Let me see if I understand this. It's his birthday, and you're going to buy yourself golf clubs? As a birthday present for him? Am I missing something?

📱 I quit playing years ago, and on more than one occasion Larry has said he wished I would start playing again. So for his birthday, I will. I think it is the perfect gift — not only because it is something I know he wants, but more importantly by having something to do together, it might help our marriage.

📱 It kind of makes sense now that you explained it, but I'll never understand how your mind works.

📱 I am trying to focus on what is important. What is so confusing about that? Go back to your American Express receipts. EOM

Over the years I had noticed that Black never really celebrated her birthday, and it wasn't until the last few weeks that I understood she looked at it as a personal celebration and not an annual event that required cards and gifts. It was a strange way to think of a birthday, but the more I thought about it, the more it made sense — at least for Black. I, on the other hand, live in a house with small children and will continue to celebrate birthdays with cakes, balloons and presents.

☎ Got a minute? I'm still thinking about your birthday gift for Larry.

☎ Why?

☎ You must admit, it's an unusual thought process.

☎ Not really. If something is important, and during the course of day-to-day living it gets ignored, you sometimes have to stop and specifically focus on it. That is all I am doing.

☎ I guess that makes sense. Not everything on my list of values (and no, I haven't finished it yet) comes up on a daily basis, but I never thought of making up a situation to force the issue. Surely it should just happen naturally.

☎ I feel like we are talking in circles. Especially since we have already acknowledged that life often gets in the way. I do not want to go through your list, but can you give me an example of something you think is not getting the attention it deserves?

☎ I'm embarrassed to admit it, but two that immediately come to mind are charity and my marriage.

☎ Nothing to be embarrassed about — I think we all tend to neglect our marriages at times. And as far as charity, I know you have donated used clothing and Natasha has even donated some of her toys. It sounds like it is a function of wanting to do more. I bet if you sat down as a family and talked about it, you could come up with plenty of ideas. And create another list.

☎ The last thing I need is another list, but I understand what you're saying.

☎ The key is by reviewing your list you will be reminded to focus on these things, which in turn will motivate you to do something. I know you sometimes get wrapped up in creating an attractive list vs. a functioning list. You need to remember this list will probably never get items crossed off, because it is not a checklist as much as it is a thinking process.

☎ Which is why I'm struggling with it. This list affects everything I do. Every day.

☎ I understand. And you may need to create other reminders for more specific objectives. It might be something as simple as displaying a few pictures of the girls or one of your "happy family" photographs next to your computer, so that you can see them when you are scheduling your time or paying bills. After all, pictures speak louder than words.

☎ It's hard to remember values when I'm staring at numbers, even with a photograph on my desk.

☎ Then use financial pictures — charts and graphs. For example, a bar chart showing where you stand against budget or showing how much you have saved towards one of your goals.

☎ Great. Something else to learn to do.

☎ Not really. Both Microsoft Excel and Microsoft Money can do it for you. In fact, you might consider reducing one of the bar charts to wallet-size and putting it next to your credit cards. Or use a picture of a dream ranch or do a "mock-up" of the girls in college graduation gowns. A picture would be a quick reminder of what is important and may make you think twice before spending money on things you do not need.

☎ Funny you should mention that. When I was working on my American Express receipts this morning, I was trying to figure out a way to get back into thinking more and spending less. When we first attacked my credit cards, I took your suggestion and used a Sharpie to write the interest rates on all my credit cards as a reminder. The problem is I use American Express because I know it has to be paid-in-full every month, but since there's no interest rate; it's the only card without a visual reminder. Maybe I should just write "College" or "Retirement" on the card.

☎ Whatever works. The key is there are many things that can remind you of what is important as long as you are receptive to the hints. Even those "warm and fuzzy" inspirational e-mails that people send to all their friends. I actually have printed a few and put them in my "Blue Book."

☎ I know. I saw them when you first showed it to me.

☎ Whatever.

I went and found several photographs that would be perfect reminders of our goals and put one in my wallet next to my credit cards, as well as a few in my monthly budget file. Besides making me smile, they remind me of some of my long-term goals before I hand over my credit card or refine our monthly budget. In fact, sometimes when I take pictures I even think about whether or not they'll make good "goals and objectives" reminders, which in itself helps me to remember what's important. As Black keeps telling me, whatever works!

Family Meetings — Learn To Communicate and Learn To Listen

One of the many things I learned during the last few months is the importance of communication. However, talk about something which gets lost in day-to-day living! We barely seem to find time to talk about daily events, let alone hopes and dreams.

- Got a minute?

- Maybe. Depends on the topic. If you are calling about hopes, dreams or birthday gifts, the answer is no.

- None of the above. I like your idea of sitting down as a family and discussing important issues, like charity. Plus, it will help the girls learn the value of communication. However, I don't want them to think I am lecturing them. Any ideas?

- Call a meeting. That is what I used to do in the corporate world. I would hold a monthly staff meeting with everyone in my department, whether or not there were specific issues or problems to discuss. I would order in pizza or sandwiches for lunch, and we would talk about different things that were impacting the department. Most of the time it was to provide everyone with an understanding of what each of us was working on and/or things we would like to do or do better. There was no right or wrong. It was an informal forum for discussing things where no one felt threatened or was on display.

- Did you have an agenda? Or was it a free-for-all?

- A bit of both. If there were any specific issues that needed to be addressed, it would be on the agenda; otherwise, it was less structured. And I would usually start the meeting by stating one positive thing the department had accomplished since the last meeting. Then we would go around the table, and everyone would give a brief update of their projects and whether they had issues for discussion or areas of concern. We would write them down and then discuss them. I would end the meeting by coming up with an action item to be accomplished prior to the next meeting.

- Sounds great for a business meeting but a little too formal for a family.

You asked a question, and I gave you a suggestion. I did not say it was the perfect solution, but I do think it has potential. I need to talk to Larry about some things that are on my mind, so this "Family Meeting" concept might be useful. Let me think about it and get back to you.

I know I have often questioned how Black's mind worked, but one of the things I like best is that many of her ideas are not things I'd ever think of doing. Sometimes I'm not sure whether they're things anyone else would ever think of doing either. But I was intrigued by the idea of a family meeting — not to mention curious how she planned to use the concept for her own purposes.

E-mail From: Black
Subject: Have A Fun Family Meeting!
Sent: Tuesday, April 20

I know the staff meeting structure sounded very formal, but when I started thinking about it, I realized it might not take much adjustment. What made the business meeting seem so formal was the subject matter — if we had talked about fun things and hopes and dreams, it would have been a lot less "structured" than discussing specific business projects. And so, keeping that in mind ...

Meeting Structure

1. Start with you or Nick complimenting everyone else at the table about something they have done since the last meeting. Let everyone have a turn at complimenting everyone else. Keep it brief. (I am guessing you never read Ken Blanchard's *One Minute Manager*. I wonder if he did a home version.)

2. Then see if either of the girls has anything she wants to talk about (issues for discussion) or questions about anything (areas of concern), and talk about them. Keep in mind the girls are young, so initially they might not have anything to bring up, but after a few of these meetings they may surprise you. (What is that quote about "out of the mouths of babes?")

3. You (and Nick) can use it as an opportunity to talk about any of the topics you feel are being neglected. Unless the girls bring up additional topics, I would focus on a single topic for any given meeting. (I have included topic selections below, but I am sure you will start your own list.)

4. Make sure everyone gets to say something, and keep in mind you and Nick should not dominate the meeting. Teach them (children and husband) how to listen as well as how to communicate.

5. If anything negative comes up, focus on what to do to fix the problem or prevent it from happening again. Do not let this become a gripe session.

6. End the meeting by deciding, as a group, on a fun event for the family to do together.

7. Make sure to schedule the next meeting, but let the girls know they can schedule an "emergency" mini-meeting if they have something they want to discuss as a family.

Possible Topics (When appropriate, add "Why" as a follow-up question)

- Specific Values (from your "secret" list)
- Family Projects: Charity-related or Savings Goal (something small for the house/family)
- What was the best thing you did this week?
- What is one thing you would really like to do?
- What is the one thing you would wish you did not have to do?
- What is the most interesting thing you learned?
- Who is your best friend?
- The question you would really like an answer to is ...
- If I had all the money in the world, I would ...

One thing I would suggest is that you have a chat with Nick beforehand, so he knows what you intend to bring up and he does not feel unprepared. You could also use that as a way to bring up issues with him in a non-confrontational manner.

E-mail From: Red
Subject: Have A Fun Family Meeting!
Sent: Tuesday, April 20

I can't believe you came up with this so quickly. It sounds like it could actually be fun. I assume this is something Larry and you have done with the girls.

E-mail From: Black
Subject: Have A Fun Family Meeting!
Sent: Tuesday, April 20

You must be kidding! I can only remember a few occasions when Larry was forced to sit down as a family to discuss a specific issue, and he could not wait to get it over with. (For example, when I set up a Family Foundation to teach the girls about charity.) However, I tried to do it informally when we had meals together. It actually was a good way to "catch-up" on the girls' lives since we only saw them on alternate weekends.

E-mail From: Red
Subject: Have A Fun Family Meeting!
Sent: Tuesday, April 20

Makes sense. You said you needed to talk to Larry about some things. So are you going to schedule a "fun" meeting?

Not to start with, but I am going to try and bring up the subject of us trying to talk more. I think I will introduce the concept by finding out what he does at work in terms of staff meetings. Our marriage seems to be more of a business relationship than anything else, so that may be the best way to approach things.

Somehow I think your meetings will be more fun! EOM

No wonder all her suggestions seemed so businesslike. It seemed as if Black and her husband were well-suited for one another because they both looked at everything from a business perspective. But I couldn't help but wonder if that was the root of some of her issues — the lack of a more personal relationship. But as I thought about it, I realized the key wasn't a function of warm and fuzzy vs. pragmatic. It was more a function of understanding what would work best for everyone involved.

Recognize Warning Signs And React Calmly

IM How was dinner? Any progress on the talking front?

IM What was I thinking? I know better than to try and have an impromptu conversation with an engineer.

IM Why do I think this isn't going to be good?

IM I mentioned you were trying to focus on what is important in life and told Larry about my idea to use a Sharpie to write interest rates and goals on your credit cards. He said that would never work for me because my American Express card is black and so I would not be able to read it.

IM That was a clever comment.

IM I agree. I laughed and said I could always use a white Sharpie. Then he looked at me and in a very stern tone said, "What would be your goal? To see how much you could spend in a month?"

IM Was he serious? Has he ever mentioned your spending before?

IM He was VERY serious. To the point it caught me totally off-guard. He has never said anything about my spending, other than to joke around and say if my American Express card ever got stolen, he would not report it because he knows the thief would spend less than me.

IM So what did you say?

IM The smart-ass in me wanted to say that would be an interesting experiment, but given the tone of his voice I knew better. For a fleeting moment I thought about trying to explain how I shopped out of boredom, but I decided tonight was probably not the night for a serious discussion. Something about how he instantly went from a humorous comment to such a serious mood concerned me.

IM But what DID you say?

IM I started babbling on about you and your credit cards. And how sheltered you were. And how little you knew about finances ... blah-blah-blah.

IM Gee, thanks.

IM No, thank you. It gave me a logical transition from his comment. Otherwise, if I had actually answered his question, it could have ended up an ugly evening. However, it made me aware my spending is apparently an issue with him and something we need to talk about. Next week I will remind him of the comment and suggest we talk.

IM Whoa! You have been saying you need to talk to Larry about things, and now he gives you a topic you can use to open up communications, and you are going to wait until next week? Sounds like you are avoiding the issue.

IM Not avoiding. Temporarily postponing. He is supposed to close on the high-rise this Friday, so that may be the real issue since it was my idea to buy the third unit and the architectural plans are fairly elaborate. Anyway, I am supposed to go to the track to test this weekend, and although it is cheap compared to a race weekend, it is not free. I hate to bring up the topic of my spending habits and then immediately go off to play with my Ferrari.

IM So you admit your spending habits could be considered excessive?

IM Definitely. But I also know why I spend money, which means I understand the conversation will be about more than just money. Which is why it needs to wait until we can sit down and give ALL the issues the attention they deserve. And that definitely was not tonight, not when we had been drinking and not in response to a snide comment about my American Express. Which reminds me — did you ever figure out why your American Express bill was so high?

IM Yes. Because I procrastinated and let it get out of control.

IM How bad was it?

IM Medium bad, but not as bad as I expected. There were several items for the house that I had forgotten about, but they were within budget. However, I did find spending in a few categories, especially eating out, had crept back up and exceeded the budget. No real disaster, although we have to rein in our spending again.

IM You have been spending a lot of time dealing with the house and the move, which explains why this routine task did not get done as quickly as you would have liked. But it certainly does not sound like it was "out of control."

IM Maybe that was a slight exaggeration. But that doesn't change the fact I'm annoyed at myself because the extra money we spent was pure waste and could have been avoided if I'd been paying attention.

IM When it comes to wasting money, you are a mere amateur. I am a professional. Just ask Larry. However, you need to give yourself some credit — you realized you needed to monitor expenditures more diligently; you caught the early warning signs and took control of the situation.

IM I think you're just being nice and probably think I'm stupid, but I'll admit I feel better having done it and knowing the truth.

IM You forget ... I do not "do" nice. I think you did the things that were highest priority first and, unfortunately, some other important, but lower priority, items were delayed. I do not think you are stupid, but stubborn does come to mind. I still think you should automatically download your American Express receipts.

IM I disagree. Manually entering the information helps remind me of where our money is going and that's one of MY reality checks on life. Just like you with Make-A-Wish. Which is just one more reason I need to try and make it a daily habit. Night-night.

And I believed that. Plus, as Black pointed out, it allowed me to recognize warning signs and react calmly, which was such a nice change from all the firefighting I initially had to do. I was determined to make sure things did not get out of control, and I knew that meant I'd probably need an assortment of reminders.

Try To Remember Important Things Every Day

E-mail From: Black
Subject: Daily Reminders
Sent: Wednesday, April 21

Save this e-mail as proof I admit when I am wrong. I changed my mind about you manually inputting your American Express charges. When I thought about it, it made perfect sense. For me, my American Express charges are just numbers that prove money cannot buy happiness, but it sure can disguise unhappiness. Anyway, I know I said Make-A-Wish is my reality check, and it is, but sometimes we all lose track of what is really important and need more frequent reminders.

I know you plan on having a "Values and Priorities" list and I think that is a great idea, although I am not sure how you plan to use/review the list. Occasionally I save meaningful e-mails in my "Blue Book," and there are a few quotes and greeting cards with words of wisdom in there too. They are in a section marked "Daily," and although I do not look at them every day, I do read them on a fairly regular basis.

This week I have been thinking about my Mission Statement. Typically, when I did this in corporate life, the first step was a fairly long narrative of where the company started, a summary of how and why it evolved as it did, and where it was going and why. It was a tedious process, requiring multiple gyrations, to condense it into a single sentence or even a short paragraph. I have started doing that for my personal Mission Statement. It is a very interesting process to put the words to paper, and has made me think about so many things. Many of which I have not thought about for a long time and yet poured out of me over the weekend. And just like your list is currently a work-in-progress, I think my Mission Statement will remain that way too. At least for a while.

However, it has given me an idea that I think would work for each of us and goes back to a very simple concept from our childhood. A journal or a diary. I have added a recurring daily task to my Franklin Planner called "Thought for the Day." Every night I am going to reflect on my day — think about the highlight of the day, what gave me joy, what made me pause and think, or maybe even what I could have done better or differently — and note it in my journal. I went online to Levenger (the company where I found the Circa binders) and ordered a five-year journal that only has room for a few sentences for each day, which means we would have no excuse for not being able to find the time to write something.

I used the term "we" because I ordered one for you. My treat.

Black told me to save this e-mail as proof that she'll admit when she's wrong. No way! I was going to save it because it was proof of her softer side. And I loved the idea of a journal, although I wasn't sure I needed something else to add to my daily list of things to do.

IM   I'm surprised you're up so early this morning based on how late last night, or technically, how early this morning you sent that e-mail. Want to talk about it?

IM   Not really. I thought it was self-explanatory. I will let you know when the journals arrive.

IM   Will you let me know when you complete your Mission Statement? Any chance you would let me read it?

IM   Sure. You plan to write one after you finish your "Values and Priorities" list?

IM   Nope. I'm just curious about yours.

IM   I suppose you are going to ask to read my journal, too? Not sure why though, my life is pretty much an open book.

IM   No kidding. It's like a Judith Krantz or Danielle Steel novel!

IM   Does the heroine always live happily ever after in those books? FYI, that is a rhetorical question — I do not want to know how my book ends. My life is better than a novel. My life is real. And I have things to do. EOM

Boy, this morning's IMs were certainly full of understatements, but the one that really hit home was about her life being real. I could tell she was in the midst of questioning things about her life and the choices she had made, and yet she still seemed so optimistic about the future. Maybe it truly was as simple as remembering the positive instead of fearing the negative. It would be nice to think so.

16

I Have Three Children
If You Count My Husband

E-mail From: Red
Subject: Your advice on the girls?
Sent: Wednesday, April 21

I know there's a lot going on in your life right now. Probably more than you're willing to let on. You seemed to be in a hurry to get offline earlier today, and I wasn't sure whether it was because you were busy with other things or because you wanted to avoid certain topics.

I've been thinking about my "Values and Priorities" list and your idea of a family "Board Meeting." I really like the idea, especially because it includes the girls. However, to be honest, I'm not sure I'll ever get around to doing it. Do you have any other suggestions?

E-mail From: Black
Subject: Your advice on the girls?
Sent: Wednesday, April 21

I am trying to get ready for a 9:00 meeting downtown with the architects. Larry is closing on the high-rise on Friday, and the next step is to select the construction company. I will call you from the car.

Even before Nick was fired, I often wondered and worried about the best way to raise our children. But when he got fired, so many other things diverted my attention. Now that things were settling down and my responsibilities had increased, I needed to make sure the girls weren't getting short-changed.

Munchkin Management

I've always believed that home is a child's first school, because that's where the foundation of their social and emotional skills and values is established. This "at home" education is as important, and maybe even more important, than many of the subjects children are taught in school. This isn't meant to undervalue the importance of a school education, but instead to stress the importance of a complete education.

Although we entrust teachers with our children's formal education, it doesn't mean we can or should ignore our own responsibilities as parents.

📱 Hello. This is the evil Stepmom here to answer all your child-raising questions. How may I help you?

☎ Very funny.

📱 I cannot believe you think you have been neglecting the girls. If you need proof, look at your Franklin Planner and all the things related to them.

☎ But those are mostly activities. I want to find a way to teach them about the more important things. Like the life lessons I have learned since Nick was fired.

📱 Children are like sponges and absorb everything around them, so whether you realize it or not, you have already started teaching them what you have learned. Not to mention that you have been doing "warm and fuzzy" with them since they were born.

☎ That's all fine and good, but I need more specific suggestions. You're very pragmatic. How did you handle Larry's girls when you became a stepmom?

📱 First, you need to remember I had the luxury of easing into the role because Larry only had possession of the girls on alternate weekends and school holidays. When we were dating, I only made "guest appearances" because I did not want to intrude on their relationship with their dad. And because I had no desire to be a full-time parent, I made it very clear I was not trying to replace their mom.

☎ That too is all fine and good, but not very helpful.

📱 Patience, grasshopper. You also have to remember that when I first started dating Larry, his girls were 7 and 9, so I skipped over the phase you are in. I had dated men with children, but none as young as Larry's, so I was not quite sure how to deal with them. So I decided to treat them like little people. In fact, that is why I started calling them the "Munchkins," like the little people from *The Wizard of Oz*.

☎ I always wondered about that. Were you the good witch or the bad witch?

📱 Neither. I was probably more like the Mayor of Munchkin City. Since I was used to working in a corporate environment, I applied the same people skills.

☎ You're kidding, right?

📱 Not really. For example, anytime I was put in charge of a new department or hired new employees, I tried to be patient because I realized people need time to adjust to a new environment and/or new responsibilities. I did not expect them to "get it" immediately. I always tried to pose things as a request vs. making a demand. And I would ask them what they needed help with vs. waiting for them to have a problem. I took the same approach with the Munchkins.

☎ That makes a lot of sense. And what about when Larry and you decided to live together?

📱 Same basic approach. Plus, by moving into a new house, it provided the perfect opportunity to establish ground rules. I even created a document called "Rules of the House."

☎ You had a list of rules? I love it! Can I get a copy?

📱 The point is not the list, but the concept. I figured they needed to know what was expected of them in our house vs. what they might do in their mom's house or had done in their dad's house. The rules also provided consistency — they knew they would not change each weekend depending on my mood or memory. All the rules were reasonable. In fact, most were common sense.

☎ Such as?

📱 Flush after you use the toilet. Brush your teeth every morning and night. The piano can only be used with permission.

☎ Those are rules in our house, too, but they seem simple enough that I wouldn't think you needed a formal document.

📱 True. But I knew employees basically wanted to please management, so I figured kids wanted to please their parents. I presented most of the rules as things to do — not things not to do. For example, instead of saying "no screaming in the house," I said, "loud screaming is to be done outside only." I looked at the rules as an opportunity for them to achieve and succeed, not as a set of restrictions. It also allowed me to teach them priorities. For example, homework had to be done first thing on Saturday, and there was no television or other activities until it was finished.

☎ Now I'm starting to understand. And what happened if they broke any of the rules?

📱 Initially they were reminded of the rule and soon they all became habits, but I never focused on punishing them for breaking a rule. Quite the opposite — they earned their weekend allowance by following the rules. I always found it more effective, with the girls as well as employees and even Larry, to reinforce positive behavior rather than punish bad behavior. It can be as simple as a "thank you," complimenting them on their efforts or maybe even reward a job well done.

☎ For someone with no prior training, you seem to have caught on to the parenting job pretty well.

📱 How difficult is it to be honest and upfront with people about expectations? And explain what they need to do or not do? And acknowledge their efforts? I hate to state the obvious, and I know there is a lot about being a parent that I do not have a clue about, but like I said earlier … children are just little people.

Black, as always, explained things in a straight-forward, no-nonsense way. I liked her idea of treating kids as "little people." And although initially I was looking for specific suggestions, this conversation made me step back and look at the big picture. Treat children with respect and honesty, trust them with responsibility and give them credit for understanding and doing the right thing. I had never consciously thought of child-rearing that way, but when I began to think about it, I realized that this was how I had always tried to treat children, my own as well as others.

Monkey See — Monkey Do

And so I began to think back over the last few months and how I had handled my children during our crisis. Black's comments about children being like sponges and absorbing things reminded me of the first days of my crisis when I was trying to learn the most basic financial concepts. Black had made what I thought was a flippant comment about my lack of financial experience being attributable to my childhood, but after some nagging on my part, I finally got her to spend (I think she'd use the word "waste") a day explaining that concept to me. Since then I have come to see that so much of what we do as adults is a function of what we were exposed to as children.

📱 I am on my way home. Any more questions on topics I am not qualified to answer?

☎ How was your meeting?

📱 That I am qualified to answer. Productive. Next step is interviewing contractors. Any other questions?

☎ Yes. I have a "do as I say, not as I do" question.

📱 A philosophical question or one about a specific disconnect?

☎ A disconnect?

📱 Sorry. Oilfield lingo. When drilling a well, if the pipe did not line up, there would be a "disconnect."

☎ Great. And what does that have to do with this conversation?

📱 A "disconnect" sums up some situations perfectly. Like when there is a gap in logic. Or when words and actions do not match.

☎ Got it. Well, at least in terms of words and actions, I think I do. Not sure I understand the drilling part. Anyway, I think you just answered my question.

📱 You did not ask a question.

☎ I was going to ask you how you deal with conflicting messages. For example, when we were growing up, Mom's words regarding what was important were very different than her actions. I was going to ask how to make sure the girls don't get confused. But now the answer is obvious — make sure the words and actions match.

📱 Exactly. You have to "walk the talk."

☎ Another tee-shirt slogan?

📱 No. Another throwback to my corporate life. It meant that your actions better support your words, whether they are directed at your employees, your board of directors or the investment community. Because at the end of the day there is nothing more influential than the power of example. Funny thing is I have come to realize it is even more important in your personal life.

☎ Care to expand on the personal life part?

📱 The lessons you teach by example will have a greater impact than "teaching by preaching," which is what happens when you use "do as I say, not as I do." A phrase, as you know, that I have always found very annoying.

☎ Then why do you always use it on me?

📱 I think "always" is an exaggeration. But when I do, it is either because our circumstances are not the same and so the actions need to be modified, or I am intentionally making a "less than prudent" decision and do not want you to follow my lead.

☎ Why would you make an intentionally stupid decision?

📱 There is a huge difference between a stupid decision and a "less than prudent" decision, but that goes back to my risk/reward tolerance level.

☎ So are we now talking about your personal life?

📱 This conversation started with you asking how to make sure you are setting a good — and consistent — example for your girls, and I answered your question. This is about you. Not me. Any other questions?

☎ Not right now, but maybe later.

📱 Yes, you are very consistent on that front.

The more I thought about it, the more obvious it became. I realized that I was setting some good examples for the girls, although I might not be verbalizing the lessons I was teaching them. I also saw (to my surprise, I might add) that sometimes one of the girls was the teacher and I was the student. Either way, the bottom line was that I wanted to make sure the importance of all these lessons wasn't missed.

E-mail From: Red
Subject: Words OR Actions?
Sent: Wednesday, April 21

I decided to go back and work on my "Values and Priorities" list in light of our conversation about having words and actions match, and realized that sometimes there might only be words OR actions. I know words alone won't make as strong an impact. There will be times I'll have to make a conscious effort to set a good example. However, there will be times when there are only actions. Then what?

I don't want philosophy, I need specific suggestions, so let me give you a few specific examples:

Situation One: Right after Nick was fired, Natasha wanted to go to Mad Potter to make pottery and I was uncomfortable spending the money. You suggested a painting session at home instead. I doubted that would satisfy her, but she was thrilled with the idea. The whole family ended up participating and everyone had a great time.

Situation Two: Recently, Natasha wanted to go to Chuck-E-Cheese — more to play the arcade games than to eat pizza, so I suggested that we go to the park instead. We had a great time and this is the unbelievable part — on the way home she told me that the park was a lot of fun, even more fun than Chuck-E-Cheese would have been, and that she wants to do it again. Soon!

In both situations there was a great lesson to be learned by all of us: It's the time we share together, not the amount of money we spend together, that's most important. How do I make sure the girls (and Nick!) get the message?

E-mail From: Black
Subject: Words OR Actions?
Sent: Wednesday, April 21

For years, or at least the past few months, I have been telling you that money cannot buy happiness. Philosophically you may have known that, but experiencing it proved it. It also demonstrated the best way to teach the girls (Nick will be a harder "sales job") about important values is by showing them.

E-mail From: Red
Subject: Words OR Actions?
Sent: Wednesday, April 21

I understand all that. And I know actions speak louder than words. My question was: What do I do if there are only actions? How do I make sure they get the message?

E-mail From: Black
Subject: Words OR Actions? BOTH!
Sent: Wednesday, April 21

Tell them! Next time you are all doing something fun at the house or you go to the park, casually bring up the "lesson" in conversation. It is as simple as thinking out loud.

It works for financial things too. For example, I know you shop at different grocery stores for different things based on price and selection. Whenever you are shopping with the girls, think out loud. Verbalize your decision process. This will work not only at grocery stores, but whenever or wherever you are spending money.

And tonight, before you leave for our Wednesday night out, casually mention that this is your escape time, similar to when Woof hides behind the couch.

E-mail From: Red
Subject: Words OR Actions? BOTH!
Sent: Wednesday, April 21

Don't you ever get tired of pointing out the obvious to me? Anyway, that all makes perfect sense. I like your idea of thinking out loud. And as part of this learning process, I think YOU should take Natasha shopping and "think out loud." And I would love to tag along. I'll even bring the popcorn.

E-mail From: Black
Subject: Words OR Actions? BOTH!
Sent: Wednesday, April 21

No way I am taking Natasha shopping with me. I remember the first time she saw my tattered Dolce & Gabbana jeans, and she told me they were "broken." I could not figure out how to explain to her that (1) I bought them that way and (2) I paid a lot of money for them. When I realized I could not explain it to her, it made me realize how foolish fashion can be. Fun, but still foolish.

I remember that day. Natasha was honestly questioning Black about her jeans, and Black responded, "I know they are broken, but I think they are fun. Sometimes I do silly things just for fun!" Thinking back, it made me realize how easy it would be to explain some of my actions. This would guarantee the words and actions match.

This approach can also be applied to habits. For instance, I'm pretty organized. I usually put the mail directly on my desk vs. dropping it on the kitchen counter, there's a hook for the car and house keys, etc. Besides the fact I can find things when I need them, I'm hopeful the girls will learn to do the same. However, if I was the type person who just threw everything everywhere, then I shouldn't be surprised if my kids can't find their shoes when I'm trying to get them out the door! Now don't get me wrong — I know that my kids will be messy because it's part of their job description. But I'm also optimistic that by setting a good example I'm increasing the odds they'll pick up some of my better habits — if not today, then maybe tomorrow.

☎ Got a minute? I need to make a confession.

☎ For that I'll make time.

☎ I was thinking about my "Rules of the House." I added a rule "no television or videos between the hours of noon and 5:00 p.m. without special permission." It was really more for Larry than the girls, although everyone benefited.

☎ You call that a confession? I wanted something a little — no, make that a lot — more interesting!

☎ Sorry to disappoint, but I wanted to bring to your attention that some of the rules and examples you use for the girls can also apply to husbands. In fact, I created this rule because I was annoyed with Larry. On the weekends we had the girls, he would play golf early in the morning while they were still sleeping, and when he got home he would sit on the couch watching television all day while the girls were upstairs in their rooms. He basically had no interface with the girls except for meals. I did not want to get into a discussion about my opinion of his parenting efforts, so instead I figured out how to stop him from watching television all day. I positioned it as he needed to set a good example for his girls.

☎ Very clever. Did it work?

☎ Even better than planned. Besides the fact it forced Larry to do more with the girls once they finished their homework, the "no television hours" provided the girls with time to read, play games or merely daydream.

☎ I'm impressed. With the idea, not the confession. Unless, of course, you want to explain why you didn't want to talk to Larry about parenting issues.

☎ Hey, do as I say, not as I do.

I knew better than to try and continue this conversation. The important thing was that the more I realized my kids would play "Monkey See, Monkey Do," the more I paid attention to what I was telling them (and Nick) with my words. And my actions.

Thinking Out Loud — Requires Thinking First

And then there are times when words need to stand alone.

📱 Have a few minutes?

☎ Maybe. Depends on the topic.

📱 No real topic. I arrived late for school pickup, so I'm stuck in the back of the line and don't have anything to read.

☎ So in other words you need to waste some time and called me. Thank you so much. Have you thought about using your car as a place of quiet and solitude? A place to escape. Or hide.

📱 Tried that. Doesn't work well. Too many windows.

☎ I was being sarcastic.

📱 I wasn't. In fact, the first few days after Nick was fired, I often escaped to the privacy of my car to have a good cry. I didn't want the girls, and to some extent Nick, seeing me upset since I wasn't sure how to explain things to them. H-E-double-hockey-sticks — at that point I didn't even understand!

☎ What did you just say about hockey sticks???

📱 Sorry, it's a habit. I do not say "hell" in front of the girls.

☎ Anyway, I do remember your initial crying escapes, but it was not long before you explained the situation to the girls.

📱 We really didn't have any choice — they were going to notice that Nick was no longer going to work. I remember you telling me to calm down and think through what we were going to tell them, instead of doing an impromptu speech.

☎ I did? I remember telling you to calm down, but that seemed to be my response to every topic. But that now seems years ago ... not three months ago.

📱 I already knew that children count on their parents for the truth, but you made me realize I didn't have to go into all the details of the situation for the sake of honesty and truth. That I only needed to provide age-appropriate information. It was a valuable lesson that I still use.

☎ Funny the things we remember. I forgot exactly what we discussed, but I remember thinking about Mom and the bum on the street.

📱 I don't think I ever heard that story, but since we're wasting time — go for it.

☎ I was probably about 5 or 6, and Mom had taken me into New York City for the day, and we walked past a homeless person. He was living in a cardboard box in a doorway. I remember asking Mom about him, and she explained he was there because he did not have a job. I never thought about it again until Nick was fired.

📱 Why? Did you think we were going to be homeless?

☎ No, but it made me realize what an impact that image and Mom's associated explanation made on me if I remembered it decades later. Imagine if Daddy had ever lost his job. I probably would have thought that meant we were going to end up living on the street. What a scary thought to put in a child's mind.

📱 It's strange how certain memories stick with you. I remember you telling me not to use the word "fired" because the girls might confuse it with guns or a firing squad. It's important to remember to look at things from a child's viewpoint. Which is just one more reason why I always need to carefully think about what I say to the girls before I actually say it.

☎ True, but keep things in perspective. Do not overanalyze everything. What is that quote about paralysis from analysis? Sometimes I think the reason Larry and I never talk about anything important is because he chooses his words so carefully and puts so much thought into it that it could take days to have a 15-minute conversation. Whereas I am the total opposite. Sometimes the first time I realize what I am thinking is when I hear the words come out of my mouth.

📱 I'll try to find someplace in the middle.

☎ Or at least something positive. You do not teach children by showing them what not to do. I never had to teach children how to carefully cross the street, but I know I would not demonstrate the concept by showing them a dead squirrel in the middle of the road!

I don't know where Black comes up with her analogies, but they're almost always amusing. And this one is going to be hard to beat. But it reminded me of how we explained moving to the girls. We told them the truth but kept it simple and emphasized the positive. Rather than explaining we were moving to a neighborhood with better public schools rather than continuing with private school, we positioned it so that from our daughter's eyes she'd be able to walk every day to a new "big-girl school." And when Black reinforced our message by telling Natasha she always enjoyed walking to school and sometimes even got to bicycle there, Natasha became even more excited about this new opportunity.

It's funny. Once I started calmly thinking about things, it seemed easier to find the words. Granted, whenever it came to significant issues, I'd talk to Black first so that she'd give me her pragmatic outlook and then I'd personalize it by adding the "warm and fuzzy." It was obvious that the key was thinking first.

Teaching Children About The "Magic" Of Money

📱 Hey. Glad I caught you. Natasha and I are in Target, and she wants a new Barbie doll and clothing. I told her I'd give you a call and see what you think.

☎ Why are you getting me in the middle of this? Is this some kind of setup?

📱 You're right. I'd love to buy the girls all the things they want, but I don't have endless supplies of money. I know I hand them a card at the checkout counter, but then the card company sends me a bill in the mail, and I have to send them money. It's not a magic card. What do you think?

☎ Let me guess ... she is listening to your side of this conversation.

📱 Yes.

☎ Does she get an allowance?

📱 No.

☎ Do you have enough money in your household budget for the doll but not the clothing? Do you know for sure, or do you have to go home and check? Explain your answers to me.

📱 That's true. Every month I know I'll want to buy the girls things, and so I put money in my budget. It's late in the month, and I'm not sure how much money is left. I know there's enough for the Barbie doll, but I don't think there's enough for the clothing.

☎ Budget is not a word she probably understands. Make it sound special.

📱 I don't think Natasha knows what a budget is. That's a very big-girl thing. I was much older than Natasha when I first learned about money and budgets.

☎ No kidding ... it was only a few months ago. I dare you to tell her the truth about that!

📱 Really? So you think she is old enough?

☎ Chicken! Budgets may be a little confusing, but an allowance might be a great way to start teaching her the value of money.

📱 So you think Natasha is old enough to learn about budgets? And maybe even get her own money? Are you sure?

☎ Anything else you want to say to Natasha while you are using me as a foil?

📱 No, that was a really good idea. I'm so glad we called you. Thanks.

OK, so maybe it was a little contrived, but it did serve my purpose. I was proud of the fact I had thought of the ploy. I'll admit I only planned on using the conversation to explain that credit cards are not magic money cards. I realized it would be hard to explain not having enough money to buy things because the girls never see us use cash in stores — only plastic. (They probably also think ATMs are magic money machines. At some point I'll need to explain that to them, too.) I knew I'd eventually need to introduce the concept of allowances, and later budgets, but since this opportunity had presented itself, I took full advantage of it.

E-mail From: Black
Subject: Allowances
Sent: Wednesday, April 21

That was a very clever maneuver you used at Target. I figure you are now going to ask me about allowances, and so I will tell you what I did with the Munchkins.

When I entered the picture, the girls had limited money at their disposal — basically Christmas and birthday gifts from relatives and a weekly allowance from their mom, although the girls said that she sometimes forgot to give it to them. Larry tended to buy them things when they asked for them, but I thought it would be better to give them an allowance. However, I was afraid to give them money for "doing nothing" because I did not want them to have an entitlement attitude, so they earned their allowances by following the "Rules of the House."

And before you ask how much we gave them, I need to tell you the amount was probably more than they really needed, but there was a reason for that. Although Larry paid substantial child support, we wanted to make sure there was extra money available for things that were important to the girls. Things they, and they alone, decided they wanted. In addition, rather than giving them cash, I set up an allowance account (and report) on Microsoft Money so they could see the total grow.

Using their allowance helped instill in them the value of money, since when they wanted to buy something, they would be spending their own money. They seemed to always think carefully about what they bought. I might add that it is interesting to see what they find important enough to buy for themselves.

E-mail From: Red
Subject: Allowances
Sent: Wednesday, April 21

I suspected there would be an e-mail waiting for me by the time I got home. Thanks! I know your situation is different from mine because you don't have the girls all the time, but I was thinking about tying their weekly allowance to household chores. What do you think?

E-mail From: Black
Subject: Allowances and Household Chores — 2 separate concepts
Sent: Wednesday, April 21

I think I am surprised you are online in the afternoon, but in response to your allowance question here are some ideas to consider first:

- If they do not need or want the money, does that mean they can skip chores that week?

- Do you ever want to hear "how much will I get paid?" if you ask them to do something?

- If you believe the girls should have a certain amount of responsibility around the house, then you should not tie chores to their allowance. (If they do not do their chores, do not take away their allowance. Instead, have them lose some of their privileges, like watching television or going to McDonalds.)

- Plus, if you want them to learn to manage their money, they have to know what they will be getting on a regular basis, which is another reason why their allowance should be kept "separate" from household chores.

E-mail From: Red
Subject: Allowances and Household Chores — 2 separate concepts
Sent: Wednesday, April 21

I only got online to quickly check e-mails before I started the girls' dinner. I thought I asked a simple question, and I get a list of bullet points! But you're right — I never thought about any of those things. I just thought it would be a good idea to link money and responsibility. I guess we can discuss this more tonight at dinner, although I'd prefer to hear about your weekend.

E-mail From: Black
Subject: Allowances and Household Chores — 2 separate concepts
Sent: Wednesday, April 21

Two more points and then I will let you go:

- Linking money and responsibility is a good idea, but I think it might be better to teach them the idea of working for your money vs. getting rewarded for something you should do anyway. (Rockefeller had an interesting approach to allowances. I will send it to you later.)

- You decide tonight's topic of discussion. I can talk about anything. And as you know, I rarely think before I speak, so no advance warning is necessary. EOM

E-mail From: Black
Subject: Rockefeller: Teaching the Value of Money
Sent: Wednesday, April 21

I know you are already offline, but I wanted to send this now while I was thinking about it.

When I was setting up the Family Charitable Foundation to teach the Munchkins about finances and charity, I researched wealthy families. I remember reading how billionaire John D. Rockefeller taught his children to value money. He raised vegetables and rabbits so his children could work and earn money. The kids were given a small weekly allowance and had to earn the rest of their money. All five boys were required to keep personal daily account books, give 10% of their income to charity and save 10% of their income. John D. obviously realized the importance of having his kids understand and value money.

P.S. — I wonder what his approach was to his wife's allowance.

I didn't get to read that last e-mail until after dinner, and by then I had learned more about Black's recent weekend away and the self-analysis she was doing in terms of her life. And the trade-offs she had made. And how money sometimes creates more problems than it solves. We never got to a movie, but as my friend Chris had said, Black's life is like a movie. On the surface it looked like a love story, but in reality it was a suspense novel because only time would tell where the next chapter would lead.

IM I'm surprised you're online. You OK?

IM Yes. Did you get my Rockefeller e-mail?

IM Yes. But with all that is going on in your life right now, how can you focus on stuff like that? Allowances can wait.

IM Life does not wait for you to figure it out. Life goes on. With or without you. The fact I have a lot to think about does not mean all I will do is think about things. If you want to discuss allowances or other financial topics — great. If not, good night. I am talked out on the warm and fuzzy topics. And the meaning of life. And the pursuit of happiness.

IM Sorry. On many fronts. And by the way, I too would be curious to know how Rockefeller handled his wife's allowance. I certainly like his approach to teaching kids about money and saving. However, since I'm not planning on raising rabbits or radishes, do you have any other suggestions?

IM The key was Rockefeller made his boys work for their money, he did not just hand it to them. I guess in that sense Larry is making me work for my money too. However, if you want specific suggestions for the girls, let me think about it and get back to you. I warn you there will be a lot of "do as I say, not as I do." Or maybe a better phrase would be "do as I wanted to do." EOM

I knew it was important to teach the girls about the true value of money. They needed to learn what money can buy — and what it can't buy. And although I felt like I had only recently learned that lesson, I could see it was a lesson that Black was relearning. Or maybe remembering was a better word.

E-mail From: Black
Subject: **Kids & Money ... ADULTS TOO!**
Sent: Wednesday, April 21

Allowances
An allowance is a good way to start learning about money and building healthy financial habits. From there, children can easily figure out that if they want more money, they have to come up with a way to earn it.

Earning Additional Money
Rockefeller made his boys work for their money. To some extent, I did the same thing by making the Munchkins earn their allowance by following the rules; however, the rules included some chore-type items. (Things like they had to make their beds every morning, they had to straighten their bathroom, clear the kitchen table.) But keep in mind they earned the allowance on a daily basis, so it was more like they were getting paid for doing that day's job.

The problem was we only had them on alternate weekends, so I did not have many opportunities to teach them the relationship between money and the value of service — in other words, service of greater value warrants a larger reward/payment. Part of the problem is Larry acts as if menial tasks are beneath him, so I could only imagine his response if I said I would let the girls "earn" more money by doing things that the maid or landscaper would typically do.

As far as specific suggestions for you, find jobs around the house that would not normally be their responsibility. Let them know it is something you would pay them to do, or help you do until they are old enough to do it alone. That way, they are not required to do it, but it is an option if they want to earn more money. For example: putting away groceries, sorting laundry, spring-cleaning closets, weeding the garden, washing the car.

Communication — Children
Try to explain money as a commodity (like the food in your pantry) with some to be used now, some saved for later. Just because it is there, it does not have to be used all at once. Remember, money is a tool, not an objective — so accumulating money is not really the lesson. Over time you can talk about more aspects of the true value of money — sometimes by "thinking out loud" and other times with a deliberate discussion.

One of the topics I listed for the Family Meetings was "If I had all the money in the world, I would ...." Maybe some of the financial issues can be dinner time discussions. Start out by making it a game with Nick. Ask him "What would you do if you found $10?" Then increase the number. To $100, then $1,000. If you play in front of the girls, they will want to play along. This will also teach all of you about communications and responsibility and make everyone realize financial decisions affect the entire family, not just the person spending the money.

Plus, it would be a great exercise for you and Nick as it lets you learn how to talk about money in front of the girls. As an aside, some people think one parent worrying about not having enough money or complaining the other spends too much is "talking about money." Wrong!

Larry and I never really talk about money in front of the girls. (Hell, we never really talk about money — period! See my next section.) It is one of my pet peeves, because I feel the girls have no concept of money. In the long run, he is doing them a huge disservice, especially since they stand to inherit millions. Talk about perfect prey for shysters. In fact, that is one reason I set up the Family Charitable Foundation — to educate the girls. Unfortunately, Larry is not helping me to get the girls to work on it, although all it requires him to do is to let them know it is important. I have already done all the work, and we all know it is not like I need more experience dealing with charity, tax accountants and lawyers!

Communication — Spouses
Couples talk about many things before marriage, but the meaning of money is typically not one of them. The fact Larry and I signed a prenuptial agreement only acknowledges we knew money was an issue. But it did not mean we discussed the value of money. And I am guessing Nick and you have not had that discussion either. But it is never too late. You just have to

be careful — it is a very complicated topic because it addresses deeper issues. (I can give you more first-hand knowledge after I try to discuss my American Express spending with Larry.)

As I told you earlier tonight, Larry and I are very different in many ways. Different is not necessarily bad, and everyone knows the cliché "opposites attract," but I think one of our fundamental issues may be money. I look at money as a medium of exchange. You use it to buy goods and services, both for yourself and others, which in turn can bring you pleasure or at least satisfaction. Plus, it can provide you with a sense of security and/or independence. Larry, like many successful businessmen, uses money as a way to measure his "success" (his definition, not mine) compared to other people. It is as if his net worth is his self-worth. The sad part is he never seems to enjoy anything his money can buy.

Lessons To Be Learned

Enough about Larry and me. The point I am trying to make is that the topic of money is very complex, and it is very easy to have words and actions disconnect. We each know what should be important, but sometimes we might not want to admit (to ourselves, let alone others) that our intentions are not quite as good as we know they should be. So first you must be honest with yourself.

To say there are many lessons to be learned — not only for children, but also adults and spouses — is an understatement. Good money management demands dedication, determination and discipline. But it is also important to remember money can bring pleasure. Money is not magical. Money itself should not be a goal. If you save every penny, you and your kids may learn to save, but you might never learn how to enjoy the money you have.

On a more practical level, you need to find a way to allow the girls, over time, to take control of their financial future. Spending teaches a child about choices. Some choices are better than others. If they make mistakes early, they will learn early. If they wait until later in life, as you did, mistakes can be more expensive and traumatic. By teaching them early, they will learn financial skills and, more importantly, they will learn life lessons.

It is never too early to start teaching children about money and money management. And it is never too late for us to learn more.

IM Good morning???

IM Why the "?s"

IM I just read your e-mail. All I can say is wow! It's a lot to absorb. Plus I'm not sure whether you're addressing my questions or your own.

IM Both. I was already thinking about many of the issues anyway; all I did was put them down in an e-mail. No big deal. Remember, financial priorities are merely the monetary representation of your personal values.

IM That's a mouthful. Anyway, your e-mail gives me a lot to think about, and when I have some quiet time, I plan to re-read it and give it careful thought. Specifically, how to implement some of it into our everyday lives.

IM Quick question. Did you get an allowance as a kid?

IM Yes. Just don't ask me how much or how old I was. Why do you ask?

IM I can not remember whether or not I did, however, I do remember Mom allowing me to "earn" gold jewelry by getting As in school. Makes me think of that old joke about where diamond jewelry comes.

IM Don't know that one, but it can't be as funny as your clothing budget! I still laugh thinking about the fact you never knew it was a punishment.

IM My budget, whatever Mom's intention, was still brilliant. I remember when I got older and wanted more than I had in my budget, I lied about my age and got a job. Obviously, I never minded budgeting as I made a career out of it. You want something to laugh about ... how about the fact Mom used to let you clean the toilets as a reward for being good.

IM Hey, I thought it was fun. All those bubbles and slopping around the water with a brush. Sawyer would love it!

IM If you say so. I still enjoy working with numbers. Do you still enjoy cleaning toilets?

IM I refuse to answer. Now let's go back to budgets. Do you think Natasha's too young to learn about them?

IM Only one way to find out ... try teaching her. She is not old enough to be a clothes-horse like me, but maybe you could start with a toy budget. If nothing else, it is a good way to practice arithmetic. And I would suggest you use real money instead of plastic. It will expose her to coins and currency. (Curiosity Question: Why do pennies, nickels and quarters get progressively larger, but dimes are the smallest?)

IM That's a great idea! Especially since no one in this family ever saw a budget, let alone had to stick to one, until fairly recently. Maybe I should sit Natasha and Nick down at the same time and talk to them about their respective budgets.

IM I suspect you are kidding, but actually that is a good idea. But I warn you — Natasha might catch on quicker to the concept of a budget than Nick.

IM Do you think you could ever live on a budget again?

IM Depends on the number, but in theory ... yes. EOM

It had taken me over 40 years to learn about financial matters, including budgets, but it never would have dawned on me to have a budget if money was plentiful. But I now knew, regardless of how much (or how little) money was involved, it was never too early (or too late) to learn. As I thought about it, I realized that teaching the girls about budgeting could accomplish several things besides the obvious arithmetic practice. It would save money because it would control spending. It would avoid endless battles because it would put an end to the constant requests to buy things. And a budget, combined with an allowance, would give the girls money to buy what they want and at the same time they would learn to make financial choices.

I decided to use the idea of "Monkey See, Monkey Do" to explain to the girls (and Nick, too, if he would listen) how I was on a budget, using my grocery budget as an example. I would start giving Natasha an allowance, and do the same for Sawyer when she is older. I wanted to introduce them to the concept of money. And values. This was an opportunity to teach them financial and life lessons — a better gift than anything I could ever buy them.

Kids Need Time To Play, Dream And Explore

As I thought about budgets and allowances and how to prioritize spending, I thought back to when Nick was first fired and how I wanted to cut out all nonessential expenses. At the time that included Natasha's swimming lessons. But Black stopped me and explained that it was important to maintain the girls' routine as much as possible. She made me realize that the girls would notice if their usual activities were significantly different, so I tried to not disrupt their everyday lives. This approach was further collaborated when my friend Chris, who is a teacher, told me that a routine makes children feel that their world is safe, dependable and consistent. Looking back, I saw how important (and true) that was, and I wanted to make sure it continued to get the attention it deserved.

☎ Busy?

☎ Yes, busy waiting on Larry's attorney to call me back about the closing documents. Why?

☎ I'm planning to introduce Natasha to the idea of budgets and so added that to one of my Franklin Planner lists. It made me think about the importance of having a routine, of managing my time and making sure to prioritize everything I have to do. I think I need to figure out how to teach the girls those lessons, too. What do you think?

☎ You mean get Natasha to start writing lists? Like you do? How about before she starts playtime you could have her write a list of all the games she wants to play and then prioritize them? And then if there is any time left, she might actually have a chance to play. What a great idea!

☎ I asked what I thought was a fairly straight-forward question, and I'm getting a typical smart-ass comment.

☎ Your question was rather vague. If you are asking whether you should introduce the girls to the idea of time management, the answer is yes. If you are asking whether you should teach them about writing lists, I will say, "Monkey See, Monkey Do." You are a compulsive list-writer, so I think the lesson you need to focus on is how to keep list-making in perspective.

☎ For the record, I wasn't referring to lists. I was thinking more about routines and schedules. And priorities. Does Franklin Planner do a kids version?

☎ I have no idea. What specifically are you trying to accomplish?

☎ Making sure the girls have a routine to their life. For example, even though Nick no longer goes to an office, we still save the weekends for doing things as a family. Part of that's because Natasha goes to school during the week, but I still plan to maintain that routine this summer.

☎ I am still not sure what you are trying to accomplish. I hope you are not planning on over-scheduling their time. I often think the Munchkins have too much of a routine. Or maybe I should say there is too much on their calendars. Between attending class, school activities and cheerleading practice, Wednesday dinners with Larry, alternate weekends with us and other scheduled items, they do not seem to have any time earmarked to be kids — to play, explore, dream, or just do nothing!

☎ Luckily my girls' schedules are much simpler than that. Or at least they are right now. I guess I was thinking more along the lines of daily routines. For now I'd be happy with some kind of after-school routine for Natasha. Or maybe I should say revising the current routine, which consists of her getting a snack, watching TV, and then, at some point, we get into a battle when I ask her to shut off the TV to work on her reading before dinner.

☎ And they wonder why kids today do not get enough exercise. Did you know the best way to grow a couch potato is to place it in front of a television at an early age?

☎ Clever, but try getting a child to turn off Scooby-Doo.

☎ I know better than that. Once you let her turn it on, it is not fair to ask her to turn it off until the mystery is solved. Even though you already know the evil monster is a mere mortal in a disguise, who would have gotten away with the crime if it had not been for "you meddling kids" or something like that.

☎ Excuse me, but how do you know so much about Scooby-Doo? Please tell me it has something to do with Brittney and Chelsea.

☎ Yes. It used to be their favorite television show. Although the plot of each episode seemed to follow a tried-and-true formula and the ending was predictable. Once they started watching it, they had to watch it to the end. I think the fact the show managed to meld comedy, adventure, mystery and horror into a cartoon that appealed to children, yet was accepted by parents, was extremely creative. And having the ages of the characters change, they were able to maintain and even increase their fan base. Even today, nostalgic adults enjoy the show.

☎ Great. Why are you siding with Natasha on this one?

☎ I am not taking sides. I am saying if you let her turn it on, she should be allowed to watch the entire show. Imagine watching a Hitchcock movie only to have someone turn it off ten minutes before the end. But why not have Scooby help you get Natasha to do her homework?

☎ Now that's a mystery I can't wait to see you solve. And am I the villain?

☎ Remember I told you one of my "Rules of the House" is no Saturday television or other activities until homework was finished? Modify that slightly, and let Natasha earn her television time by doing homework first.

☎ That's sounds good, but in reality she needs a break between school and homework.

☎ Then have a time limit of how much television she can watch before homework must be started. Or make it a trade. Maybe minute for minute. And build up a television-watching account.

☎ I like the time limit idea. I could make it a new rule. Right now Natasha's only homework is reading, so even if I limit her TV time, she can still do her homework and even have time left over to do other things. And although Sawyer isn't in school yet, she's still at an age when she listens to Mommy, so setting up a maximum TV time and redirecting her to other activities would probably be pretty easy. Then, hopefully, this will become more of a habit as she gets older. The problem will be getting them to turn off the TV when they can see that Nick is watching TV!

☎ Do not forget that I was able to get Larry to follow the television rules by explaining that he was a role model for the girls. I am not sure it would have worked with him on a daily basis, but it did on Munchkin weekends.

☎ How could I forget that? I thought it was very clever. Any other husband tricks you want to share?

☎ "Tricks" makes it sound like I am training a dog. And lately I feel there is a lot of truth to the saying "you cannot train an old dog to do new tricks!" However, I will try to come up with some ideas for the girls.

I was still concerned about her situation with Larry, but I wasn't going to ask any more questions on that front. Plus I understood there was a limit to how much re-training you can do with a husband. However, I was confident she'd have some useful suggestions in terms of the girls.

E-mail From: Black
Subject: Time Management for Kids
Sent: Thursday, April 22

Here are a few suggestions off the top of my head. The warning that comes with this e-mail is the Munchkins were 7 and 9 when I first met them. Since Natasha is not yet 6 and Sawyer is not yet 2, I have no experience with kids that age!

Calendars/Schedules

- For each girl print a blank daily calendar that shows the days of the week on one axis and the hours of the day on the other.
- Fill in the blanks with EVERYTHING that has to be done. For Natasha, that might include homework, school, meals, sleep, etc. For Sawyer, you might want to use pictures as well as words, and the tasks might be simpler. (Brushing your teeth, getting dressed, etc.)
- The girls can then see where their time goes and where there is free time.
- If you want to control television time, allocate a portion of their free time to their favorite shows.
- You might also want to earmark "veg" time — daydreaming, reading or just doing nothing.
- Set up a reward program for keeping to the plan. Anything except money. (Maybe bonus television time, a movie or picking a favorite restaurant, etc., after keeping to the plan for five days.)

Task Lists

On Munchkin weekends, I would make sure to include a few things on my Daily Task list for the girls. It might be things we needed to discuss or shopping they had mentioned they wanted to do. Or sometimes it was time blocked off to go to a movie or the golf course. The important thing was there were items designated with an "M" for Munchkins. I also included some "L" items for Larry.

On either Friday night or Saturday morning, we would talk about our plans for the weekend, and I would find out how much homework they had to do. Sometimes I would have to modify my initial plans, but all in all it was a very good system. I left a printed copy of my list on the kitchen counter where everyone could see it. During the course of the weekend we would accomplish most, if not all, of the items. After a while, the girls started mentioning things to put on the list for next time. As they got older, they even had me buy them organizers so they could start keeping track of their own calendars and lists.

☎ I saw your e-mail. The part about the girls makes perfect sense. But I especially like the part about creating a list of things for Nick to do.

☎ I do not need to tell you that Nick, like any other husband, will not be happy with a daily "to do" list. However, what I found was that when I included Larry's "honey-dos" on my list, he saw he had so few items in comparison to me, he usually did not gripe. Plus, he knew he was doing it in his capacity as a role model, not because I was nagging him. And he only had to do it two weekends a month. I am not sure how well this would work on a regular basis, but I guess you have nothing to lose by trying. You might want to start out with just weekends.

☎ It's worth a try. I think adding everyone to my weekend list might be a great way to introduce the concept.

☎ Just be careful that you do not become too list- and schedule-oriented with the girls and Nick. I know you and I love our lists and tend to be overly organized and goal-driven, but be careful not to overload them. Sometimes I find the Munchkins have too much they are trying to get done in a limited amount of time.

☎ Until the girls are older, I doubt I'll have that problem.

☎ You mean they never get so wrapped up in something that you can not get them to stop?

☎ Yes, that often happens when they're painting or playing outside. What do you do then?

☎ At that point, we look at what else needs to be done and decide if anything can wait. If it is a choice between schoolwork or a fun project, the answer is easy, although I use those occasions to get them to really focus on the school work so if time permits, we can get back to the "fun."

☎ Like a bribe?

☎ Like I always say ... whatever works. However, there have been times when it is all school work, which means everything was important and had a deadline. Then I had to go against my nature as a perfectionist and teach them to prioritize — that not every-thing had to be "done to the max." But I used those occasions to explain we needed to start working on the big projects well before their due date.

☎ Says the woman who wrote her MBA thesis the night before it was due!

☎ To be accurate, it was the day and night before. It was turned in on time and nothing was neglected ... except for a night of sleep.

☎ Fine. So, do you ever use your "eating an elephant" analogy with them?

☎ Not that I can remember, but they did learn a lot from our vacations.

☎ Huh?

☎ The girls used to laugh at me because they knew I made hotel and flight reservations months, sometimes even a year, in advance. As the vacation would get closer, I would start making dinner reservations and booking any activities the girls wanted to do. I explained it was because we traveled at the same time so many other people do — when school is out — and that I wanted to make sure we could accomplish everything on their vacation wish list. After the first few trips, they saw how smoothly things went and began to understand the many advantages of planning ahead. And they stopped laughing.

☎ Let me guess, you gave them a printed itinerary.

☎ Of course, although it might not include everything I had planned because sometimes there were surprises. But even on vacation I tried not to over-schedule them. I made sure they had free time to relax or sleep late or add something else to the schedule. And that is not something that applies only to vacations ... you always need to make sure children have time to sleep. And time to daydream.

☎ What about me? I'd love to have more time to sleep and daydream. Not to mention time to eat all those bonbons that Mommy seems to think I eat by the dozens in my spare time!

☎ Sounds like a personal problem.

I have always been one of those annoyingly organized moms with my schedules and "To Do" lists. It's just the way I am, and so it was no surprise that I wanted to use some of these same skills to help my girls learn to organize themselves and their time. However, I initially didn't consider the amount of time and effort it would take to set up and implement these strategies. For example, one Saturday Natasha had two birthday parties at the same time. It would have been easier and quicker for me to pick one. Instead, I took the time to sit down with her and discuss the options — go to one early enough to get to the other or just pick one to attend.

Even little kids can be taught the basics of organizing and prioritizing. For example, I made cleaning up a game by asking Sawyer if she could pick up all her crayons and coloring stuff before I finished singing the alphabet song. The ideas are limited only by my imagination, and I keep everything age-appropriate and FUN!

Raising Your Husband As An Adult

My children, as Black had said, were indeed sponges. They were anxious to learn. And to please. I wished I could substitute the word "husband" everywhere this chapter refers to children. In some ways, they are a lot alike; however children are far more excited about learning. And certainly easier to "train."

IM You're online early this evening.

IM Quick dinner. I told Larry I had to review all the documents on the high-rise one more time tonight since closing is first thing tomorrow morning.

IM Then I will leave you alone.

IM Not necessary. Truth is, everything is ready to go. Larry was in a pissy mood all day, so I am trying to avoid him. I do not know what I would do if he was home all the time like Nick.

IM Tell me about it! I'm not sure which is the harder adjustment — having no money coming in or having Nick home all day.

IM I loved the fact Daddy worked from home. But it would partially explain why Mom slept late in the mornings and spent most of the day out of the house running errands.

IM Maybe. But Daddy being home was what we were used to, not a change in the routine.

IM I thought the girls had adjusted to Nick being home and that when he is in his workroom they leave him alone.

IM They have. And they do. I'm the one that's having a hard time adjusting. When we first sat down and talked with the girls about our new situation, I explained how they could help — not only by letting Nick work when he was in his office, but also by giving me more quiet time to handle new responsibilities.

IM Have they done that?

IM Yes. They seem to have adjusted to the fact that the pattern of my day and my availability to them is different. Not less, just different. Of course, they don't realize many of the traditional household responsibilities, like the finances, have moved from Nick to me, but they do like the ones that have moved in the other direction. Natasha loves the fact Nick handles some of the morning and afternoon school runs.

IM OK, let me see if I understand. The girls have adjusted to the changes. And Nick seems to be trying to help out more because he is around more. You no longer seem in a panic about everything. So what exactly are you having a hard time adjusting to?

IM Never mind. I'm just tired. I think I'll try to get to bed early tonight. Night-night.

There was no way I was going to admit the truth — the whole truth — to Black. I found having my husband in the house was a mixed blessing. I thought it was great that the girls and I got to see him more, but it was also difficult in that my expectations of him were probably unrealistic. Because he was at home, I expected him to automatically pick up more of the household chores. At times I fell into the trap of thinking that Nick was a mind reader and should know what I needed him to do and when. But the truth was he usually considered my requests reasonable and tried to help.

For me, the key was to have realistic expectations and try to look at things as opportunities, not as problems. And, most importantly, to keep the lines of communication open on all issues. I learned to try to emphasize the positive and use some of the skills that applied both in dealing with children and in the corporate world.

A Small Team Can Accomplish Big Things

I learned the best way to raise my children in times of crisis is no different than any other time — it's a matter of keeping all my priorities in perspective. Working together as a family we've been able to accomplish so much more than if I, or Nick and I, had tried to do this alone. And it wasn't as if there were any magic tricks. Everything was common sense. Well, it was, once I stopped to think about it.

As I have said before, I had come to see that so much of what we do as adults is a function of what we're exposed to as children. But now I realized there was a second part to that concept. One that was even more important. I now know that what our parents were like is entirely a matter of luck, but what our children are like is greatly influenced by their parents — which is entirely within our control. And it's our responsibility as parents to do the best possible job we can.

17
My Dozen Commandments

 Hello. Just checking in.

 I was surprised you weren't online this morning.

 I was, but you were still getting your beauty sleep. I got an early start since the closing was this morning.

 How did it go?

 OK, I think. Larry was still in a bad mood. One of the women from the mortgage company was amused that I was reviewing all the mortgage documents and then handing them to Larry to sign. She made a comment about how it must be great to have such a competent wife. Larry stared at her with such contempt that everyone at the table fell silent.

 Are you serious?

 Wish I was. I defused the situation by saying, "Yes, I am very good at spending his money. And buying three adjacent high-rise units at the same time is such an efficient way to do that. I guess I can skip Neiman Marcus today. Maybe even for a week!" Everyone laughed, and then I focused on getting the rest of the documents signed as quickly as possible.

 So what do you think is going on with Larry?

 Not exactly sure. It might have been the fact he took out a mortgage to buy the units instead of paying for them outright, but that was purely an investment decision in terms of mortgage rates vs. having to sell stock.

 I'd be thrilled to know we could qualify for millions of dollars of mortgage, let alone be able to buy it outright! You'd think Larry would be happy.

 Yes, you would. He is worth over $100 million, and yet he does not seem to enjoy life. Maybe he is starting to realize money cannot buy happiness. On second thought, nah!

 He must know that.

I am not so sure. I can remember vividly a Saturday night at Tony's with Brittney and Chelsea when they brought up the subject of the Golden Rule. Larry half-jokingly made his usual comment, "He who has the gold rules," and Chelsea proudly corrected him and explained it was "Treat others as you would have them treat you." The girls and I kept talking about it, but I honestly think Larry does believe what he said. And his actions do support my theory. Anyway, I think both statements are accurate, but I am not in the mood for a philosophical conversation. I have too many other things to do before I head to the track this weekend.

 I guess that means you don't want to discuss my "Values and Priorities" list.

 You have an uncanny knack for the obvious. I will put that on my list of things to do ... right after poke myself in the eye with a sharp object.

Although I would have loved to talk to her about my list, I knew she needed to escape to the track this weekend. So I decided I'd leave her alone, which left me time to think things through on my own.

Is "What" Or "Why" More Important?

On numerous occasions, Black had made me realize that thinking out loud was important and could apply to almost any topic. And I think it's important to teach not only what we believe, but also why. Recently, I had been seriously assessing my personal values and priorities. And now I was at the point where I wanted to make sure that I was teaching my children what I truly believed was important. And why.

Values And Priorities To Teach My Children

Lately, I had started jotting down notes and ideas, and threw them together in a large envelope. When I finally sat down to organize them, there were so many different issues I decided to physically cut them into separate pieces of paper. After sorting them into small piles based on the general concept or example, I then came up with a "commandment" for each pile. It reminded me of Black's elephant analogy, but in reverse. I was starting with lots of small pieces, trying to reconstruct the elephant. Or at least make sure the elephant had all the important body parts.

As I entered each individual Post-It Note and scrap of paper into a Microsoft Word document, I thought about Black's comment about how it took only 10 commandments to cover everything important. I kept rearranging and consolidating my thoughts, and although I wasn't able to be that concise, I was happy to get it down to 12. I knew that I'd continue to review and modify the list, and it would always be a work-in-progress, but it still was a valuable reminder of the ideas and concepts that I feel are incredibly important to teach my children.

1. Develop Self-Esteem and Self-Worth

- ☐ Focus on strengths, not weaknesses. Talk about what can be improved.

- ☐ Avoid embarrassing the girls out of anger or to make a point. It can lead to a lack of self-confidence and can hurt the bonds of trust.

- ☐ Give the girls the freedom to attempt something new and/or difficult, even if they may fail. Remember that we learn from our mistakes as well as our successes. The key is to emphasize they'll never succeed if they don't try.

- ☐ Explore new ideas to widen their (and my) horizons. Develop the confidence to admit there are things you don't know.

- ☐ Catch them doing something right! And praise, praise, praise! (Apply this to Nick, too!)

  Note: With the exception of Black, I can't think of anyone who doesn't like to be recognized for doing something well.

2. Be Responsible for Your Actions

- ☐ Household chores remind us that the family has needs in addition to our own personal desires. Learning to balance our needs against those of the family is a great way to learn responsibility. And teamwork.

- ☐ Let the girls know what I expect of them. Equally important, make sure they understand there are consequences for not doing what's expected. These consequences should be fair and clearly explained in advance.

3. Know "Right" from "Wrong"

- ☐ Because this is so obvious, it's easily overlooked — so make sure to explain how to tell the difference between right and wrong whenever possible.

- ☐ Whenever possible, encourage the girls to do the right thing by presenting them with more than one option and discussing the differences and potential outcomes.

4. **Have Honesty and Integrity**

   ☐ Never lie to the girls. (This excludes "little white lies.") Make sure they see me being honest with others — family, friends, salespeople, waitresses, etc.

   ☐ If they get caught lying, make them realize that it's unacceptable behavior.

   ☐ When we play games, I try to make sure they understand it's important to play fair. Not change the rules as we go along. And no cheating.

5. **Learn Compassion and Sharing**

   ☐ Let them know it's OK to feel and display emotions. Make a conscious effort to teach them to use words like sad, angry, frustrated, happy, proud.

   ☐ Teach the girls how to share with each other, which gives them the skills to share with others.

   ☐ Show the girls they can make a difference in the lives of others.

6. **Demonstrate Respect for Others**

   ☐ Encourage the girls to care about how other people feel by demonstrating interest and concern about their feelings. Frequently ask them how they feel — about themselves, about their friends, about school, about everything! And discuss why.

   ☐ Apologize to the girls (Nick too, I guess) whenever appropriate. And do it in a timely fashion.

   ☐ Teach them how to say no politely, but also help them understand that saying no isn't always an option. In addition, teach them how to accept and respect it when someone else says no.

7. **Be Dependable**

   ☐ Teach the girls the importance of keeping a promise. And that it doesn't matter the magnitude of the promise, whether arriving at a birthday party on time or clearing the dishes every night, but rather that their word is good.

   ☐ Make a point of demonstrating how and why people count on us.

   ☐ Include the concept of dependability when dealing with routines and schedules to show how it makes things work better.

   ☐ Acknowledge and thank the girls when they act responsibly.

8. **Learn Self-Discipline**

☐ Find ways to stay calm when angry. Understand and explain it's normal to sometimes get angry or irritated, but how you handle those feelings is very important. And that some ways are better than others. And some are totally unacceptable.

☐ Have everyone in the family designate a quiet area where they can go when they're upset and need their own space. And make sure to respect that space.

9. **Stress the Importance of Good Manners**

☐ Appropriate behavior, and especially good manners, are some of the best qualities I can instill in my children.

10. **Learn To Make Decisions And Solve Problems**

☐ Give the girls choices and teach them to make decisions even if it means a bit of extra work in the short-term. Teach them how to think about the pros and cons of any given decision.

☐ At the same time, be careful not to give them too many choices. Keep the choices age-appropriate, both in terms of numbers and types of choices.

☐ Ask the girls questions to help them solve problems on their own. Avoid the easy route of making their decisions for them; otherwise, they'll never learn this critical skill.

☐ Encourage them to express their preferences and let them know you understand their position and that it's important — even if Mommy or Daddy's final decision isn't their preferred outcome.

11. **Resist Peer Pressure**

☐ Teach my daughters to stand up for what they believe in and to have the strength not to follow the crowd. (Since I tend to avoid confrontation, I might need to use Black as an example.)

☐ Be available and open to discuss issues.

☐ Remember courage and perseverance are by-products of self-esteem, confidence and a sense of self-worth.

12. Value Relationships

- ☐ Teach them the value of relationships — both friends and family.
- ☐ Stress the importance of having friends. Explain to have a friend, you must be a friend.
- ☐ Explain that even though outside friends are very important, the best friends my girls will ever have are each other.
- ☐ Understand and experience the unconditional love of parents.

I know every day there are countless opportunities to engage my girls in discussions on important issues and teach them valuable lessons. If I try to live by my values, Natasha and Sawyer hopefully will follow my lead. And if I want to teach values, I must do it by example. I know that it's hard to remember to focus on these things when I'm trying to juggle getting the girls to school, grocery shopping, doing the laundry, helping with homework and all the other million and one tasks that have to be done every day. Which is why I needed to create this list. But once I did, I found that I was addressing many (but not all) of the items out of habit. I found that a relief, but more importantly, I found that gratifying.

18

Whine Or Lemonade? Your Choice

📱 Hello. Just letting you know I am off the track and heading to the hotel.

☎ You sound really happy. It must have been a good day.

📱 I am. It was a great day. I love being in my race car.

☎ I know, and I think that's wonderful. Any special plans for tonight?

📱 No. This morning when I left the house, Larry said he was going to come up for dinner, but I just spoke to him and now he is not coming. Something is not right.

☎ It's odd that he changed his mind. Did he say why?

📱 What was odd was that he said he was coming at all. He never joins me on car-related weekends. Anyway, he said he did not feel like making the drive. He babbled something about having fallen asleep on the couch after playing golf and had not yet packed.

☎ It was raining most of the afternoon; maybe he was drinking at the golf course and now doesn't want to make the drive.

📱 I understand, but it is only 4:30 and he is only an hour away. He was explaining too much, which is why it rang untrue. I asked him what was wrong, and he said "nothing." His tone of voice was strange. He was acting unusual last night, too. I thought he would have been excited about closing on the high rise, but he did not even mention it. There is definitely something going on.

☎ Well, at the risk of you saying I'm over-reacting do you think you need to go home tonight instead of spending tomorrow at the track?

📱 You are right — you are overreacting. First of all, if he has been drinking, I definitely do not want to go home. And even if something is bothering Larry, it does not mean he will talk about it. So as far as leaving early … whatever is going on can wait one more day. Being at the track tomorrow will not change anything.

☎ If you say so, but what if he's upset about your spending habits?

📱 Based on his recent snide comments, that would not be a surprise. Which is why I am going to attempt to broach the subject after this weekend. Meanwhile, tomorrow is a customer day, which is the cheapest track time available. Unless, of course, I wreck the car.

☎ That's not funny.

📱 If Larry thinks racing a Ferrari is expensive, fixing a Ferrari is even worse. I remember when I blew the engine. I did not have the heart to tell him how much a new one cost, so I paid for half of it from my own money. Even then, Larry thought the cost of half an engine was expensive!

Black never ceases to amaze me. She knew, or at least she thought, there might be trouble brewing on the home front, and yet she could remain calm and pragmatic. How did she do that?

So, What Exactly Does Money Buy?

I thought about her last comment — that she had paid for half a Ferrari engine without letting Larry know about it. I didn't even want to think about how much that cost, but it must be important to her if she paid for it herself. Black spent a lot of money, no question about that, but like she said when she was talking about allowances — it's always interesting to see what people find important enough to buy for themselves.

📟 What are you doing online?

📟 Checking e-mails before dinner. And you?

📟 Same same.

📟 Can I ask you a question?

📟 You just did.

📟 Cute. You said you paid for half your engine yourself instead of having Larry pay for all of it. I'm sure an engine is incredibly expensive, so that seems like an awful lot of money to spend if you didn't have to.

📟 Trying to find out how much a Ferrari engine costs? Trust me; you do not want to know.

📟 No, I'm trying to figure out why you spent your own money. Or at least why you didn't tell Larry you were paying for half of it yourself.

📟 Many reasons, but it all boils down to the fact that Larry and I never really talk about money. (Snide comments do not count.) In fact, when I decided to buy the vintage Porsche race car, I told him about it once it was on the trailer heading to Texas. But I quickly added that I had bought it with my own money.

📟 You did? Why? It must have been expensive.

IM It was something I needed and wanted. Before you ask – the Porsche 356 is twitchy so it teaches you car control. Plus the car is significantly less expensive to run than the Ferrari, so "seat time" is much more cost effective. Anyway, I knew Larry would pay for it if I said it would make me happy, but I felt guilty having him buy me another race car.

IM So did the car make you happy?

IM Trying to trick me and get me to admit money can buy happiness? Money alone will not make you happy, but it can allow you to do things which bring you pleasure. And satisfaction. And fulfillment.

IM Is that how you rationalize your spending? And your racing?

IM Interesting questions.

IM You're avoiding the questions.

IM No, I'm avoiding the answers.

IM Fine. So much for your "my life is an open book" attitude.

IM No. Yes.

IM ???

IM I answered your questions. No — my overall spending is related to boredom. The money is filling a void … not making me happy. Yes — racing makes me happy. For many reasons. I have thought about it a lot in the last few weeks. The key is knowing why you are spending money and what you are getting in return.

IM And what have you figured out?

IM That racing is an analogy to life.

IM I can't wait to hear this! Please go on.

IM When you race, you have to keep your eyes up and look down the track. You look way ahead in order to be prepared. There is not much you can do about the next corner because it is coming too quickly. It is a commitment you have already made. You see it in your peripheral vision, but you are focused on the things you can change. On the next lap, you focus on improving what you did last time. For example, if you screwed up a corner, you do something differently. You learn from your mistakes.

IM And when do you stop and smell the roses? And enjoy what you have?

IM Every time I climb in the race car. Every time I hit a perfect apex. Every time I improve my lap times. Every time I think about how fortunate I am to be able to race.

IM Pretty expensive roses!

IM Agree. But we can afford it, so it is not wasted money … unless of course I do something stupid and wreck the car. Which may explain why I am not faster. I never really put the car at risk. I guess I am trying to race cost-effectively.

IM Sorry, but there's no way you're going to get me to believe there's a cost-effective way to race a Ferrari! So don't even try. Go to dinner.

Look At The Bright Side

I had tried to stop comparing my life with other people's lives and for the most part I was feeling successful. I was confident my values and priorities had improved during the last few months, but I knew my perspective still needed work.

IM I'm surprised to find you online again.

IM Why? Typical Saturday night. Done with dinner and no one to talk to once I get home. Only tonight home is a hotel and there is no one snoring on the couch.

IM Sorry.

IM No reason to be. Everything will work out. One way or another.

IM That's what you told me when Nick was fired. In fact, you went so far as to say you thought it was the best thing that ever happened to us. Did you really mean that, or were you trying to make me feel better?

IM Maybe not THE very best, but it was definitely a good thing. What is that cliché about when life hands you lemons ... make a lemon drop martini?

IM Gee, and I always thought you were supposed to make lemonade! But are you saying that because you're trying to find a positive side or because you genuinely believe it?

IM Both. It does not cost anything to look on the positive side of things, but focusing on the negative can definitely have a steep price. Think about where you might be if you had chosen to wallow in your misery rather than taking a proactive approach. Think about where you are today and your outlook for the future. If Nick had not gotten fired, what would have made you look at your priorities? Not to mention your spending habits and all the other lessons you have learned. Do you think you would be in the same place? Doubtful. So yes, I genuinely believe it was for the best.

IM You're very philosophical tonight. So you really believe things happen for a reason?

IM Absolutely, although at the time we may not understand the reason. One day we may be able to look back and understand why things happened. Or we may never understand. Regardless, life goes on. And you need to make the most of each and every day.

IM OK, Miss Eternal Optimist, that's all fine and good. But what do you do on the days when you can't see the bright side? Then what?

IM Then imagine how things could be worse and be thankful for the fact they are not. Like I tell Mom when she is looking for sympathy and starts whining about problems or ailments ... "look on the bright side, at least you are not dead."

I doubt our mom appreciates that sentiment, but it's a pretty memorable statement and it did make me think. It was a matter of whether you choose to focus on what you think is missing from your life or what positive things actually exist. A very simple perspective to understand, but not always so easy to remember. Or apply.

Financial Lessons: Understand The Basics

There are times I wonder if I tackled the financial issues in the most logical order, but the truth is I didn't have many options. I felt like I was fire-fighting — dealing with the biggest financial fires first and then moving on to the smaller ones — until everything was under control. In many ways, though I definitely didn't see it that way at the time, I had the luxury of having my priorities set and was forced to take specific actions one right after another. I didn't have to ask myself, "Where do I start?" or "What next?" Plus, because I started out financially naïve, it meant I was working from a clean slate; I didn't have any preconceived notions on how to do things nor did I have a "know it all" arrogance.

I can't begin to list everything I learned about finance and financial decision-making, nor can I attempt to explain the best way to learn since there are so many different ways: ranging from family and friends to magazines and books to classes to financial advisors. I was incredibly lucky to have Black. Early on, Black had told me that the good news was my financial learning curve was steep. Of course, I initially panicked because I thought that meant it was going to be difficult to learn, thinking steep mountains are the most difficult to climb. Then she explained it meant I'd learn a lot in a very short time because I'd learn the basics quickly. More advanced topics would take more time. I didn't believe her at first, but once I understood the basic concepts and gained experience and confidence, new financial concepts did seem more straight-forward and logical. It also helped that I didn't have to deal with all of them on a regular basis. However, understanding the underlying fundamentals made most of the routine financial decisions so much easier.

I certainly don't pretend to be a financial expert now, but I'm no longer a financial ostrich. And the most important lesson I could ever teach anyone else is to learn the basics. And preferably before you're in a crisis mode. I can't begin to say how many times I have uttered or thought the words, "if I had only known ..." Although there's nothing I can do about the past, I can try to make the future better, based on the financial knowledge I have today. And, perhaps most importantly, I can definitely make sure that Natasha and Sawyer are better prepared than I was to face their financial future.

Life Lessons: Understand What Is Important

The financial lessons were numerous and significant, but pale in comparison to the life lessons I learned. Losing a job is never a good thing (I know Black would probably argue with this statement), but it forced me to focus on my personal values and priorities. It made me realize what was truly important. Eventually it became obvious that it was the personal things that should drive the financial decisions, not the other way around. Which is the way we had been living our lives. It was a major change, but one that made sense and ultimately felt good. But it's also one of the hardest things to do on a daily basis. It's so easy to get sidetracked by the demands of daily life and not focus enough attention on values and priorities.

My girls have always been the most important thing in my life. Sometimes I think Nick gets short-changed, or may feel like he is a second-class citizen, but he puts up with it admirably because of his love for the girls. The crisis made me focus on Natasha and Sawyer even more, because I didn't want them to feel neglected or confused while we were making changes in our daily life. Along the way I tried to explain the changes to them in such a way as to also teach them values and what was truly important — by both my words and actions.

It also made me understand that the family needed to be working together — all of us as a team, as well as Nick and me as a partnership. During the years Nick was building his corporate career, and especially after the girls were born, it was easy to put our relationship on the back burner. But now the key to our success would be our ability to communicate and to make sure our priorities were still compatible. And I knew if we could work together through the bad times, we'd be better positioned to enjoy the good times.

True Colors Come Out In A Crisis

Something even more important than specific lessons came out of my crisis. Black and I had started to become closer in the years after I moved back to the States, but something truly amazing happened when Nick got fired and I turned to her for help. It started with advice and understanding. And then it grew into something more powerful and long-lasting. It was a new respect and appreciation. I learned the true value of family and friendship. The security of knowing that someone would always be there for me, no matter what, and that they weren't judging me or focusing on my weaknesses. And I found someone I could trust to point me, and on occasion push me, in the right direction if I lost my way.

📱 Hello. Just checking in to let you know I am off the track and heading home. It was another great day. A really great day.

☎ You sound very excited. And happy. I'm glad. Have you talked to Larry? Are things better?

📱 I only spoke to him briefly this morning since he was already at the golf course. He seemed OK, but the reality of the situation is that there is not much I can do about it. Except deal with it. However, this weekend was just what I needed. It was a great escape.

☎ Please don't tell me this was another lifesaving weekend!

📱 No, just a continuation of the other one. Remember when I told you that as long as you and Nick's priorities and dreams are compatible, as long as you can find a way to communicate and are willing to be open and honest with yourselves, as well as each other, then the two of you have a shot at happiness?

☎ Yes, I remember all that. I also remember that whenever I try and talk about you and Larry, you always seem to turn the conversation around and make it about me and Nick.

📱 Whatever. My point is that relationships are continually tested. And they take work. Sometimes more work than other times, but work nonetheless. The key is both parties need to focus on the positive and learn how to deal with the negative. And hopefully the good will more than offset the bad. No relationship is easy. And none is perfect.

☎ Yes, I know. Life isn't a fairy tale. You've made me painfully aware of that.

📱 Someone had to. But if it makes you feel any better, I bet even Prince Charming wakes up with morning breath.

☎ It's bad enough that I have to admit life is not a fairy tale. Don't spoil the fairy tales, too! So how do you know when you've found happiness? Or is it just an elusive dream you keeping working towards?

📱 What do you want? Street signs? There are signs that will lead you to Paradise, Texas, but when it comes to happiness, you are on your own.

☎ Thank you. I know I can always count on you for sarcasm. And do you expect me to believe there really is a city called Paradise?

📱 Believe what you want.

And so I let the conversation end. I knew the more I asked and the closer I got to sensitive subjects, the more flippant the remarks I'd receive. OK, so Prince Charming might have morning breath. But I decided to look on the bright side; at least she didn't tell me George Clooney did, too.

19

There Is No Conclusion ...
Because Life Goes On

You asked, "How do you know when you've found happiness?" And my reply was "When it comes to happiness, you are on your own." Although you accused me of being sarcastic, I was not. I was being serious. Very serious. It is something I have always known and have been thinking about a lot lately.

- Happiness is a state of mind. It is a feeling of contentment, of looking forward to the future, of enjoying where you are today.
- You control your own happiness. You cannot expect other people (or things) to make you happy. You have to take responsibility for your life and whether or not you are "happy."
- Similarly, you cannot make other people happy. You may be able to create an environment that allows them to be happy, but you cannot force them to be happy.
- Today's dreams can be tomorrow's realities, but only if the dreams are realistic. If your expectations are unrealistic, you will be disappointed. And to further complicate the situation ... reality is not only a moving target but also a work-in-progress.
- People talk about the pursuit of happiness, which sounds like an oxymoron to me. If you chase it, it will elude you. You have to remember to stop and enjoy. Take time to be happy.
- Life is a journey ... NOT a destination.

The specific things that make people happy may differ from person to person, but I believe the process for finding happiness is the same for everyone. The problem is that some people do not take the time to think about it. Or at least not honestly.

And that is the end of my philosophy class on happiness. It has been a long weekend, and to quote Scarlett from *Gone With The Wind*, "tomorrow is another day."

If Black had sent me this e-mail before Nick had been fired I'd have agreed with her theory, but not really thought much more about it. Although I might have thought it was easy for her to be philosophical about happiness given her financial situation. She never had to worry about anything.

And if Black had sent it during the first month or so after Nick had been fired, I'd have said I had no time for theory and needed specific advice. And more money in the bank. At the time I was too pre-occupied with chasing false dreams and dealing with financial emergencies to even think about happiness. I was focused on survival. I wasn't ready to believe that life is a journey. I wouldn't have seen that sometimes we're in such a hurry rushing towards the future that we forget to enjoy the present.

Since Life Is A Journey — Enjoy The Trip

It had taken me a while to understand the value of the "bumpy road" and the fact it would help me to appreciate smoother travels. I had also come to understand that the road might not always be smooth, but that, too, was OK. More importantly, I could look to the future knowing that the roads I have traveled help prepare me for whatever lies ahead. Once I could look back with a better understanding of where I came from, I could also look forward with less fear and trepidation. And I certainly need reminders to focus on what's most important. But I knew I could periodically go back to Black's advice. Almost like a refresher class.

Earlier in the evening I had completed my Sunday night review of my lists. As I looked back over my assorted lists, some more important than others, I realized how far I had come in the last three months. My "Values and Priorities" list was still a work-in-progress, but I planned to send it to Black once I felt it could withstand her scrutiny. I knew she would accuse me of having an uncanny knack for the obvious or some other smart-ass comment, but the bottom line was that she was greatly responsible for making me realize what was genuinely important. I was indebted to her. I had no idea how I'd ever repay her, although I knew she wasn't expecting anything (nor would she even want the recognition) in return.

Life Happens Even When You Make Other Plans

And I was finally ready to agree that Black was right when she told me Nick getting fired was one of the best things that ever happened to us. Because I knew, without doubt, that so much of what I learned about life I learned when my husband got fired. It was a rude awakening, but it was what I needed. I'm not sure I would have seen the reality of my life any other way. And now, as an ostrich standing tall, I finally understood that my happiness would come from the journey — not the destination. And from the people whom I love who would be by my side along the way. I knew the road would be bumpy at times, but I made a pledge to myself that I would try my best to remember everything I had learned and enjoy the ride. Bumps and all.

I went to sleep that night feeling like my life finally had some semblance of reality and balance, and I was looking forward to enjoying it. And sharing my newfound optimism with Black. But as I had already learned, and would probably be reminded of again and again in my life — life has a way of interrupting our best-laid plans. And the interruption came fast and furious Monday morning.

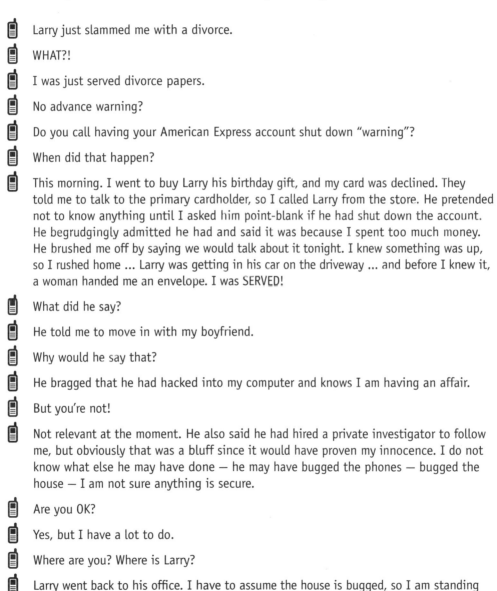

Larry just slammed me with a divorce.

WHAT?!

I was just served divorce papers.

No advance warning?

Do you call having your American Express account shut down "warning"?

When did that happen?

This morning. I went to buy Larry his birthday gift, and my card was declined. They told me to talk to the primary cardholder, so I called Larry from the store. He pretended not to know anything until I asked him point-blank if he had shut down the account. He begrudgingly admitted he had and said it was because I spent too much money. He brushed me off by saying we would talk about it tonight. I knew something was up, so I rushed home ... Larry was getting in his car on the driveway ... and before I knew it, a woman handed me an envelope. I was SERVED!

What did he say?

He told me to move in with my boyfriend.

Why would he say that?

He bragged that he had hacked into my computer and knows I am having an affair.

But you're not!

Not relevant at the moment. He also said he had hired a private investigator to follow me, but obviously that was a bluff since it would have proven my innocence. I do not know what else he may have done — he may have bugged the phones — bugged the house — I am not sure anything is secure.

Are you OK?

Yes, but I have a lot to do.

Where are you? Where is Larry?

Larry went back to his office. I have to assume the house is bugged, so I am standing on the driveway. I do not know if you can bug cell phones.

📱 Do you want me to come over?

📱 No. I need to get the Ferrari and my jewelry somewhere safe. And then call my attorney. I do not know what is going to happen next.

📱 Is there anything I can do?

📱 Not that I can think of. At least not right now. I will keep you posted, but I will probably be out of pocket most of the day. If you do not hear from me, do not worry. I will call you later. This will all work itself out. One way or another.

But how was I not supposed to worry? I thought back to all the times during the past three months when Black had said, "This is not about me, this is about you." But now it was about her. And whether she had the ability to continue to look at life as pragmatically as she had in the past. Part of me believed she would deal with this as she had everything else — head-on, like a bull in a china cabinet. But the warm and fuzzy part of me couldn't stop worrying about her. I hoped she'd be OK, and that I'd be able to help her in some way. But only time would tell …

....

....

....

....

....

....

....

....

....

....

....

....

....

epilogue

Red: Always One More List

As I review my Franklin Planner, the changes in my life become even more obvious. I always had plenty of lists, but now in addition to being better organized, they more accurately reflect what I honestly want to accomplish. Instead of overbooking my calendar, or the girls', I try to treat many of the lists as a menu of projects rather than things that must be done. I try to keep in mind that the world won't stop if I don't accomplish everything on my list. And that 5, 10, 20 years from now, it won't matter what I did on any given day, but rather in how I approached my days and whether I made time for things that were truly important.

I decided to put together one more list. It would be one I could review whenever I needed help remembering the glass is half-full. Unlike the long list I had made of all my notes, this consisted of only seven items. I had to chuckle to myself because I knew if I shared these with Black, she'd ask me if these were my answers to the seven deadly sins.

Whenever I review this list, I realize that all seven points still hold true.

1. Take My Head Out Of The Sand

Whether financial or personal — avoiding the truth won't change the facts. It certainly will NOT make the situation better. Nor will it make the situation go away. Problems will lie dormant only until such time as they're too big to continue ignoring. Acknowledging a problem (and the earlier, the better) is a HUGE first step towards doing something positive.

2. **Eat The Elephant One Bite At A Time**

This applies to many large issues or projects. Situations which become bigger the longer I delay addressing them. Which then can become another excuse for not dealing with them. A vicious circle! But I can tackle/deal with/solve anything; I CAN eat an elephant, just not all at one time. I initially applied this concept to our financial situation and later used it for less urgent projects, such as the girls' scrapbooks. Now I find myself using this concept whenever I have large tasks to tackle that in the past I'd have kept postponing.

3. **Communication Includes Dialogue**

I've talked a lot about communication, and there's no question that it's absolutely critical to any relationship. But now I've added the word "dialogue." A cooperative spouse is great, or a close friend, a sister (!) — anyone who will listen and be available to bounce ideas around. I'm lucky to have Black in my life, but if I didn't there are support groups. I would never try to get through a crisis alone.

4. **Be Honest With The Mirror**

I have made a commitment that I'll try to be honest with myself — about what's important to me, what will make me happy (I don't mean winning the lottery), what I want from life. I need to be open to the thoughts of friends and family (NOT society at large) about what's important to them, but I treat them as a "menu of options" — not definitive answers. And I remind myself I might be looking at Astroturf.

5. **It's Just Stuff And Fluff**

Spending time and money chasing "things" is a waste of time and money. (Beyond basic needs, of course.) Besides, it isn't a good example to set for children. At the end of the day, the most important things are my beliefs, my values, my priorities, my loved ones, my memories. The things money cannot buy. The rest is just fluff.

6. Slow Down And Enjoy

Life can change in an instant — a spouse gets fired, a family member gets seriously ill, a loved one dies — so I have to enjoy what I have and the people in my life. Spend less time "doing" and more time "enjoying." Read one less e-mail. Play a game with the girls. Shut off the TV at dinner and have a conversation. Have coffee with a friend. Make sure to take the time to unwind. And to dream.

7. Crisis = Opportunity

Finally, I have given myself the gift of believing that everything happens for a reason, even if I can't understand why at the time. If I allow myself to treat a crisis as a potential opportunity, I might find myself one day in the future saying, "I'm so glad that happened because if it hadn't then: I might not have learned something. Understood something. Gotten to the place where I am today."

Black: I See Elephants On My Horizon

The purpose of this epilogue is to look back and reflect. But if you think I have the time, or the inclination, to focus on anything other then the future right now, then you do not know who I am. I have more important things to deal with. EOM